Subversion Version Control

BRUCE PERENS' OPEN SOURCE SERIES

http://www.phptr.com/perens

Subversion Version Control

Using The Subversion Version Control System in Development Projects

William Nagel

PTR **Prentice Hall Professional Technical Reference**

Upper Saddle River, NJ • Boston • Indianapolis • San Francisco
New York • Toronto • Montreal • London • Munich • Paris • Madrid
Capetown • Sydney • Tokyo • Singapore • Mexico City

Many of the designations used by manufacturers and sellers to distinguish their products are claimed as trademarks. Where those designations appear in this book, and the publisher was aware of a trademark claim, the designations have been printed with initial capital letters or in all capitals.

The author and publisher have taken care in the preparation of this book, but make no expressed or implied warranty of any kind and assume no responsibility for errors or omissions. No liability is assumed for incidental or consequential damages in connection with or arising out of the use of the information or programs contained herein.

The publisher offers excellent discounts on this book when ordered in quantity for bulk purchases or special sales, which may include electronic versions and/or custom covers and content particular to your business, training goals, marketing focus, and branding interests. For more information, please contact:

U.S. Corporate and Government Sales
(800) 382-3419
corpsales@pearsontechgroup.com

For sales outside the U.S., please contact:

International Sales
international@pearsoned.com

Visit us on the Web: www.phptr.com

Library of Congress Cataloging-in-Publication Data

Nagel, William A.
    Subversion version control : using the Subversion version control system in development projects / William Nagel.
       p. cm.
    Includes index.
    ISBN 0-13-185518-2 (pbk. : alk. paper)
    1. Computer software–Development. 2. Open source software. I. Title.
    QA76.76.D47N35 2005
    005.1–dc22

                                                                                    2005005872

For information regarding permissions, write to:

Pearson Education, Inc.
Rights and Contracts Department
One Lake Street
Upper Saddle River, NJ 07458

ISBN 0-13-185518-2
Text printed in the United States on recycled paper at Courier in Stoughton, Massachusetts.
First printing, May 2005

To Sara,

and the wonderful life we'll have together

Contents

Preface

I was first introduced to version control (and CVS) in college, about the same time I was introduced to Linux. At that time though, most of the projects I worked on were small and generally involved only a couple of developers. So, although version control would have been useful, I never took the time to really use it; my knowledge of CVS remained limited to what little I needed to know to check out the occasional bleeding-edge project on Linux (which seemed necessary a little more often in those days). As my college career progressed, the projects I worked on became more involved, and I began to learn about "software engineering." The instruction I received on software engineering never really covered version control in any depth though, and despite the increased size of the software projects I was working on, I never delved into using a version control system to keep track of things. I wanted to; I thought CVS was a neat idea. I just never invested the time necessary to learn how to set it up and use it. Then came my first major team project. It was a real-world project, with real-world clients, and its completion was required for graduation. Finally, I had an excuse to really give version control a try. I presented the case for CVS to my teammates and (although there was some small resistance) convinced them that we needed to use it. It was a success. By the end of the project, I was fully sold on the necessity of version control in any future projects, however big or small. I loved CVS.

After school came the real world, and the love affair with CVS didn't last long. As I learned (mostly through trial and error) how version control systems should be used, CVS steadily became more and more inadequate. I could see its potential, but it didn't measure up. Code was lost, fits were thrown, and hair was pulled. Still, CVS was the best free, open source version control system out there, and as an entrepreneur trying to keep a start-up company going, free was a required feature. Then someone told me about a new version control project called Subversion, so I went to its site and took a look. It seemed intriguing, but it wasn't quite up to the point where I could trust it for my code—and I barely had time to eat back then, so getting involved in the project's development was out of the question. Instead, Subversion went on my back burner and I moved on to other things.

Several months down the road, I saw that Subversion had become self-hosting. "Well," I thought, "If they trust it with their own code, maybe it's time to take another look." Rolling up my sleeves, I sat down to play around with it. Once again, I had fallen in love. Subversion was everything CVS could have been. It was stable, it was flexible, and it didn't eat my code. Thus, after a suitable period of testing, CVS was unceremoniously chucked and replaced by Subversion. I've never regretted the change. In fact, the only thing regrettable is the hours of my life wasted fighting with CVS.

Writing the Book

When I was first approached about writing a book on Subversion, my first thought was, "Why?" There's already an excellent Subversion manual, written by several of the principle Subversion authors (who presumably know more about Subversion's inner workings than I do), and it's freely available at that. So, I almost turned down the opportunity to write this book because I couldn't imagine why anyone would want to read it. What could I possibly add that wasn't already written? Then I got to thinking back to my college days, when I learned version control through trial and error (mostly error). I had the manual to CVS, but it covered how to use CVS, not how to use version control. It was a good manual, it just wasn't complete. The Subversion manual is similar; although it is far, far better than the documentation available for CVS, it's still primarily a technical manual. As a technical manual, it is excellent. As a guide to realizing Subversion's full potential in relation to your software development project, it isn't complete. Therefore, I've written this book to be the guide I never had when I was learning how to use version control.

Of course, this book aims to cover the nuts and bolts of Subversion as completely as possible—you can't very well use Subversion to develop software if you can't use Subversion—but it does so in the context of how to do the things you want to do in day-to-day software development. The book also goes a step further: It explains how to expand on the built-in capabilities of Subversion to make the system work for you. In some places, that takes the form of example scripts or configurations. In others, it is merely ideas that you can expand to fit *your* software development process. This is not a book to sell a process. I do make suggestions here and there of what I think will work in certain situations, but you don't need to buy into my "exhalted process" to get the most from this book. Instead of showing you how you should develop your software, I show you how Subversion can make your process easier.

The Layout of the Book

The book is split into five sections, each covering Subversion from a different perspective.

Part I: An Introduction to Version Control and Subversion

This first part looks at Subversion from the beginner's perspective. It explains what version control is, why it is useful, and how Subversion fits into the version control world. It shows you how to install and set up Subversion, and it walks you through Subversion's essential features.

Chapter 1 An introduction to the essential concepts that make up a version control system.

Chapter 2 An introduction to Subversion's features and how they compare to some other common version control systems.

Chapter 3 A basic guide to installing Subversion on Linux, Windows, and Mac OS X.

Chapter 4 A tutorial walkthrough of Subversion, from creating your first repository to basic branching and merging.

Part II: Subversion from a Client User's Perspective

The second part of the book examines Subversion from the perspective of the client user. It takes a detailed look at using the most important Subversion client commands, as well as properties, user configuration, and integration with a variety of external tools.

Chapter 5 Walk through a Subversion working copy and the commands used to interact with it. Most of the common Subversion client commands are covered in this chapter.

Chapter 6 How to use the Subversion tools to work with properties attached to versioned files.

Chapter 7 A look at Subversion client configuration and customization for an individual work environment.

Chapter 8 An overview of many of the client tools that Subversion can integrate and interact with.

Part III: Subversion from an Administrator's Perspective

This is a look at Subversion from the admin's perspective. In this section, I talk about repository administration and organization. I show how to use automation to help integrate Subversion into your development process, and I examine the nuts and bolts of such things as repository security and migration from another version control system.

Chapter 9 Tips on repository organization, as well as how to migrate an old repository to Subversion with minimal loss of history and metadata.

Chapter 10 Basic repository administration: security, backup, and repository maintenance.

Chapter 11 An in-depth look at automation in Subversion, using hook scripts, metadata, and the Subversion API. Includes a number of example scripts that you can use in your project.

Part IV: The Software Development Process

This part takes a look at Subversion from the project manager's perspective. It looks at the software development process and how Subversion can fit into a variety of different types of projects, with many different policies and philosophies.

Chapter 12 An overview of different policies adopted by many development projects and how Subversion can be used to complement those policies.

Chapter 13 An examination of the software development process and how Subversion can be integrated into that process.

Chapter 14 Case studies that examine both archetypal and real-world projects and their use of Subversion.

Part V: Reference

The final section is a Subversion command reference. When you need to look up something quickly, it can be difficult to sift through paragraphs of expositional language. This section takes the essential technical information from the Subversion commands and makes it easy to find quickly.

Acknowledgments

I would like to thank everyone who made this book possible. First, my parents for giving me the support to become the person I am today, and for not dropping me off at an orphanage (however tempting the option may have been). And the rest of my family and friends—especially my lovely fiancée, Sara—who never ceased to support me, no matter how many times I said, "Sorry, I can't. I have to work on my book." I'd also like to thank my coworkers at Stage Logic who never complained when I fled work early or skipped out on a few days. I'd especially like to thank Ralph Rodkey for helping me to research some of the Windows-specific aspects of Subversion; Drew Hintz for loaning me his laptop to play around with Windows myself; and Zach Lute, because I told him I would, even though I can't remember why.

I am grateful to Martin Streicher of Linux Magazine for giving me my first opportunity as a published writer, and for giving me the opportunity to write the article on Subversion that ultimately led to this book. I am also grateful to Jill Harry at Prentice Hall for giving the opportunity to write this book and for supporting me the whole way. Of course, she couldn't have done it alone, so I'd also like to thank Brenda Mulligan, John Fuller, Robin O'Brien, Ebony Haight, Lara Wysong, Kelli Brooks, and the rest of the Prentice Hall team who have worked very hard to make this book a reality.

This book is not just the work of one mind, either. Without the many who reviewed and commented on my book along the way, it would be a much lesser book. I would like to thank Michael Ching, Stuart Robertson, and Gustavo Niemeyer for their reviews of the book's concept. I'd also like to thank Michael Ching and Gustavo Niemeyer, as well as Ben Reser and Chris Pavicich for their invaluable input on the book after it was written. I'm also grateful to thank Mike Treaster for his commentary on several early chapters from the perspective of a non-version control expert; to Jason Reese for his commentary from the perspective of someone who thought version control was a song by Prince; to Jim Markham for his valuable input on the book's layout and writing style in the early chapters; and to Ted Gould for reading those early chapters, even if he never got around to actually telling me what he thought.

Many thanks also goes out to those people who contributed their real-world experiences to allow me to prepare the case studies near the end of the book: Mark Grosberg of Glade-Soft, Felix Collins of KeyGhost, Robert Allan Zeh of Error Free Software, Mark Bohlman of Teledata Communications, Ron Bieber, Chris Wein, and John Szakmeister. And, of course, many thanks goes to Stuart Robertson of Absolute Systems for his contributions of the RSS feed script and Samba/Windows Domain Controller configuration steps.

Without Subversion, this book would not be. So, a sincerely grateful thanks goes out to everyone who has contributed to Subversion and made it the great version control system that it is today.

I've tried hard to ensure that everyone who helped me with this book has been thanked. However, I may have inadvertently left someone out. To that person, I extend an extra thanks for putting up with my faulty memory.

Finally, thanks goes to K.C. Sanborn, whose continued inability to grasp the concept of a SCSI bus has helped me keep a proper perspective on the place of computers in the world.

Part I

An Introduction to Version Control and Subversion

Chapter 1

An Introduction to Version Control

"Hey, Jane, could you send me a copy of those changes you made last Tuesday?"

"Bob, this function doesn't work anymore. Did you change something?"

"Sorry, I can't seem to find those old classes. I guess you'll just have to re-implement them."

"Ok, we've all been working hard for the last week. Now let's integrate everyone's work together."

Do any of these comments sound familiar? If you've ever worked on a disorganized project, they may very well be frighteningly common. They're key indicators of a process where information is not under control, and in software development, information control is crucial to a successful project. It is crucial because that's what software development is. Any nontrivial software project is a complex system, often involving numerous different developers. For all of those developers to accomplish something, they must know what they need to accomplish, and that is very difficult to accomplish without controlled distribution of information between developers.

Organized software development involves a large bag of tools and techniques. At the core of those tools is the ability to keep the source code—without which, software development is simply nothing—maintained and accessible to the people who need that access. Enter the version control system, which assumes the role of tracking, maintaining, and storing the revision history of a development project's source.

Version control is not a simple task, nor are all version control systems created equal. In the world of open source, the Subversion version control system is rapidly emerging as a major contender for not only open source development projects, but also small, medium, and maybe even a few large software companies. For instance, the open source Samba project has begun using Subversion, as has the Apache Software Foundation. Additionally, although there are no numbers showing just how many commercial companies are using Subversion, the Subversion Web site contains numerous testimonials from users who have successfully deployed Subversion in a commercial setting. Also, according to Jason Robbins at `tigris.org` (the site hosting the Subversion project), the version 1.0 release of Subversion in February of 2004 sparked an enormous increase in downloads of Subversion (more than 29,000 in May, 2004, for example).

To help you to make the most of this rising star, I will not just show how to use Subversion in this book. I will instead show you how to use Subversion effectively as a core part of your software development process, through examples and explanations of things you will actually do during real-world, every-day usage of the system, as well as ideas for integrating Subversion into your total development process.

Before learning how to use Subversion, it is imperative that you have a solid grasp of the basic concepts of version control. If you have used a version control system extensively before, you may want to skip to Chapter 2, "An Introduction to Subversion." If you would like to learn more about what typical version control systems can do, and how they can benefit your process, please read on.

1.1   What Is Version Control?

Most major software development projects involve many different developers working concurrently on a variety of (overlapping) sets of files, over a long period of time. It is therefore critical that the changes made by these developers be tracked, so that you can always tell who is responsible for any changes, as well as what your source files looked like an hour ago, a week ago, or a year ago. Furthermore, it's just as important (if not even more important) to be able to merge the contributions of those many developers into a single whole. This is where a version control system comes into play.

The basic functionalities of any version control system are to keep track of the changing states of files over time and merge contributions of multiple developers. They support this, for the most part, by storing a history of changes made over time by different people. In this way, it is possible to roll back those changes and see what the files looked like before they were applied. Additionally, a version control system will provide facilities for merging the changes, using one or more methods ranging from file locking to automatic integration of conflicted changes.

1.2   Why Use It?

You know what version control is; why do you need it? Especially for a small team project, what benefit does a good version control system provide that outweighs the cost of setting up and learning how to use it? Let's look at some of the reasons why version control is critical in any development project, small or large.

1.2.1   Data Integrity

A good version control system helps to protect the integrity of your data. By keeping a revision history, there is no worry that if code is removed in an edit on one day, it will be lost when it is determined a week later to have in fact been necessary.

Having a central project repository can also help with data backup. If developers regularly commit their data to the versioning system, it can be backed up nightly in one chunk and offloaded to backup storage, with few worries that weeks worth of unfinished data will be sitting on a developer's desktop, waiting for the inevitable hard drive failure.

1.2.2   Productivity

By freeing developers from the drudgery of by-hand integration of work, a version control system can greatly increase productivity. As projects grow larger than one or two people, even the most well organized of processes will lose countless man hours toward integrating the work of multiple developers. With a version control system, developers are able to test changes against the latest work of their peers, identifying and fixing conflicts before they become unmanageable. They are also able to experiment more easily, free to branch and modify code without worrying about whether their changes will affect the stability of the main project or the work of others. If an experimental change breaks something, it can quickly and easily be rolled back or compared with the original code to see what changed.

A version control system also protects against productivity lost to re-implemented work, not only by avoiding losses of data that was incorrectly deemed to be unnecessary, but also by making each developer's work readily available to other developers on the project. If developers are able to easily see where the others working on the project are going with their work, they will be less likely to duplicate effort. Even in a well-organized project, it can be easy for two developers working on closely related sections to accidentally implement the same piece of functionality. If all developers regularly commit their work to a repository, this becomes much less likely to happen.

1.2.3   Accountability

In any development process, it is important to know exactly who added each bit of code to a project, as well as when they did it, and who has made modifications since then. This sort of fine-grained accountability is important not only for technical reasons (for example, who to go to if a section needs to be fixed), but also for purposes of legal defense. In recent times, there have been a number of high profile cases, involving both open source and closed source projects, that have hinged around allegations of source code being illegitimately placed into other projects. In light of the potential liability that the maintainers of a project could have in these sorts of cases, having a version control system that makes each contributer accountable for his own contributions seems to be a prudent precaution to take, especially if you are maintaining an open source project, where little may be known about the contributer, and money to fight a legal battle may be tight or nonexistent.

1.2.4   Software Engineering Process Support

Good software (even open source projects) are developed with a software engineering process. By software engineering, I mean the application of disciplined development policies aimed at ensuring that the end product of the process will meet the desired goals in a timely manner, and with the highest possible standards of quality.

A good software engineering process involves a number of different processes and policies, such as good overall project design, peer review of project components, tracking of bugs and other issues, and quality assurance testing. None of these are explicitly supported by most version control systems, but many version control system features (such as hook scripts and logs) can be an important tool in supporting a project's software engineering policies. For example, a version control system (VCS) may be set to automatically e-mail an issue tracking system in order to report a bug fix, or a system could log peer reviews, and through the use of hook scripts, disallow any code that hasn't been peer reviewed to be merged onto the project's main source trunk.

1.2.5   Development Branching

As projects progress over time, branches will naturally occur. Old releases will need to be supported with bug fixes. New projects may be spun off from existing code bases to serve emerging markets. Whatever the reason, branches will happen, and unless the relationship between branches is carefully maintained, they will tend to diverge irreconcilably. Issues that are fixed in one branch will go unfixed in another. Features implemented in a divergent branch will be unusable in the main trunk. In general, keeping even a semblance of consistency between different branches of development will be a maintenance nightmare.

If used in an organized and consistent manner, the branching features built into most version control systems can greatly reduce the headaches associated with maintaining divergent branches of development on a project. By using the commit logs generated by the system, as well as its capability to merge changes from one branch to another, changes that are applicable to multiple branches can be cleanly implemented on a single branch and then applied to the other branches. Similarly, a new feature added to a branch can be migrated to other branches where it may be useful.

1.2.6   Record Keeping

A version control system will help to enforce policies that can ensure a project keeps quality records for later use. In addition to the aforementioned records of who committed each change, repository commit logs are invaluable for storing plain-English descriptions not only of what changes were made in a given commit, but why they were made. In many cases, commit logs can even be verified against certain patterns, to enforce guidelines for logs entries that are in place for the project.

In addition to providing a record of what has gone into each commit, logs kept by a version control system can be used for a variety of applications. For example, they could be used to create a changelog at a release, or to automatically tie into an issue tracking system.

1.2.7   Distribution of Work

In our modern Internet age, life is becoming more and more distributed, and nowhere is this more true than in software development. Open source projects are (almost by definition) developed in a distributed nature, by developers all over the world, but even in the closed source corporate world, distributed development can be a major issue. Regardless of whether a developer is telecommuting from across town or an outsourcing firm in India, distributed development can be difficult to deal with.

Version control can make dealing with distributed development easier, by automating much of the workload of exchanging and merging the work of different developers. As developers work on their projects from remote corners of the globe, the repository makes the latest work of their coworkers readily accessible at any time. Combined with good communication habits, using something like e-mail or instant messaging, distributed development can become almost as painless as being the next cube over.

1.2.8 Rapid Development

Recent software development methodologies have been moving toward rapid, flexible development, with processes like Extreme Programming (XP) and Agile Development being adopted with increasing frequency. These rapid development methods accentuate policies of small incremental change and frequent refactoring, which cry out for version control. By using good version control practices, a project will maintain extremely useful code histories that delineate the many twists and turns rapidly developed code can take. Additionally, the central repository of a version control system is perfect for automating the frequent systems builds called for by an Agile process.

1.3 The Elements of Version Control

So, version control is, in its essence, exactly what its name purports it to be: the tracking, controlling, and merging of different versions (called revisions) of a project over time. In practice, as with almost anything, this is not nearly as simple as it sounds. Version control systems are complex software tools with a wealth of different features that vary widely from system to system. Conceptually, though, they are in fact fairly simple, and most version control systems can be grasped with an understanding of a few basic concepts.

1.3.1 The Repository and Working Directory

Most version control systems store versioned projects in a central repository. The repository may simply be a structured directory on a server with each versioned file stored separately, or it may be a database containing entries for the various files in a project. It may even be a complex distributed system that redundantly stores the versioned project all over the world.

Regardless of what the repository looks like, the one commonality among version control systems is that developers do not work directly on the files in the repository. Instead, they have some sort of working directory accessible from their development machine, where they can make local modifications.

Working directories generally allow individual developers to work locally, adding and testing changes as necessary, during the development process. Once a change or set of changes is deemed complete, the developer is able to commit the changes back into the repository, where they become a part of the project.

Once a change has been committed to the repository, the other developers working on the project are able to update their working copies to include the latest versions of the project's files. This allows the other developers to test the new changes with the uncommitted local modifications in their own working directories, and fix things as necessary—or demand that the developers responsible for the modifications fix their changes, as appropriate.

1.3.2   Revisions

Version control systems don't just store the most recent state of a project. Instead, they store a history of changes to the project over time. Whenever a developer commits changes to a project, those changes are stored in a *revision*. Depending on the version control system, revisions will either be global points that refer to the state of the entire repository at a given point, or they will exist as file-level revisions that refer to the state of an individual file.

In a file-level revision system, each file has a revision history independent of the rest of the project. For example, let's say a repository consists of `foo.c` and `bar.c`. If `foo.c` has had ten different modifications committed, the version control system may give its revision as ten, but lists `bar.c` as only being at revision five (if that is the number of modifications committed for `bar.c`). This sort of revision scheme tends to be unwieldy, and can make it difficult to keep track of the overall state of the project at a particular point in time. For instance, being required to know that the repository consisted of revision 5 of `bar.c`, revision 10 of `foo.c`, and revision 8 of `ReadMe.txt` at 3:26 PM last Tuesday would be a nightmare. To make the tracking of project states easier, most version control systems allow you to refer to revisions by the state they existed in at a given date and time, or a specific tag. Tags are essentially snapshots of the repository at a specific point, which can be used as a reference (I talk more about tags in a little while).

Other version control systems (such as Subversion) have revisions that are global across the entire repository. In this type of system, a modification committed to a single file would increment the revisions of all files in the repository. Thus, "revision 10" would refer to a snapshot of the whole system at the time of the tenth commit. Figure 1.1 shows an example of a repository that uses global revision numbers. You will notice how the revision number increases by one each time a commit occurs, even though the files are not the same for each commit. This gives a huge advantage over file-level revisions, because you no longer have a need to keep track of the relationships between different revisions of different files. Consequently, explicit tags tend to become less necessary. For instance, with a file-level system, you might make a tag before every significant feature, to allow you to roll back the whole repository to a consistent pre-change point. When you have global revisions, though, each revision is essentially a tag itself. This makes it much easier to move the entire repository between revisions, or to compare revisions.

The differences between two revisions of a repository are often referred to as *changesets*. In addition to allowing a developer to retrieve specific revisions from a repository, most VCSs allow the retrieval of changesets. The changesets can usually consist of either changes to the entire repository between two revisions, or changes to a specific subset of files in the repository. Some VCS implementations will also allow one or more revisions

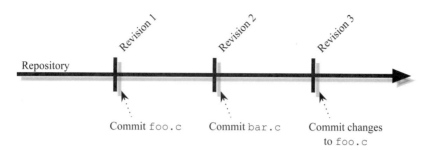

Figure 1.1. A repository with global revision numbers.

to be grouped into a changeset that can be used later to roll back changes to a repository or apply those changes to a different repository.

1.3.3 Logs

Keeping track of code changes is important. However, to truly keep an organized development process going, it isn't sufficient. It is useful to know that three lines of code were added to a source file, but what you really want to know is *why* those lines of code were added, and what logical change that addition makes to the project. That might not be too hard to discern if the change is small, as with three lines, but if ten thousand lines are added, using a diff to figure out what changed may be practically impossible.

One way to keep track of logical changes would be to keep notes on what is happening in source code comment blocks. This keeps the information close to the source, but it quickly becomes unwieldy. Comments can be hard to find, if someone simply wishes to know what changed from one version to another. Additionally, logical changes that require many small changes scattered throughout the project are especially difficult to document concisely in source code comments.

Moreover, keeping track of logical changes can be invaluable when debugging a project. In any actively developed project, it is inevitable that mysterious bugs will appear in places that worked fine just a few days ago. When that happens, the first thing you'll want to do is figure out what changed since the point where the project last worked. If you don't have a good set of logs showing the logical changes made in that period of time, figuring out where the offending modification lies may be an arduous job.

It would also be nice to be able to compile a change log, showing changes that have occurred from one project release to another. Keeping track of this in source comments would also be extremely difficult, and would probably require some sort of special tagging to allow a script to extract changes. Another option would be to keep track of the changes that occur in a separate file. Such a file would be hard to maintain, though, and could easily become out of sync and inaccurate. A much better solution to tracking logical project changes is to include a log along with each repository commit. The log would allow developers to enter the reason and substance of the change they are committing, in plain English.

Not surprisingly, any version control system worth using keeps logs that can easily be used for exactly the purposes described in the preceding. When a developer commits a set of changes to a repository, the VCS will either read the log entry to attach to the commit from an external source like a text file or command line parameter, or it will present the developer with a text editor so that she can enter the log entry right then. If the log entry is well structured, it can be used down the road to do things like automatically create a changelog or list of fixed bugs.

1.3.4   Tagging

As I discussed earlier, most version control systems provide a means by which you can tag revisions, so that they can be referred back to at a later date. This frees the developer from reliance on references with poor contextual relation, such as revision numbers or dates. Tags can be placed at development milestones, to allow development in a project to continue, without hurting the ability for someone to later go back and see a snapshot of the project's source at that milestone. For example, if a tag is placed at each project release, it is easy to go back at a later date to search out the cause of a bug that has been discovered, even if the current code of the project has diverged and no longer contains the portion of the project where the bug occurred.

1.3.5   Branching

Tags are useful, but what happens when the code that has been tagged needs to change, thereby diverting from the main development trunk, such as in the preceding bug fix example? It's not sufficient to simply find the cause of a bug that has been discovered in a previous release. In most cases, you will also want to fix that bug and release a patch to your users. Typically, version control systems will support this type of divergence by allowing you to create parallel paths of development for the repository (or a subset of it). These parallel paths are usually referred to as branches.

At any given revision, a branch can be created, with development continuing from that point in two parallel paths. Each branch can be worked on independently, and changes committed to one branch will not affect any other branches of the project. Later, if the developers decide that a change made on one branch would be useful on one or more of the project's other branches, it is usually possible to merge all or part of two branches together.

You can see an example of a repository that has branched in Figure 1.2. In this case, a branch was created after the version 1.0 tag was created at the release of the product on the main branch, which has allowed the version 1.x release of the project to continue making releases (1.1, 1.2, and so on), which the main project branch moves on to develop release 2.0.

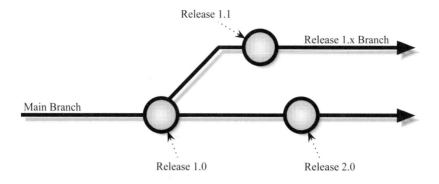

Figure 1.2. A repository with branches and tags.

1.3.6   Locking versus Merging

Up to this point, the discussion has focused mostly on the work of a single developer when using a version control system. In a real development environment, though, a project can easily involve dozens of developers working on the same general area of a system. Good practice dictates that in the best of all worlds, no two developers will ever be modifying exactly the same part of a system at the same time. In reality, however, most of us don't actually live in the best of all worlds, and a multitude of practical reasons can lead to two developers needing to make changes on the same source file at the same time.

When the division of work on a project collides at one spot, there needs to be a way to arbitrate who can modify the offending file or section. There are two primary ways in which version control systems tend to handle these collisions: file locking and merging. Most version control systems will use one of those two methods most of the time, but many use a hybrid system that allows some combination of both methods to be used. Because of the inherit limitations of locking (as discussed shortly), most modern VCSs will support merging. There are many locking only systems, but they are almost universally older and obsolete (with the notable exception of Microsoft's Visual SourceSafe, which is still used by many development shops).

In a file locking system, the developer locks a versioned file when beginning to make changes. While the file is locked, no other developer will be allowed to make any changes. Then, when the developer has finished, the changed file can be committed back into the repository and the file can be unlocked.

The upside to file locking is that it enforces very organized division of work, in order to minimize the number of times where two developers need to modify the same source file or section simultaneously. It can also work better than merging when working with files that are not easily merged automatically, such as graphics, or files in proprietary binary formats. On the other hand, locking can disrupt development if progress is blocked by two developers competing to work on the same file. The problem can be magnified further if one of those developers forgets to unlock the file when finished. In general, locking scales very poorly and is unworkable for broad use by projects involving more than a few people.

The second method for handling collision avoidance/resolution is the use of automatic or semi-automatic file merges. In this model, developers can modify files in their working copies of the repository without regard for what others are doing.[1] Then, once the developers have finished making their changes, they can commit those changes, and the version control system will check to see if there are any collisions caused by two people simultaneously editing a file. In many cases, the system will automatically merge two files together; but if it can't, most systems will provide the developer making the commit with information about the conflicted area, to allow the developer to merge the changes by hand.

The main advantage of a merging system is that it frees developers to work independently of other developers. This is especially advantageous in projects where multiple developers are likely to be working in different areas of the same file simultaneously (since most version control locking is at the file level). It also scales better than locking, but it can cause problems if communication between developers is poor, since frequent collisions requiring hand-merging can lead to delays and wasted/duplicated effort.

Of course, neither locking or merging is a perfect approach to the integration of multiple developers. For instance, file locking doesn't provide any assurances that other sections of the project won't change in a way that is incompatible with the changes made to the locked section, but similarly, file merging only catches conflicts that occur in the exact same location of a given file. In light of these granular deficiencies in the methods used in version control for managing integration, every version control system also relies on the developers themselves to use the tools given to them alongside good practices that will help ensure smooth integration of multiple developers. For instance, in most version control systems, the recommended best practice is to always update your local working copy and test it with the changes from other developers before committing a new revision to the repository.

1.4   Summary

As you have seen, all version control systems provide a means to keep track of the changes made to a collection of files over time; and since software development is usually a collaborative effort, they also provide facilities to merge the efforts of multiple developers. Branching and tagging features of many VCSs allow the paths of development on a project to be marked at critical points, as well as to branch off into different paths, for such cases as fixing bugs on previous releases or allowing a developer to add and test new functionality without breaking the main development trunk.

The benefits of using a version control system are many, and its use is critical for any project of larger than trivial size. Beyond the obvious benefit of code tracking, a good VCS will improve data integrity and record keeping, as well as aid developer productivity and accountability for individual contributions. The VCS also allows projects to distribute

---

1. *Can* and *should* are two different issues completely. Developers should always communicate with their fellow developers to know what they are working on.

work more effectively over a large number of developers, and facilitates many of today's rapid development processes, such as XP and Agile Development.

Now that you have a firm grasp of the general features and benefits of version control, you can turn to Chapter 2, "An Introduction to Subversion," where I show how the Subversion Version Control System implements the basic version control features, and how those features measure up to Subversion's predecessor CVS.

Chapter 2

An Introduction to Subversion

In 1986, Dick Grune introduced the Concurrent Versioning System (CVS) as the first version control system to support development of multiple files concurrently by multiple developers, using the merging paradigm to combine those developers' work together when they committed to the repository. From there, CVS went on to become immensely popular, especially among open source projects, where it is the nearly ubiquitous choice for version control. Despite its popularity, though, CVS has started to show its age, and suffers from many shortcomings that can make it difficult to use. So, in an attempt to overcome these shortcomings, the Subversion project was started in 2000, and in February of 2004 was released as version 1.0. Since that release, Subversion has increased rapidly in popularity, and appears to be poised to succeed at its goal of replacing CVS.

2.1 Why Subversion?

Subversion may be successful, but does that mean it's right for your project? If you're currently using CVS, the answer is almost certainly yes; if you're not using CVS, the answer very well may still be yes. Of course, choosing a version control system for a project is a big decision, and making big decisions based solely on "because that book-author-guy said so" isn't usually a good idea (and could be grounds for firing if the project is your job). So, since you don't want to take my word for it, let's examine why Subversion (which is also known as SVN) may be a good choice for a software development project.

2.1.1 A Software Engineering Tool

Software development is a craft, on par with the finest woodworking or most intricate mechanical clock. Every craft, however, reaches its highest potential when it moves beyond mere craftsmanship, and becomes an engineering discipline. Although it is still in its infancy, the discipline of *software engineering* aims to elevate software development to the level of the other engineering practices. Part of a good engineering process, though, are tools that enable that process, and Subversion is one of those tools.

Subversion is hosted (as an open source project) by `tigris.org`, an online community designed to promote the development of open source tools for software engineering. As the Tigris mission statement says, open source development has contributed much to software development tools and practices, and will almost certainly continue to do so in the future. This gives Subversion a focus that promotes its viability as not just a repository for source code, but a full-blown tool for software engineering. Because Tigris is an active community, dedicated to the success of the projects hosted there, it is likely that Subversion will continue to evolve over time into a powerful tool for software engineering. Tigris is funded by CollabNet (`www.collab.net`), which is responsible for funding Subversion's initial development. In fact, many of the core Subversion developers are employed full time by CollabNet, to work on further Subversion development.

Already, Subversion is a flexible tool, capable of supporting many aspects of organized software engineering. Much of this book, in fact, is dedicated to showing how Subversion can fit into a variety of different development processes.

2.1.2 Open Source Solutions

I grew up in a small town surrounded by farmland, and even though I've never worked on a farm, when you live near them long enough you can't help but learn a few things. One of those things you learn is the importance of diversity. A smart farmer never stakes the entire future of the family farm on a single source. For example, if you grow corn, you grow a variety, to minimize the chance that a disease or insect will come through and kill the whole crop. Genetic diversity in the fields makes the whole stronger and more resilient.

When I first learned about open source software, I quickly realized that it follows the same principle of the farmers who plant a variety of corn in their fields. By allowing a menagerie of software developers to contribute to a project, the project is strengthened, and becomes much more resilient to hardships over time. An open source project is significantly less likely to succumb to the economic equivalent of an insect swarm, which helps to ensure not only the quality of the product that evolves, but also the longevity.

Subversion is licensed under an open source license similar to those used for the Apache Web server and the BSD operating systems. In short, the license states that you are free to do whatever you want with it, as long as you give credit to CollabNet, which currently holds the copyright for Subversion. Unlike the GNU Public License, used for Subversion's predecessor CVS, Subversion does not require you to distribute code for any changes you make—although contributing changes back to the Subversion project helps ensure that they remain compatible with the rest of the system as new versions are released, as well as provides others who may have similar problems to solve the benefit of your brilliance.

So, in addition to it being free of charge, exactly what direct benefit do you as the end user gain from Subversion's open source license? I want to avoid philosophical discussion of whether you have a right to open source software or of the supposed "evilness" of closed source products. There are, however, a number of practical benefits to SVN being an open source project.

By being open, Subversion positions itself to be a standard in version control and has a good chance of succeeding at overthrowing the reigning de facto standard, CVS.

Standards, of course, are generally a good thing to deal with. It means that even if your other tools don't currently support SVN, the odds are that they will in the future; or if they don't, someone will develop a third-party solution to adapt your current tools to Subversion. It also means that more people will know how to deal with Subversion. For open source projects, this increases the number of people who will know how to use Subversion, which will hopefully help increase the number of people willing to get involved in the project and contribute code. Conversely, if your project is internal or closed source, the increased number of people who know how to deal with Subversion will still help, by decreasing the likelihood that developers will have to be explicitly trained in SVN's use by their employers.

The open nature of Subversion also makes it very integrable. The core of Subversion is, in fact, a set of libraries with a well-documented, open application programming interface (API). This API allows developers to write custom clients for Subversion, integrate it into another tool, provide a GUI, or even automate some of the process of interacting with an SVN repository.

2.1.3   Major Features of SVN

What, exactly, can Subversion do? What features make it stand out against other version control systems? What features foster familiarity by being similar to other version control systems? How do these work together to form an excellent version control system? To answer those questions, let's take a look at the highlights of Subversion's feature list, and how many of those features stack up against other version control systems, such as the venerable CVS, Microsoft's Visual SourceSafe, or GNU's Arch.

Basic Operation

The basic interface to Subversion is very similar to CVS. The primary method of interfacing with Subversion is through the command line (although there are some very good GUI front ends available), and by design, SVN has very similar command-line operations to CVS. Commands have not been needlessly renamed, and for the most part, if a user is familiar with how to do something in CVS, doing the same thing in SVN will have similar (if not identical) syntax. In fact, unless there was a compelling reason for changing the syntax, Subversion uses identical command syntax for all of the Subversion features that have a CVS counterpart. Of course, with Subversion's much larger feature-set, Subversion has many commands that don't have a CVS counterpart, but the basics are extremely easy to pick up and the overall command-set is still reasonably small and easy to learn. Even if you aren't coming from a CVS background, the concepts are similar to many other version control systems, and the differences should be easy to learn. This clean, simple approach sets off Subversion from another common open source VCS, Arch, which has a complex command-set and a paradigm vastly different from that of CVS or Subversion.

Like many common version control systems, Subversion uses a client-server paradigm, where a central repository sits on a server and clients check out local working copies where they can modify things as much as they like. When a modification is complete, changes between the repository and the working copy are merged, and the modified version is committed back to the repository.

Repository Flexibility

Subversion allows for great flexibility in layout of repositories, by keeping revision histories for both files and directories across moves, copies, and renames. This may not seem like a big deal if you're not familiar with other version control systems, but copy, move, and rename functionality is a feature sorely lacking in many popular version control systems. Most notably, CVS is notoriously inflexible when trying to modify an existing repository's structure. It does not allow files to be moved, copied, or renamed without splitting the file's history (so that you need to know its old name to see its old history). Worse, CVS doesn't allow directories to be moved around (or even deleted) without editing the repository directly. Similarly, moves, renames, and copies are difficult in Microsoft's Visual SourceSafe, although not quite as bad as CVS. On the other hand, with Subversion, you can move, rename, and copy files and directories as much as you like without any worry that you will lose (or split) your history or corrupt older revisions.

Atomic Commits

Subversion uses transactions whenever it modifies the database. When a commit starts, Subversion marks the current state of the database, then makes its modifications. That way, if a crash (or bang or boom) interrupts the commit, there is no risk that the database will be corrupted. When it is resumed, the database will automatically be restored to its state before the commit began.

This is another feature sorely lacking in many older VCSs, such as CVS or Visual SourceSafe. If a network glitch or software crash causes a commit in either of those systems to fail, the repository can be left in a corrupted, unstable state, which may require the repository to be restored from backup.

Branches and Tags

Most version control systems allow for the revision trees of individual files and directories to be branched and tagged. Subversion, on the other hand, does not explicitly support this. In fact, SVN has no built-in concept of either branches or tags. Instead, it provides *cheap copies*. When a developer uses the `svn copy` command, Subversion does not make a copy of data contained in those files. Instead, it just marks the location of the new file and links it back to the history of the original file, up to the point where the copy is made. From that point on, if changes are applied to the copy, a new path of revision is created for the copy, independent of subsequent revisions applied to the original file.

Using this paradigm, a branch can be created by simply copying the directory (or file) to be branched. Usually, this is done into a directory named `branches`, so that it is always clear to users that they are dealing with a branch of part of the repository's main trunk. There is no enforcement of this in Subversion, though, and in Chapter 9, "Organizing Your Repository," I talk about a variety of different approaches that you can take when deciding where to place branches, to best fit a project's style of development.

Similarly, tags are also created by making a copy, usually in a `tags` directory. Like branches, this makes for a wide latitude of flexibility when dealing with how tags are used. The downside is that there is no built-in enforcement to make sure that tags stay tags, and don't inadvertently become branches when someone makes a change to them. It is possible, though, to enforce tag policies using either Subversion's support for hook scripts,or (if you are using Apache as your server) permissions on the `tags` directory to disallow changes to files in the `tags` directory after they have been created.

Binary Files

Versioning binary files is a more difficult task than versioning text files. With a text file, the file data itself has meaning to a human being, which makes it easy to merge files or examine their differences. With a binary file, though, you need an external program to interpret the file and present it in a manner that has meaning for a human. This makes it difficult for a version control system to automatically perform merges or present diffs, because it has no context for performing merges properly and no way to present the result of a diff in a meaningful manner. Instead, diffs will result in incomprehensible binary data, and merges will likely result in corrupted files that cannot be read by the proper external program. However, versioning of binary files is not hopeless, because they can at least be stored in a versioned manner that allows different versions to be retrieved and compared with external tools. Anyone who has ever used CVS to version binary files, though, knows that it handles them quite poorly. So poorly, in fact, that it doesn't store differences to versioned binary files. Instead, it just stores an entire new copy of the file whenever a binary file is committed. Subversion improves on this by using a binary difference function for all files, which allows binary files to be versioned the same as text files.

Subversion still doesn't have any direct support for automatically merging binary files (which would be nearly impossible anyway, unless SVN could understand the binary files). It does, however, have much better support for resolution of merges that can't be handled automatically. When a merge conflict occurs, Subversion provides complete copies of both versions of the file, which allows the user to easily use an external editor to manually merge the conflicted file.

Symbolic Links

Release 1.1 of Subversion adds the capability to version symbolic links from UNIX systems —like GNU Arch and unlike CVS. If a user is working on a UNIX-like system, he can add symbolic links to the repository, just as he would any other file, and the repository will retain the link information for any other UNIX user who checks out a working copy of the repository. (Windows users will not get symbolic links, because Windows does not support UNIX-style symbolic links.)

Conflict Resolution

Subversion and CVS both use a paradigm of making modifications and then merging them with the modifications others have made, instead of the file locking paradigm used by many other VCSs like Visual SourceSafe. Resolving conflicts in merges when using CVS can be a bit messy, though. When CVS fails to automatically merge changes between the working copy and the server, it replaces the conflicted file in the working copy with a version of the file containing diffs of the two different versions. If the conflict was large, the resulting diff can waste hours while the developer tries to sort through the changes; and because the local changes are not backed up, there is no way to revert to the pre-conflict state of the working copy without sorting through the diff. Subversion, of course, can't prevent conflicts from happening anymore than CVS can, but it does handle them better when they do happen. If a conflict occurs, SVN replaces the offending file with one containing diffs, just like CVS; however, it also adds temporary versions of the file with the local version, the server version, and the local version prior to any changes. These extra files make resolving conflicts significantly less painful, and once the conflict has been settled, a call to svn resolved removes the extra files.

Storage

Subversion has a flexible repository backend that allows different types of repository storage systems to be plugged in, transparently to the client. Originally, the only actual repository storage system that was available was the Berkeley DB database system. As of release 1.1 of Subversion, though, a filesystem-based backend (FSFS) is also available as part of the core Subversion system. Instead of storing the entire repository database in a single monolithic database, like the Berkeley DB backend does, the Subversion FSFS storage uses individual files for each revision in the repository. So, when you commit revision 3529, there will be a file named 3529 created, which holds all of the changes for that revision, regardless of how many versioned files were changed in that revision.

Network Protocols

Subversion provides two servers for communicating with the repository via different protocols. The first server (known as svnserve) uses an SVN-specific network protocol that requires a dedicated server and open port, which allows a Subversion server to be set up quickly and easily. svnserve also supports Inetd access, or tunneled-SSH style access. The other server is a module for the Apache Web server, and is based on the Web-based Distributed Authoring and Versioning (WebDAV) protocol, with a few extensions for version control-specific operations. By using this standard protocol, served over HTTP via Apache, there is no need to open a special port on the server. Because WebDAV support is built into a variety of file managers on different operating systems, it is also possible to get limited access to interact with a repository directly through the Gnome Nautilus file manager on Linux, the Microsoft Windows Explorer, or any other WebDAV client. If read-only access to the repository head is all that is required, you can even access the repository through a Web browser with no special clients or setup required.

Data Transfer

Subversion reduces much of the overhead that is associated with communications between the client and server, through a couple of methods not used by many older VCSs, such as CVS. For starters, it only transfers file differences both from client to server and from server to client, whenever possible—unlike CVS, which only transfers differences when going from server to client. Subversion also caches a lot more information locally, which allows it to avoid network communications altogether in many instances. It even stores a full copy of the working directory as of the last update, to allow the user to make comparisons with local changes without contacting the server.

Properties

One of Subversion's powerful, unique features is its support for file and directory metadata in the form of properties that allow the user to store arbitrary keyword:value data pairs that can be associated with a particular file or directory. This makes it easy to store whatever file metadata makes sense in your development process. Additionally, Subversion defines several special properties that it can use internally to provide some extra functionality, like keyword expansion or end-of-line interpretation.

Hook Scripts

Subversion supports a broad array of hook scripts that are run in response to a variety of SVN actions, such as before or after a commit or property change. These scripts are given access to relevant information about the action that is taking place, as well as the capability to examine the repository. Hook scripts can be a powerful tool for automating tasks or enforcing policies. Although they are supported in one form or another by most version control systems, the Subversion support for hook scripts is much more flexible than that found in many others. CVS, for instance, provides commit scripts with little information about the commit being made, such as the target branch for the commit.

Full-featured API

Subversion features a very complete API, which developers can use to easily and elegantly create new client interfaces, to create new Subversion servers, or to integrate Subversion into other development tools. In fact, the standard Subversion client tools, as well as the SVN servers, use these same APIs to communicate with each other, the Subversion repository, and a local working copy. Additionally, the interfaces are available with language bindings for a number of different programming languages (such as C, C++, Java, Perl, and Python), which allows interfacing programs to be written in whatever language best suits the problem at hand (and the developer's expertise).

2.2 Limitations of Subversion

Subversion is a powerful version control system, but it does have its limitations and is missing some features found in other popular version control systems. You can compensate for some of these limitations with external tools that can work with Subversion, and implementations of some of the other shortcomings are planned for future versions of SVN. It is also possible to work around some of SVN's limitations with clever uses of hooks and properties. In fact, workarounds for many of Subversion's limitations are discussed throughout this book.

The following features are some that are either missing from Subversion, or severely limited in their implementation.

Locking

Subversion currently has no support for file locking,[1] to prevent more than one person from working on a particular file at a given point in time. In most cases, locking isn't the desired behavior anyway, so this is not a major missing feature. It can become a problem, though, when dealing with binary files that are not easily merged. Locking can be partially implemented through properties and hooks, but the result is somewhat fragile. According to the Subversion developers, however, locking is on the list of features to be implemented in the next few releases of the system.

Distributed Repository

Some version control systems (such as the open source Arch system) have support for distributed repositories, which can be extremely important for some larger projects, especially open source projects. Subversion does not currently have any support for distributed repositories, but there is a secondary project, called SVK, that does provide a distributed wrapper for a Subversion repository. There are also some ways to do hot backups of a repository to provide some of the redundancy afforded a distributed system, as is discussed in Chapter 10, "Administrating the Repository."

Visualization Tools

In terms of ease of use and comprehensibility, Subversion's copy paradigm is far above the branching and tagging functionality built into CVS. In its current implementation, though, the copy paradigm makes tracking the path a file takes, as it branches and merges over time, difficult at best. In fact, Subversion puts the task of tracking file history trees on the shoulders of the user. In order to maintain information that should be available automatically, the Subversion user must manually track using information entered into the logs at commit time.

For example, look at the complex repository tree in Figure 2.1. The svn log command would make it easy for me to see all of the changes that were made to the third revision on the main trunk of the repository, but if I want to see that two of the changes occurred on the main trunk and two occurred on branch 2, it would be impossible, unless I had the foresight to keep careful notes in the log entries about which branch a change occurred on.

---

1.   Locking support is planned for version 1.2 of Subversion, however.

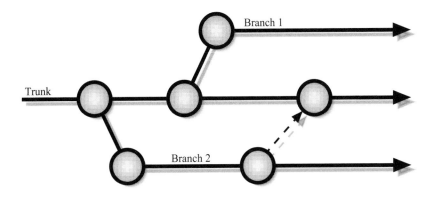

Figure 2.1. Subversion fails to provide the capability to visualize a complex branching tree like this.

Merging History

Merging of changes in Subversion works much the same as in CVS. A user makes changes, and then prior to committing those changes, uses Subversion to merge changes committed by any other developers. Subversion, like CVS, uses a bit of logic to merge together trivial changes and those that don't overlap, while punting anything more complicated to the developer. In this sense, it is equally as good as CVS, which in most cases is good enough. In fact, by giving the developer more information when it does punt on a merge, SVN is better than CVS.

Where Subversion falls short is in another case where merging occurs: merging between branches. When Subversion merges between two branches, it merges all of the differences between the first location and the second location into a third location in the working copy of the repository. This means that if a developer wants to merge changes made on a branch back into the main trunk (or to another branch), the developer needs to specify the differences in revisions on the branch, where the changes to be merged occurred. Unfortunately, this means that the user must keep the accounting information describing when the branch was created (and when it was last merged) in order to ensure that the correct data is merged. Failure to keep track can result in undesired behavior. For instance, you can end up "undoing" a change, if you accidentally remerge a section of a file that has been removed since the first merge. Duplicate merging can also result in spurious conflicts if remerged sections have been modified instead of removed.

2.3   Summary

Meant to be a replacement for the aging CVS, Subversion is a major step forward for open source version control systems. In general, Subversion improves upon the many annoyances of CVS, and does things in a more flexible and powerful way. Some of Subversion's improved features include its handling of branches and tags via a file copy paradigm, its improved merge conflict resolution, its pluggable repository database architecture, and its use of HTTP/WebDAV for network communications. Additionally, Subversion provides new features not found in CVS, such as properties that can be attached to versioned files, and powerful hook scripts that can be run in response to a variety of actions.

Although Subversion does have its limits, such as a lack of locking, poor merge history storage, and no distributed repository, they are well outpaced by Subversion's strengths in most project situations, and are almost universally issues that are also present to one degree or another in CVS. Some of Subversion's shortcomings are handled better by other open source version control systems, such as Arch, but feature-for-feature Subversion is on par with any other open source system available. Many of the features missing in SVN can also be gained through the use of external tools that are available (or currently in development).

In the next chapter, I will go into detail about installation and setup of Subversion on a variety of operating systems.

Chapter 3

Installing Subversion

The purpose of this chapter is to show you how to install and set up Subversion. Subversion runs on a variety of operating systems and distributions, and to describe all of the idiosyncrasies of installing on all of those systems would take a book of its own. Instead, I will describe how to install Subversion on a couple of typical systems, with some advice on things to look out for when doing your own install. When you are done with this chapter, you should have enough of an understanding of the installation process to be able to perform your own install. If you already have Subversion up and running, you can skip ahead to Chapter 4, "Basic Subversion Usage."

3.1   Installing on Linux

As with many open source projects, the primary platform of installation for Subversion is Linux. Although Subversion is far from a second-class citizen on other operating systems, such as Microsoft Windows or Apple's Mac OS X, Linux is where it feels most at home. Of course, Linux is not a single entity. There are, in fact, a wide variety of different distributions, each with its own slightly different filesystem layouts and package management systems for installation of software. As I said in the chapter introduction, describing all of these different distributions is well beyond the scope of this book. Instead, in this section I will show you how to compile and install Subversion from source, which should work for most Linux distributions. If you would rather install binaries with your distribution's package management system, you will find that there are binary packages available for most of the major distributions on the downloads page for Subversion.

3.1.1   Subversion's Prerequisites

In order to make compiling a Subversion client easy, Subversion includes most of the dependencies it needs for the client in the Subversion source distribution. On the other hand, if you want to compile a server, there are a number of different prerequisites that you need to install first. Which prerequisites you use depends on exactly which features of Subversion you need. If you read on, I describe each of the packages that you may need to install, as well as the functionality they provide and where you might find them.

Apache Portable Runtime Libraries

The Apache Portable Runtime (APR) libraries are a set of libraries that provide a cross-platform abstraction layer for developing software that will work the same on a variety of different operating systems. Subversion is built on top of APR, and makes heavy use of the library, which helps ensure that SVN runs on the variety of platforms it supports. APR is therefore a core library for SVN, and is required when building the system.

The APR libraries are available for download from a variety of mirrors, which can be reached from the Apache project's Web site, at `apr.apache.org`. Downloading the APR libraries is not usually necessary though, because the APR source necessary for compiling Subversion is included in the Subversion source distribution. Most compiled binary distributions of Subversion also include the necessary APR libraries, so installing them separately will likely be unnecessary.

Apache Web Server

Subversion uses the Apache Web server as one of the two servers it supports for allowing remote access to the repository. If you want support for using the Subversion extensions to WebDAV for accessing the repository, you will need Apache. If you would rather use the Subversion custom-protocol–based svnserve, or only want to use Subversion on the local machine, you do not need to compile Subversion with support for Apache.

Most Linux distributions include Apache as a part of their core packages, and your system likely already has it installed. This may not be what you need though. Subversion requires version 2.0 or later of Apache, which is not yet in predominant use, and is often not installed. If you cannot upgrade your whole system to use Apache 2, it is possible to install Apache 2 alongside an existing version of Apache 1. I will show you how to set up such a system in Section 3.4, "Configuring to Use Apache."

If you want to download the sources for Apache to compile them yourself, they can be obtained from mirrors linked from the Apache Web site, just like APR. You can download Apache from its site at `httpd.apache.org`. The Apache Web site also provides compiled binary versions of Apache for most platforms if you need to install Apache but don't want to compile it yourself. Unlike APR, Apache is *not* included with the Subversion source and must be installed separately.

Berkeley DB

The Berkeley DB (BDB) database is an embedded database, developed as an open source project by Sleepycat Software. It is a database system designed to be integrated into other programs, and is used by Subversion for its database repository backend. Berkeley DB is only required if you are going to use the Subversion database repository. If you are instead using the new filesystem-based repository introduced in version 1.1 of Subversion, you can compile without support for Berkeley DB.

Most binary distributions of Subversion will include the necessary BDB support, so you shouldn't have to acquire BDB separately. If you are compiling Subversion from scratch, or are using an installation package that doesn't include BDB, you will need to install BDB yourself in order to have support for BDB-based repositories (most Linux distributions will already have it installed, so you might want to check before attempting to install it yourself). You can download BDB from Sleepycat's Web site, at `www.sleepycat.com`.

Neon

Subversion uses the Neon library in its client for communications with a WebDAV server. In most cases, you will not have to download this library separately, because it is included in the Subversion source distribution. If you are installing binary packages, however, you may need to install this as one of the prerequisites. The binary packages you will need, however, are in most cases available from the same place as the Subversion package that you are installing.

3.1.2 Downloading the Source

The Subversion source code can be downloaded from the Subversion project's Web site, at `subversion.tigris.org/project_packages.html`, which is where you will also find a variety of already compiled binary packages for various operating systems and distributions. Source versions are available in a variety of archive formats (tar gzip, tar bzip2, and zip).

If you're compiling on a UNIX-based system, you'll probably want to download either the bzip2 archive for the latest version of SVN (`.tar.bz2` extension) or the gzip archive (`.tar.gz`). After you have the source archive for Subversion downloaded, it's time to get things unpacked, so that you can start compiling. To perform the unpacking, you will want to send the decompressed file to the `tar` command for unpacking. The easiest way to perform both the decompression and unpacking is to decompress with either the `gzip` or `bzip2` command (depending on the compressed version you downloaded), and use the `-dc` options to tell the command to decompress the file and then send the decompressed file to standard output. A pipe can then be used to send the decompressed file directly to tar, which you'll want to run with the `xvf` options to tell it to extract the archive from a file, verbosely, and a hyphen (-) to tell it to take the archive from standard input. So, for example, if you had downloaded the `bzip2` compressed version 1.1.0 of Subversion, the command to unpack it would be

```
$ bzip2 -dc subversion-1.1.0.tar.bz2 | tar xvf -
```

The `tar` command will unpack everything into a directory named (in the case of the preceding version) `subversion-1.1.0`.

3.1.3 Compiling and Installing

For the most part, compiling Subversion is straightforward. It auto-detects the presence of the various prerequisites that are required for compilation of the server, and decides whether it can build the server. If none of the prerequisites are installed, it will just compile the Subversion client (which doesn't have any prerequisites beyond what is included with the source). To perform a basic compilation, just cd into the Subversion directory that you unpacked in the previous section and run the following commands.

```
$ ./configure
$ make
$ su
Password:
# make install
```

In most cases, this compiles everything that you need, and installs everything in /usr/local/. Notice that the last command (make install) requires you to super-user to the root user, in order to have the proper permissions to perform a systemwide install of Subversion.

Configuration Options

Sometimes the default compile and install is not actually what you want. For instance, you may not want to compile the server with all of the possible features, even if the prerequisites are installed; or you may want to install to somewhere other than /usr/local/. In these instances, the Subversion configure script provides several options that you can set when it is run. I explain the ones you are most likely to run into in the following. If you would like to see the complete list, you can run ./configure -help. To configure the Subversion compilation with one of these options, you should run the configure script with the desired option passed as a command-line parameter.

--prefix=PREFIX

The prefix option specifies where Subversion should be installed. By default, this is in /usr/local/. If you would rather install Subversion somewhere else, pass configure the --prefix option, with PREFIX replaced by the path where you would like Subversion to be installed. For example, if you are installing SVN on a system where you don't have root privileges, you can run ./configure -prefix=$HOME/subversion to have Subversion installed in a directory named subversion in your home directory.

--with-apache=PATH
--without-apache

These options tell the build scripts whether they should compile the Subversion server with support for Apache and WebDAV. The default behavior is for Apache to be included, but if for some reason you don't want Apache support to be compiled, passing --without-apache to configure will disable it. Additionally, if Apache is installed in a nonstandard place on your system, you may have to tell configure where to find it. You can do that by passing the --with-apache option, with PATH replaced by the path to where Apache is installed.

```
--with-berkeley-db=PATH
--without-berkeley-db
```

These options tell the build scripts whether they should compile the Subversion server with support for the Berkeley DB. The default behavior is for BDB to be included, but if you plan on using the filesystem-based repository storage, `--without-berkeley-db` will disable BDB (of course, you can still use the filesystem repository even if BDB support is compiled). Also, if Berkeley DB is installed in a nonstandard place on your system, you may have to tell `configure` where to find it. You can do that by passing the `--with-berkeley-db` option, with `PATH` replaced by the path to where BDB is installed.

```
--disable-mod-activation
```

By default, Subversion modifies your Apache `httpd.conf` file to enable the Subversion WebDAV module, `mod_dav_svn`, when you run `make install`. If you don't want it to make this modification, you can pass `--disable-mod-activation` to the configure script.

3.2 Installing on Mac OS X

Like Linux, Apple's Mac OS X is a UNIX-like operating system. It was originally based on the open source FreeBSD operating system, which was itself derived from the University of California, Berkeley-developed BSD UNIX. On top of the UNIX underpinnings, Apple has built its own excellent graphical user interface. Regardless of whether you prefer to deal with OS X using the GUI or from under the hood at the command line, you have options for installing Subversion that should meet your needs.

3.2.1 Installing OS X Binaries

Installing the Subversion client on OS X is trivial. The Subversion Web site provides a link to prepackaged binaries of Subversion. To install, all you need to do is download the Subversion disk image (`.dmg`), mount it, and then launch the installer package (`.pkg` extension). The installer will take you through a typical OS X install process that will set up everything to allow you to run Subversion from the command line, using `Terminal.app` or another terminal emulator.

3.2.2 Compiling Subversion on OS X

Compiling Subversion by hand on OS X should be as simple as compilation on Linux, and should follow the same process. Before installing, though, you may need to install the Apple Developer Tools, which are available for free from Apple's developer site (`developer.apple.com`). Installing the developer tools will install the GCC compiler, as well as a number of other development utilities, such as GNU Make.

3.2.3   Using Fink

An alternate way to install Subversion for OS X is through the Fink package management system. Fink provides a reasonably easy way for many open source packages (mostly from the UNIX world) to be installed. If you don't have Fink installed already, you can get it from `fink.sourceforge.net`. When Fink is installed, you can install Subversion from the command line.

To install the SVN client from the command line, open Terminal.app, and run `sudo fink install svn-client`. Additionally, you can install several other packages if you would like to get different versions of the Subversion server. Installing the `svn` package, for instance, will get you the standalone `svnserve` Subversion server, whereas the package `libapache2-mod-svn` will get you everything you need to serve the repository over WebDAV, via Apache. If you would like the Subversion documentation, you can install the `svn-doc` package.

3.3   Installing on Windows

Installing Subversion on Windows is easy to do. If you follow the links for Win32 on the SVN download page, `subversion.tigris.org/project_packages.html`, you will find a Windows installer program, which should be named something like `svn-1.1.0-setup.exe`. You can download the setup program and run it to install Subversion. It will step you through everything you need to do to install SVN and get the basic application set up (see Figure 3.1).

If you plan to set up your Windows machine to serve a Subversion repository through Apache, I suggest that you run the Subversion installer *after* installing Apache. If you do so,

Figure 3.1. The SVN setup program makes installation on Windows easy.

the Subversion installer will give you the option of allowing it to automatically configure Apache to load the appropriate modules for Subversion and WebDAV. You can also re-run the Subversion installer at a later date, if you install Apache and want to configure it for Subversion.

When installing Subversion on a Windows 2000 or XP machine, you should be able to install Subversion just by running the installer program. On the other hand, if you are installing on Windows 95, 98, or Millenium Edition, you may need to modify your `Autoexec.bat` file to properly configure the system environment for Subversion. For example, if you installed in `C:\Program Files\Subversion` (the default location), you should set up your `Autoexec.bat` file as follows.

1. Make sure that the `%PATH%` environment variable points to the directory that contains the Subversion binaries, like this:

   `SET PATH=C:\WINDOWS;C:\;C:\PROGRA~1\SUBVER~1\BIN`

2. Set the `APR_ICONV_PATH` environment variable.

   `SET APR_ICONV_PATH="C:\Program Files\Subversion\iconv"`

3. Reboot your computer.

Subversion can also be compiled from source on Windows with Visual Studio, using the Windows-specific source, available as a zip compressed download (from the same place as the `gzip` and `bzip2` source downloads). The specific instructions for compiling under Windows, though, are beyond the scope of this book. If you are interested in compiling the Windows version, the `INSTALL` file included with the Subversion source contains detailed step-by-step information about the process.

3.4 Configuring SVN to Use Apache

If you plan to use the Subversion WebDAV extensions for remote access to your repository, you have to set up Apache to load the SVN WebDAV module and tell it where to find your repository. Also, make sure that Apache has read/write access to any repositories that you want it to serve.

3.4.1 Loading the Modules

The first step is to make sure that Apache is set up to load the `mod_dav` and `mod_dav_svn` modules (`mod_dav` is not compiled in Apache by default so you may have to compile it yourself; most distributions of Apache do have it compiled already though). Subversion's `make install` command should have done this for you, but it's a good idea to take a quick look to make sure everything seems correct. The `LoadModule` directive for the SVN DAV module should be in your `httpd.conf` file. The location of the `httpd.conf` file is very system specific, and depends a lot on how Apache was installed on your particular system. In general, though, you will probably find it either in `/usr/local/apache2/conf` or somewhere under the `/etc` directory on most UNIX-based systems. If you are installing under Windows, the `httpd.conf` file should be in the directory where Apache is installed (which is probably `C:\Program Files\Apache Group\Apache2\conf`). If you have both Apache 1 and Apache 2 installed on your system, make sure that the `httpd.conf` file you are checking is the configuration file for Apache 2.

After you have found the `httpd.conf` file, you should check it for the `LoadModule` directives for `mod_dav_svn` and `mod_dav`, which should look something like this:

```
LoadModule    dav_module          modules/mod_dav.so
LoadModule    dav_svn_module      modules/mod_dav_svn.so
```

There may be other `LoadModule` directives between `mod_dav` and `mod_dav_svn`, but it is important to make sure that `mod_dav` is loaded before `mod_dav_svn`. On some systems, `mod_dav` may have been statically compiled into Apache, in which case there is no need to have a `LoadModule` directive for it.

3.4.2   Setting Up Access

In order to allow people to access your repository through Apache, you need to set up a `Location` directive to tell Apache where to find the repository, as well as what URL path to use. The `Location` directive will also go in your `httpd.conf` file, and should be added to the end of the file, to ensure that everything has been loaded properly before it is processed.

A basic `Location` directive for your repository will look something like this:

```
<Location /repos>
    DAV svn
    SVNPath /srv/subversion/repos
    AuthType Basic
    AuthName "Subversion"
    AuthUserFile /srv/subversion/svn_passwd
    Require valid-user
</Location>
```

Let's look at what each line in the preceding directive means.

The first line opens the `Location` directive. The path given after `Location` tells Apache what the URL path to the repository should be. For example, in the preceding sample directive, if your Web site were at www.example.com, the URL for the repository would be `http://www.example.com/repos`. The `Location` directive is then closed by the `</Location>` tag on the last line.

The second line of the directive tells Apache that the location you are setting up points to a WebDAV share, which should use the SVN extensions. That is followed by the third line, which tells Apache where to find the Subversion repository, which should give an absolute path to the directory that was created when `svnadmin create` made your repository.

The next four lines set up the security policies for the repository. `AuthType Basic` informs Apache that you want simple password protection, and `AuthName` is the name that should be used when requesting the password. The `AuthUserFile` gives the file that contains the valid users and their passwords. Finally, `Require valid-user` specifies that a valid authorization should be required for all operations on the repository. For a more detailed discussion on securing your WebDAV share, see Chapter 10, "Administrating the Repository."

Setting a Parent Path for Multiple Repositories

If you want to set up your `httpd.conf` file for multiple repositories, you can always add multiple `Location` directives to individually configure each repository; however, if you have a lot of repositories, that can be a major pain—especially if repositories are frequently added or removed. To solve that problem, Subversion allows you to set up a single `Location` that points to a parent directory that contains one or more repositories, using the `SVNParentPath` directive. Apache will automatically pick up each repository in the parent directory and allow clients access.

As an example, say we have two repositories named `repos_uno` and `repos_dos`. If we place both of those repositories in the directory `/srv/svnrepositories`, the `Location` can be set up as follows.

```
<Location /repos>
    DAV svn
    SVNParentPath /srv/svnrepositories
    AuthType Basic
    AuthName "Subversion"
    AuthUserFile /srv/svnrepositories/svn_passwd
    Require valid-user
</Location>
```

The two repositories would then be accessible through the URLs

`http://svn.example.com/srv/svnrepositories/repos_uno`

and

`http://svn.example.com/srv/svnrepositories/repos_dos`

respectively.

3.4.3   Using Apache 2 and Apache 1 Together

Subversion requires version 2.0 or later of the Apache Web server in order to allow WebDAV repository access. Version 2 of Apache, however, was a major overhaul of the server, and not all of the extensions supported by Apache 1 are supported under Apache 2. This means that you may find that your server needs to support both versions of Apache for different parts of your Web site. Fortunately, Apache supports running two versions side by side, and setting Apache 1 up to point certain URLs (like the path to your repository) to a running instance of Apache 2 is relatively easy.

The first thing you need to do is to set Apache 2 up to run on a different port than the default port 80 that HTTP runs on by default. A good choice here is to use port 8080. To change Apache 2's port, you need to edit your `httpd.conf` file and look for a line that says `Listen 80`, which you will need to change to `Listen 8080`. If there is no `Listen` directive in your `httpd.conf` file, go ahead and add one. That's it. You can now run both versions of Apache at the same time, and both will be accessible. Apache 1 will still be accessible as normal, and Subversion can be accessed on Apache 2 by entering the port number in the URL (e.g. `http://www.example.com:8080/repos`).

3.5   Configuring SVN to Use svnserve

If, for whatever reason, Apache is not a practical solution for allowing remote access to a Subversion repository, there is also a standalone server, which you can use in place of Apache. This Subversion server, `svnserve`, allows a client to access the repository via a custom Subversion protocol, instead of the extended WebDAV protocol that the client uses when talking to the Apache server. The server can run by itself as a persistent process that listens on a dedicated port, or as an on-demand process that is either started over a tunneled SSH/RSH session or by an inetd server.

The `svnserve` server is contacted from the Subversion client using a URL that begins with `svn://` or `svn+ssh://`, instead of the `http://` prefix used for WebDAV. Like WebDAV, the body of the URL will then consist of the server being contacted, followed by the path to the repository. If the `svnserve` process was invoked without a repository root specified, the path that the client gives must be an absolute pathname. For example, if the repository is located in `/srv/svn/repos`, you would need to use the URL `svn://example.com/srv/svn/repos`.

To increase both security and ease of use, you can give a repository root when invoking `svnserve` using the argument `--root PATH`. If a root is given, repository URL paths will be relative to that root, and unable to access anything outside of that directory. So, `--root /srv/svn` would make the preceding URL `svn://example.com/repos`.

3.5.1   Running as a Daemon

The easiest way to run `svnserve` is as a standalone daemon process, which runs in the background and listens on a port for requests from Subversion clients. You can run the server this way from the command line, by running the following.

```
$ svnserve --daemon --root=/srv/subversion/
```

The `--daemon` parameter tells `svnserve` that it should disconnect from the shell and go into the background after it starts, and the `--root` parameter, of course, gives it a root for repository URLs. In order for the server to access your repository, you need to make sure `svnserve` runs as a user who has filesystem read/write permission for your repository.

By default, svnserve listens on port 3690, and responds to requests directed at all host-names and IP addresses bound to the machine the server is running on. If you would rather have svnserve listen on a different port, you can give it a port with --listen-port=PORT, where PORT is the port to listen on. Additionally, if you want the server to bind to a particular hostname, you can give it the hostname with --listen-host=HOSTNAME.

Instead of explicitly invoking the svnserve daemon process from the command line every time you want to start it, you can also set up the server to be started as a service when your machine boots, or enters certain runlevels. Every OS and distribution handles startup services a little differently, so the specifics of setting up such a service is beyond the scope of this book, but documentation on how to set up such a service is usually readily available. If you installed a binary package, using your distribution's package management system, you may find that the hard work of setting up a service to start svnserve has already been done, and all you need is to configure it to be started.

3.5.2 Running with `inetd`

An alternate method for running svnserve is to use a UNIX inetd server to start svnserve on demand, as it receives requests from a client. In order to allow you to run svnserve this way, it has a special mode for invocation from inetd, which is specified with the command-line parameter, --inetd. When it is started this way, svnserve handles all of its input and output through stdin and stdout, which is how inetd expects to talk to services. As with running svnserve in daemon mode, you need to make sure that svnserve is run by a user who has filesystem read/write permission for any repositories the server will access.

Setting up svnserve to use inetd requires you to configure the service to react in response to an SVN request on the Subversion port (which is 3690, by default). Start by telling inetd what to do, which involves putting an entry in the inetd configuration file(s), in /etc. The exact configuration file to edit will depend somewhat on your particular inetd server and operating system distribution, but most systems use one of two methods.

Modern distributions are moving toward using the much more secure inetd implementation, xinetd. If your system uses it, you will need to add a file to /etc/xinetd/, named svn. In this file, you will need to add something like the following lines.

```
service svn
{
    socket_type = stream
    protocol    = tcp
    user        = svnuser
    wait        = no
    server      = /usr/bin/svnserve
    server_args = --inetd --root=/srv/svn
}
```

This tells xinetd that it should expect a stream of data, over TCP, and should then launch the svnserve program, with the server_args arguments, and should run it as `svnuser` (which needs to have read/write access to the repository).

Then, for `xinetd` to know when to invoke the service, you need to add the line

```
svn     3690/tcp
```

to your `/etc/services` file.

If you have a more traditional `inetd` server installed, the setup process is similar; instead of adding `/etc/xinetd/svn`, you add the following line to `/etc/inetd.conf`:

```
svn stream tcp nowait svnuser /usr/bin/svnserve svnserve --inetd --root ¬
  =/srv/svn
```

The `/etc/services` file should be set up the same.

3.5.3 Tunneling over SSH

You can also use `svnserve` by tunneling over SSH. To allow this, you need to make sure that every user accessing the repository has an account on the server that allows him to connect via SSH. You will also need to make sure that he has permission to modify the Subversion repository on the server's filesystem; `svnserve` will be invoked locally on the server with the `--tunnel` option when the user connects. Then, all he needs to do is feed a URL with an `svn+ssh://` schema to his SVN client and Subversion will handle the rest, like in the following checkout:

```
$ svn checkout svn+ssh://svn.example.com/repos
```

3.6 Summary

You should now have a clear idea of how to go about installing Subversion on your system. The number of potential system configurations on which Subversion can actually be installed is way beyond the capability of this book, but this chapter covered most of the basics, which should serve as a starting point if your particular system is in some way different. The chapter covered basic compiling and installing of Subversion on a typical Linux system, as well as installation on Microsoft Windows and Apple's Macintosh OS X. The last couple of sections in the chapter covered setting up a server for remote access to an SVN repository through WebDav, via Apache, and the standalone `svnserve` server.

In the next chapter, I will introduce the actual mechanics of a Subversion system, by walking through usage of the system, from creation of your first repository to operation of the basic client tools.

Chapter 4

Basic Subversion Usage

In this chapter, I will walk you through the basic use of Subversion, from creating a new repository, all the way through to more complex features such as creating and merging a branch.

If you are like me, you learn best by actually sitting down at a computer and getting your feet wet. To allow you to do that, all of the examples in this chapter build on each other, one right after the other, starting with a simple Hello World project. All of the examples in this chapter assume that you are in a UNIX-like environment, such as Linux or Mac OS X. For the most part, they will all work if you are running in a Windows environment, with a few minor changes, such as turning forward slashes (/) in path names into backslashes (\).

We'll start the project with two files, which make up our example project. The first file is the source for our Hello World program, `hello.c`:

```
#include <stdio.h>

int main(int argc, char** argv)
{
    printf("Hello World!!\n");

    return 0;
}
```

The second file is a makefile, which could be used with the `make` program to compile our fabulous application. The file is named, appropriately, `Makefile`:

```
all: hello.c
    gcc hello.c -o hello
```

4.1 Creating the Repository

Subversion stores files in a repository database (which is Berkeley DB by default, but version 1.1 also supports FSFS). So, the first thing to do is create a new repository where we can store Hello World. This is done using the `svnadmin` program, which is used for most server-side administrative tasks when using Subversion. The repository is created with the svnadmin `create` command. First, though, you will want to create a directory in your home directory, where you can store the repository (you'll see later why creating it directly in your home directory isn't a good idea). If you were creating a repository to use on a server, for production use, you would probably want to place it somewhere other than your home directory, such as `/srv/` or `/var/`.

In the following example, `bill` should be replaced with your username on the machine where you are creating the repository. Similarly, in all future examples where you see my username, `bill`, you should replace it with your own username.

```
$ svnadmin create --fs-type fsfs /home/bill/my_repository
```

This creates an empty repository named `my_repository` in your home directory, using the filesystem-based FSFS repository backend. By choosing FSFS instead of the default Berkeley DB backend, you don't need to worry about repository wedging, which can happen if Berkeley DB is interrupted. Although wedging is not fatal to repositories, it will leave your repository in a temporarily inaccessible state, which requires the Berkeley DB recovery process to be run in order to clear the wedge.

In most situations, you will want to create a repository on a server, and access it through HTTP/HTTPS, or the Subversion server `svnserve`. For simplicity's sake, though, we'll take advantage of Subversion's capability to communicate directly with a repository on the local machine, using a local directory path, for all of the examples in this chapter.

After you've run the create command, you can look in your home directory, and you will see that Subversion has created a directory named `my_repository`. This contains the repository database. In general, you won't directly edit any files in this directory. Instead, you will interact with it through Subversion's `svn` command. If you look inside this directory, you can see that there are a bunch of files and directories, but there is little reason for you to worry about what they are for at this point. In Chapter 11, "The Joy of Automation," you will learn how you can edit some of the files in your repository to customize Subversion's behavior.

```
$ ls /home/bill/my_repository/
README.txt  conf/  dav/  db/  format  hooks/  locks/
```

4.2   Getting Files into the Repository

Now that you have created the empty repository, it's time to get the project files into it. To do this, you need to put the files into a basic directory structure for the repository, and then import the entire structure. It would be possible to make that directory structure as simple as a single directory named `hello_world`, with `hello.c` and `Makefile` inside. In practice, though, this isn't a very good directory structure to use.

If you recall from the previous chapter, Subversion does not have any built-in support for branches or tags, but instead just uses copies. This proves to be a flexible way to handle branches and tags, but if they're just copies, there is no set means for identifying what files are branches and what files are on the main source trunk. The recommended way to get around this missing information is to create three directories in your repository, one named branches, another named tags, and a third named trunk. Then, by convention, you can put all branched versions of the project into the branches directory and all tags into the tags directory. The trunk directory will be used to store the main development line of the project.

With large, complex repositories, there are a number of different ways you can set up the directories for the trunk, branches, and tags, which can accommodate multiple projects in one repository, or facilitate different development processes. Because our test project is simple though, we'll keep the repository simple and place everything at the top level of the repository. So, to get everything set up, you first need to create an overall directory for the repository, called repos. Then, set up trunk, branches, and tags directories under that, and move the original source files for the project into the trunk directory.

```
$ mkdir repos
$ mkdir repos/trunk
$ mkdir repos/branches
$ mkdir repos/tags
$ ls repos
branches  tags  trunk
$ mv hello.c repos/trunk/
$ mv Makefile repos/trunk/
$ ls repos/trunk/
Makefile  hello.c
```

After the directories are created and filled, the only thing left to do is import the directory into our repository. This is done using the import command in the svn program.

```
$ svn import --message "Initial import" repos file:///home/bill/ ¬
  repositories/my_repository
Adding         repos/trunk
Adding         repos/trunk/hello.c
Adding         repos/branches
Adding         repos/tags

Committed revision 1.
```

The --message "Initial import" option in the preceding example is used to tell Subversion what to use as a log message for the import. If you omit the --message option when you are importing or committing files to the repository, Subversion will automatically open an editor for you,[1] which will allow you to type a log message as long and complex as you need it to be.

Now that the repository structure has been imported, you can delete the original files. Everything should now be stored in the database, and ready for you to check out a working directory and begin hacking.

---

1. See Section 7.2, "Editing the Configuration Files."

4.3   Creating a Working Copy

The working copy is where you make all of your changes to the files in the repository. You check out the working copy directory by running the svn checkout command, and it contacts the repository to retrieve a copy of the most recent revision of all the data in your repository. A local directory tree that matches the tree inside the repository will be created, and the downloaded working directory files will be placed in there.

```
$ svn checkout file:///home/bill/my_repository/trunk my_repos_trunk
A  my_repos_trunk/hello.c
A  my_repos_trunk/Makefile
Checked out revision 1.
```

As you can see, Subversion has checked out the trunk directory from your repository, creating a local working copy directory with the name my_repos_trunk, along with the files hello.c and Makefile that were stored in trunk. You'll notice, however, that the branches and tags directories were not checked out. Subversion will let you check out the entire repository at the top level, but doing so is generally not good practice. If you do, you may end up with multiple local copies of the source tree, because branches and tags are made by copying files. Instead, if you only check out the main trunk, you will ensure that you only have one version of the files at a time in your working copy. If you need to access specific branches or tags, you can either check them out on an individual basis, into their own working copies, or switch files in your trunk working copy to point to other locations in the repository (e.g. branches or tags), which I'll show you how to do in a later section.

Now, if you look closely at your new working copy, you can see that Subversion also has placed one additional directory in the directory that you checked out.

```
$ ls my_repos_trunk
Makefile  hello.c
$ ls -A my_repos_trunk
.svn  Makefile  hello.c
```

When you check out a repository, Subversion places a .svn directory in every directory of the repository. Inside these directories, Subversion places a wide variety of metadata about the working directory, including what repository the working directory comes from and what revisions of each file have been checked out. It also stores complete pristine versions of the last checked-out revision of each file in the working directory. This allows Subversion to provide you with diffs showing what changes you have made locally to a file, without needing to contact the server.

4.4   Editing Files

Now that you have checked out a working copy of the repository, it's time to edit some files. Let's say, for example, that you decide that your Hello World program needs to tell everyone about a glorious new system that you've just discovered. So, you bring up your favorite text editor and modify hello.c, so that it now looks like this:

```
#include <stdio.h>

int main(int argc, char** argv)
{
    printf("Subversion Rocks!!\n);

    return 0;
}
```

Whew! After a big change like that, it can be hard to remember everything that you've done since the repository was checked out. Sounds like it's time to learn about Subversion's query commands.[2]

Subversion provides you with a couple of different commands for querying the current state of the working directory. The first, `svn status`, shows the current status of local files. You can see whether files have been added, modified, deleted, and a number of other things. Running it on your current working directory shows that one file has changed:

```
$ svn status my_repos_trunk
M       my_repos_trunk/hello.c
```

Each output line from SVN (in this case, only one) shows the state of a file in the working directory tree, with files that haven't changed since the last update omitted. As you can see, the `hello.c` file is listed, with an `M` that informs you that the local file has been modified.

Just knowing that the file has been modified, though, doesn't tell you a whole lot. It would be significantly more useful if you could see exactly what has been modified. This is where the `svn diff` command comes in. With the diff command, you can see the difference between the local copy of the file and the last version to be updated from the repository (you can also use the diff command to compare with revisions other than the most recent, as you'll see in Chapter 5, "Working with a Working Copy").

```
$ svn diff my_repos_trunk/hello.c
Index: my_repos_trunk/hello.c
===================================================================
--- my_repos_trunk/hello.c (revision 1)
+++ my_repos_trunk/hello.c (working copy)
@@ -2,7 +2,7 @@

 int main(int argc, char** argv)
 {
-    printf("Hello World!!\n");
+        printf("Subversion Rocks!!\n");

        return 0;
 }
```

---

2. See how I set you up for that one with a smooth, effortless transition?

As you can see, the diff command gives you an overview of the changes made to the file, including both removed information and added information. The header portion of the output identifies which files have been diffed. In this case, it shows that the original file was revision 1 of `hello.c`, and all lines from that which have been removed in the latest version (which it notes, is the working copy) are marked with a - sign. Additionally, all lines added to the working copy, but not in revision 1, are marked with a +. The @@ -2,7 +2,7 @@ tells you that the diff to follow shows lines two through seven from both versions of `hello.c`. For each section of a file that has changed, the diff will show the changes, as well as a few of the unchanged lines before and after the change. These can help you get your bearings as to which section of the file it is that you are seeing changed.

4.5   Committing Changes

Now that you've made some changes to the project, it's time to commit those changes back to the repository. This is done with the `svn commit` command, as follows.

```
$ cd my_repos_trunk/
$ svn commit --message "Changed program output"
Sending          hello.c
Transmitting file data .
Committed revision 2.
```

When you run the commit command, Subversion sends the changes you have made to the repository, where a new revision is created with the changes applied to the files in the repository. As soon as the commit is complete, other users are able to update their own working copies of the repository and retrieve the updates that you have just committed.

As you can see, the output from the commit command says that Subversion committed revision two. This is the global revision number of the repository. Whenever any user commits a change to the repository, Subversion increments the revision number of the entire repository by one. This way, you are always able to refer to a snapshot of the repository at a given point in time, using the revision number. Unlike CVS, there is no need to remember that revision 10 of file A was matched with revision 15 of file B.

4.6   Viewing the Logs

After you have multiple revisions committed to the repository, you will likely find a time when you want to review the history of changes you have made. This can be done using the `svn log` command, which displays the commit logs for a file. If multiple files are given, Subversion aggregates the logs for all of the files into a single log output, showing the log entries for each revision where at least one of the listed files changed. If a directory is given, SVN will output the log information for not only the given directory, but also all files and subdirectories contained within the directory given.

You can view the log for the `hello.c` file by running the following.

```
$ svn log hello.c
------------------------------------------------------------------
r2 | bill | 2004-07-11 04:45:12 -0500 (Sun, 11 Jul 2004) | 1 line

Changed program output
------------------------------------------------------------------
r1 | bill | 2004-07-08 16:28:57 -0500 (Thu, 08 Jul 2004) | 1 line

Initial import
------------------------------------------------------------------
```

Looking at the output, you can see that it shows both of the revisions that you have committed, along with the name of the user who made the commit, the time of the commit, the total number of lines that were changed in files that were part of the commit (in this case, just one), and the log message that you gave for each commit.

4.7   Creating a Tag

It's hard to improve upon perfection, so you decide that it's time to release your Hello World application so that others can bask in its glory. You would, however, like to be able to continue work on version 2.0 of Hello World (with many new features) after you release version 1.0. To ensure that you always have access to exactly what you released as version 1.0 (in case, for example, you later find a bug that you want to fix), it would be handy to mark the revision of the repository that made up the version 1.0 release. You could do this by writing down the revision number somewhere, but the easier (and more reliable) way to keep track of the version 1.0 release is to create a tag.

Subversion has no explicit concept of a "tag." Instead, it simply uses lightweight copies of the files being tagged. So, to create a tag, you just have to use the `svn copy` command to create a copy of the files included in the release in the `tags` directory that you created when you made the initial repository. In order to avoid the expense of actually making a copy of the files in the directory (as opposed to just marking them as copied), and because you never checked out the `tags` directory into your working copy, it is best to perform the copy entirely in the repository, by running the following command.

```
$ svn copy --message "Tagged version 1.0 release" file:///home/bill/ ¬
  my_repository/trunk/ file:///home/bill/my_repository/tags/version_1_0 ¬
  /
Committed revision 3.
```

This performs the copy inside the repository immediately, and creates a new revision. You can see that the copy occurred by using the `svn list` command to see the contents of the repository.

```
$ svn list file:///home/bill/my_repository/tags
version_1_0/
```

```
$ svn list file:///home/bill/my_repository/tags/version_1_0
Makefile
hello.c
```

4.8   Creating a Branch

You should have tags pretty well down at this point, so let's take a look at branches. Say, for example, that your boss isn't yet quite as enlightened as you are, and decides you need to release a version of Hello World that touts that *other* version control system. Because you know he's heading down a dead-end path, though, you don't want to stop development on your already excellent version of Hello World. The solution is to create a branch of the project, which will allow you to take the project in a different direction, while maintaining the current development path in parallel.

Branches in Subversion are just like tags, copies of the original repository part they refer to. Therefore, you make them exactly the same way; only in this case, you will want to copy the files into the branches directory, instead of the tags directory.

```
$ svn copy --message "Created a branch of the project to make the boss ¬
  happy" file:///home/bill/my_repository/trunk/ file:///home/bill/ ¬
  my_repository/branches/cvs_version
Committed revision 4.
```

After you have created the branch, you'll need to put it into a working copy so that you can make changes to it. You could check out the branch (using svn checkout) into a new working copy. In fact, that will work just fine. There's a better solution, though. Instead of checking out a new working copy, you can switch your current working copy to point to the branch, instead of the /trunk directory that it points to now. To do this, you need to use the svn switch command. To switch your working copy to the branch, run the following command line.

```
$ svn switch file:///home/bill/my_repository/branches/cvs_version
Updated to revision 4.
```

The files in your working copy now point to the branches/cvs_version/ directory, and any changes that you commit will be applied to that directory. In this particular case, running svn switch didn't make any changes to the files in your working copy, because the branch and your trunk are identical. Had they been different, Subversion would have updated all of your working copy files to reflect the cvs_version/ directory that you switched to.

You can look at what directory you are currently switched to by running svn info. For instance, the following command line will show you that your current working copy is switched to the cvs_version branch (look at the URL line).

```
$ svn info
Path: .
```

```
URL: file:///home/bill/my_repository/branches/cvs_version
Repository UUID: 5380c965-27ea-0310-9e69-9d7dd738c2c1
Revision: 4
Node Kind: directory
Schedule: normal
Last Changed Author: bill
Last Changed Rev: 4
Last Changed Date: 2004-12-01 00:46:13 -0500 (Wed, 01 Dec 2004)
```

Now that you have switched your working copy to point to the branch, you'd probably like to make some changes to the branch. For instance, to make your boss happy, you might change my_repository/branches/cvs_version/hello.c to look like this:

```
#include <stdio.h>

int main(int argc, char** argv)
{
    printf("CVS is the best!!\n"); // Ugh! The boss made me do it

    return 0;
}
```

Then, when you commit those changes, they will be applied to the copied version of the file, but the original file will remain unaffected, as you can see in the log outputs here.

```
$ svn commit --message "Changed program output to praise CVS"
Sending        hello.c
Transmitting file data .
Committed revision 5.
```

After the commit, the branch shows the committed change.

```
$ svn log file:///home/bill/my_repository/branches/cvs_version/hello.c
------------------------------------------------------------
r5 | bill | 2004-07-12 23:32:11 -0500 (Mon, 12 Jul 2004) | 1 line

Changed program output to praise CVS
------------------------------------------------------------
r4 | bill | 2004-07-12 22:47:11 -0500 (Mon, 12 Jul 2004) | 1 line

Created a branch of the project to make the boss happy
------------------------------------------------------------
r2 | bill | 2004-07-11 04:45:12 -0500 (Sun, 11 Jul 2004) | 1 line

Changed program output
```

```
-----------------------------------------------------------------
r1 | bill | 2004-07-08 16:28:57 -0500 (Thu, 08 Jul 2004) | 1 line

Initial import
-----------------------------------------------------------------
```

But the the original `hello.c` file, still only shows the first two revisions.

```
$ svn log file:///home/bill/my_repository/trunk/hello.c
-----------------------------------------------------------------
r2 | bill | 2004-07-11 04:45:12 -0500 (Sun, 11 Jul 2004) | 1 line

Changed program output
-----------------------------------------------------------------
r1 | bill | 2004-07-08 16:28:57 -0500 (Thu, 08 Jul 2004) | 1 line

Initial import
-----------------------------------------------------------------
```

Of course, now that you're done modifying the branch, it's a good idea to switch your working copy back to the trunk. If you don't make the switch as soon as you're done with the branch, it can be all too easy to forget and accidentally apply modifications to the wrong place.

```
$ svn switch file:///home/bill/my_repository/trunk/
U  hello.c
Updated to revision 5.
```

As you can see, Subversion updates your `hello.c` file so that it represents the trunk version, rather than your modified branch version of the file.

4.9   Merging a Branch

As various branches of a repository's main trunk progress and diverge, it's sometimes necessary to use changes made on one branch in a different branch. Subversion allows you to apply these changes using the merge command. Let's say you add a line of output to the Hello World program to make it output some copyright information so that it now looks like this:

```
#include <stdio.h>

int main(int argc, char** argv)
{
    printf("Subversion Rocks!!\n");
    printf("Copyright 2004, Bill Nagel\n");
```

```
    return 0;
}
```

This change is of course committed as usual, using svn commit.

```
$ svn commit --message "Added copyright information"
Sending        hello.c
Transmitting file data .
Committed revision 6.
```

Because outputting the copyright information is something that would be useful in both your Subversion-praising version and in the CVS-praising branch, it would be nice to merge these changes over to the branch. To do this, you'll use the svn merge command.

The merge command works by taking the difference between two revisions of a file or directory in the repository and applying those differences to a location in your working directory. In this case, you want to apply the change made to the repository trunk in revision 6 to the cvs_version branch.

First, you should run svn log to check which revision(s) of the repository the change you want to merge was committed on.

```
$ svn log hello.c
------------------------------------------------------------
r6 | bill | 2004-07-13 00:23:38 -0500 (Tue, 13 Jul 2004) | 1 line

Added copyright information
------------------------------------------------------------
r2 | bill | 2004-07-11 04:45:12 -0500 (Sun, 11 Jul 2004) | 1 line

Changed program output
------------------------------------------------------------
r1 | bill | 2004-07-08 16:28:57 -0500 (Thu, 08 Jul 2004) | 1 line

Initial import
------------------------------------------------------------
```

In this case, you can see that the copyright information change was applied to the main trunk in revision 6. That means that to apply those changes to the branch version, you need to apply the difference between revision 6 of hello.c and revision 5.

The Subversion merge command takes as parameters two different revisions of a source directory, and a working copy path to apply the changes to. Although merges are relatively easy to undo, after you have run them, it is usually a good idea to execute the merge command first with the --dry-run option, which will show you the files that will be changed before it applies the change. This lets you see any potential merge conflicts before they happen, which can often make them easier to deal with, and may even allow you to eliminate the conflict before it occurs. After the merge, it is a good idea to test the merged files and make sure everything was applied correctly, before committing the merge to the repository.

To run the merge in your repository, you can do the following.

```
$ svn switch file:///home/bill/my_repository/branches/cvs_version/
U  hello.c
Updated to revision 7.
$ svn merge --dry-run -r 5:6 file:///home/bill/my_repository/trunk
U  hello.c
$ svn merge --revision 5:6 file:///home/bill/my_repository/trunk
U  hello.c
$ cat hello.c
#include <stdio.h>

int main(int argc, char** argv)
{
        printf("CVS is the best!!\n"); // Ugh! The boss made me do it
        printf("Copyright 2004, Bill Nagel\n");

        return 0;
}
$ svn commit --message "Merged with revision 6 - revision 5 in trunk/ ¬
  hello.c"
Sending        hello.c
Transmitting file data .
Committed revision 7.
$ svn switch file:///home/bill/my_repository/trunk
U  hello.c
Updated to revision 7.
```

You may notice that I explicitly stated in my log file for the merge commit which revisions were merged with the branch. It is actually very important to keep that information in the logs whenever a commit is made, because Subversion doesn't yet do any sort of tracking of merges and branches. By keeping track of the merged revisions in the logs, you can help ensure that you don't accidentally apply a merge more than once, which can have the unintended side effects of triggering spurious conflicts or even putting back changes that were taken out previously.

4.10   Handling Conflicts

Let's finish this chapter by taking a look at conflicts and how you can resolve them when they occur. Conflicts occur when Subversion is unable to merge two files together automatically. Generally, this happens when two users have independently made a change to the same area of a file. Because Subversion doesn't actually understand the files that it merges, it has no way of figuring out which of the two versions to use. Its only recourse, in this case, is to let the user solve the conflict.

Before you can resolve a conflict, you have to have a conflict. So, let's create a conflict. To start, check out a new working copy, which will represent the work of a second developer.

```
$ svn checkout file:///home/bill/my_repository/trunk/ /home/bill/ ¬
  other_dev_trunk
A    other_dev_trunk/hello.c
A    other_dev_trunk/Makefile
Checked out revision 7.
```

Then, edit the file `hello.c` in your new working copy, and change the line

```
printf{"Subversion Rocks!!\n");
```

so that it reads

```
printf("Subversion is Great!!\n");
```

After the change has been made, commit it to the repository.

```
$ svn commit --message "Changed to a more conservative phrase" /home/ ¬
  bill/other_dev_trunk/hello.c
Sending         hello.c
Transmitting file data .
Committed revision 8.
```

With your changes from the new working copy committed, it's time to go back to your original working copy. Once there, edit the copy of the file `hello.c` that is stored there, *without updating the file from the repository first.* This time, change the line

```
printf("Subversion Rocks!!\n");
```

to the third, yet equally complimentary line,

```
printf("Subversion is Awesome!!\n");
```

Now, try to commit this change to `hello.c`.

```
$ svn commit --message "Decided on a more hip phrase" /home/bill/ ¬
  my_repos_trunk/hello.c
Sending         my_repos/trunk/hello.c
svn: Commit failed (details follow):
svn: Out of date: '/my_repos_trunk/hello.c' in transaction '9'
```

Well, Subversion obviously didn't like that. The reason, of course, is that Subversion won't allow you to commit changes to a file if those changes cause a conflict with previous changes, which can happen if you try to commit without first updating the working copy to the latest revision. To resolve the conflict, you first need to update your working copy to the latest revision, using `svn update`.

```
$ cd ~/my_repos_trunk/
$ svn update
C  my_repos_trunk/hello.c
Updated to revision 8.
```

Notice that there is a C in front of the listing for `hello.c` instead of the normal U for files that have been updated. The C is used to indicate a conflict. When a conflict such as this one occurs, Subversion does two things. First, it marks the file as being in a conflicted state. Second, it creates four versions of the conflicted file, for you to use when resolving the conflict.

```
$ ls trunk/
Makefile  hello.c  hello.c.mine  hello.c.r7  hello.c.r8
```

The first file, named `hello.c` just like the original, contains the file with each conflicted area showing both possible versions of the file. The first version shown is the version in your working copy, before the conflict occurred, and begins at a «««<. The second version shown is from the version of the file that the working copy was being merged with. It begins at the ======= that separates the two versions, and ends at a »»»>. You can see an example of this diff view here.

```
#include <stdio.h>

int main(int argc, char** argv)
{
<<<<<<< .mine
        printf("Subversion Is Great!!\n");
=======
        printf("Subversion Is Awesome!!\n");
>>>>>>> .r8
        printf("Copyright 2004, Bill Nagel\n");

        return 0;
}
```

The second version of the file, `hello.c.mine`, is a copy of the file as it existed in your working directory right before the conflict. The third version, `hello.c.r7`, is the file as it existed in your working directory the last time you checked it out, prior to any local changes. The `.r7` tells you that the file is taken from revision 6 of the repository. The fourth and final file, `hello.c.r8`, is the file as it exists in the repository revision that is being merged into the working directory. Like the previous file, the `.r8` extension on this file tells you that it is from revision 8 of the repository.

To resolve the conflict, you need to modify the original file (`hello.c` in this case) so that it represents the resolved, final version of the file that you would like to commit to the repository as part of the next revision. In doing so, you are free to make use of any of the conflict files Subversion provides (either by copying information from them or copying the file on top of the existing version wholesale), as well as any data from other sources, as necessary. If you need to, to resolve a conflict, you could even rewrite the entire file from scratch.

After you have the conflicted file set up the way you want it, with all conflicting data merged or removed, you need to tell Subversion that you are done. This is done through the `svn resolved` command, which tells Subversion to remove the flag that marks the file as conflicted. Subversion also removes the extra versions of the file that it created when the resolved command is run. After the conflict has been marked resolved, you are free to commit the file to the repository.[3]

```
$ svn resolved hello.c
Resolved conflicted state of 'hello.c'
$ svn commit --message "Resolved conflicted state"
Sending        trunk/hello.c
Transmitting file data .
Committed revision 9.
```

4.11 Summary

In this chapter, you have walked through most everything that you will encounter in day-to-day interaction with a Subversion repository. The first few sections walked through the basics of creating a repository, including how to get the initial files into a repository and how to check out a working copy of the repository. After that, you learned the basics of editing files and committing changes, followed by some more advanced techniques such as branching and merging. Finally, you saw how to manually merge conflicts that Subversion can't handle automatically.

This ends Part I of the book. Now that you've gone through a thorough introduction to what Subversion is and how it works, Part II will delve in depth into the workings of Subversion from the point of view of a user of the Subversion client.

---

3. Of course, it's entirely possible that someone else may have committed yet another version of the file while you were working on resolving the conflict, which could put the file into a conflicted state again.

Part II

Subversion from a Client User's Perspective

Chapter 5

Working with a Working Copy

The primary users of Subversion will almost certainly be developers who interact with Subversion through a client program that connects to a remote repository. They will not deal, on a day-to-day basis, with any sort of server-side administration, nor will they be responsible in most cases for configuring the layout of the repository or assigning permissions to other users. They will need to deal with the fine details of modifying and maintaining source code that resides within the repository. In Part II, you will learn those details—the ins and outs of working with Subversion from the client user's perspective.

The framework that the developer works within, when interacting with Subversion, is a working copy of a repository. In this chapter, you will learn in detail how to interact with a working copy in order to facilitate development. In addition to fundamentals such as checking out the repository and modifying the data it contains, you will also learn details about some of the more advanced topics you may encounter in daily use of Subversion, like branching and merging.

Like most version control systems, Subversion stores versioned data in a central database, called a repository. The repository contains information about all of the versioned files and directories, including all changes to their contents over the entire history of the repository. When users want to examine or modify the data in the repository, they generally check out a working copy. The working copy is a snapshot of a part of the repository that a client user can manipulate locally, committing changes back to the repository at logical points.

5.1   The Subversion Client

When interacting with Subversion, the primary client program that you will end up using from the command line is the `svn` command, which provides most of the features that you will need for interacting with a repository or working copy as a client user. To run the `svn` command, you will also need to give it a subcommand such as `commit` or `update`. Each command has its own set of options that you can use to control the behavior of the command. Many of the options, though, are common to many different commands. For instance, in almost every Subversion client command, you can specify a revision (or range of revisions) using the `--revision` option.

5.1.1   Common Command Options

Because many of these options are common to a variety of commands, let's take a look at them before diving into the Subversion commands themselves. The following commonly used options are common to most commands and have usage that is worth discussing before taking a look at the commands themselves.

--message

Whenever Subversion creates a new revision, it attaches a log message to that revision that describes what changes were made in the revision, and why. Normally, Subversion will open an editor to allow you to enter in the log message, but if the message is short (or you're running the command from a script) it can be easier to specify the log message directly on the command line. To allow you to do that, all Subversion commands that create a new revision in the repository allow you to use the --message option. To specify a log message, you just give the command --message followed by a message, enclosed in quotes. For example, the following command performs a repository-side copy, and specifies the log message to use:

```
$ svn commit --message "Fixed bug #1154."
```

--no-auth-cache

Normally, Subversion caches your repository authorization information (username, password, etc.) as a convenience, so you don't have to type it in every time. Sometimes, though, you don't want that information to be stored. For example, you might be using someone else's workstation (or worse, a public workstation). If, for whatever reason, you don't want Subversion to cache your authorization information, you can turn the cache off using the --no-auth-cache option. This option will work with every Subversion command that contacts the repository.

--recursive/--non-recursive

Every Subversion command that can operate on multiple files defaults to either recursive behavior or non-recursive behavior, depending on the command. Basically, commands that can destroy data (such as svn revert) are non-recursive by default. Everything else defaults to recursive. Regardless of which default a program uses, you can override the default using --recursive or --non-recursive. For instance, the following command will revert all local changes in the trunk directory:

```
$ svn revert --recursive trunk/
```

--revision

Many Subversion commands require you to specify a specific revision in the repository, or a range of revisions. For any command that takes a revision, you can supply it using the --revision option. Single revisions can be specified by following the option with a single revision number. Or, if the command takes a range of revisions, you can give two revision numbers separated by a colon. For example, the following command will display the log messages for revisions 1 through 50.

```
$ svn log --revision 1:50
```

To make your life a little bit easier, Subversion also defines a few aliases that can be used to refer to certain revision numbers by their context, rather than their explicit number. Those aliases are HEAD, BASE, COMMITTED, and PREV. Each one can be used in any Subversion command, when a revision number is called for—although BASE, COMMITTED, and PREV can only be used when referencing a working copy because they require the working copy to give them context. The HEAD alias refers to the greatest numerical revision in a repository. This is the same for every file, regardless of when they were last committed. The BASE alias, on the other hand, points to the base revision for the working copy file or directory being referenced. So, for example, if you check out the trunk directory at revision 3497, BASE would point to 3497. If you then commit a modified file inside the trunk directory at revision 3583, the BASE for that file will point to 3583, whereas the base for the trunk directory and the rest of its contents will still point to 3497. If you later update the trunk to 3583, its BASE will then point to 3583. The remaining two, COMMITTED and PREV, are then relative to the BASE revision. COMMITTED refers to the most recent commit at or before the working copy item's BASE revision, and PREV refers to the revision prior to COMMITTED. So, for instance, if you want to show the log messages from the first revision to the most recently committed revision, you could run the following command.

```
$ svn log --revision 1:COMMITTED
```

5.1.2 Paths

In addition to options that are common across commands, the format for specifying paths in a working copy or repository are also common. For most Subversion commands, you can reference files and directories that reside locally in a working copy or in a remote repository. Working copy files/directories are referenced by giving a local path to that file (either absolute or relative to the current directory). Repositories are referenced with URLs. For instance, you might reference the trunk directory in a remote repository that is served via Apache with http://svn.example.com/repos/trunk/. Most commands will take either local paths or URLs on the command line, and in most cases you can mix URLs and local paths in the same command—to copy from the repository to a working copy, for example.

```
$ svn cp http://svn.example.com/repos/trunk/foo.c ~/repos_wc/ ¬
  trunk/bar.c
```

5.2 Checking Out and Maintaining a Working Copy

A working copy is created by checking out all or part of a Subversion repository, using the command svn checkout (which can be abbreviated svn co). To indicate the repository that should be checked out, you pass a URL that points to the desired repository along with the checkout command. The exact form that the URL takes depends on the type of server that you are contacting.

If the repository is being served by Apache, via HTTP/WebDAV, the appropriate URL prefix is `http://`, or if the connection is secured by SSL, `https://`. On the other hand, if the Subversion server for the repository is `svnserve`, you will want to use `svn://` or `svn+ssh://`, depending on whether the connection should be tunneled over SSH. Finally, if you are not contacting a remote server, but are instead directly accessing a repository that resides on the local machine, the prefix should be `file://`. The remainder of the URL follows the same standards as a URL used for any other purpose and consists of the form `username@host.example.com/path/to/repository`. Of course, the username and hostname are dropped if it is a directly accessed local repository, via a `file://` prefix. Also, remember that a local filesystem path should have an initial /, in addition to the prefixed double slash (so you should have three slashes total). This applies even for local filesystem URLs on Windows, even though Windows doesn't use the slash to indicate a root directory in the filesystem hierarchy.

You can also make a working copy that consists of only part of a repository by continuing the path in the URL out to identify the portion to check out. For example, if a repository `repos` contains a directory named `trunk` at the top level, you could check out just `trunk` by issuing the following command.

```
$ svn co http://svn.example.com/repos/trunk
A trunk
A trunk/foo.c
```

Running the preceding checkout command with that URL will check out just the `trunk` directory in the repository and create a local directory named `trunk` in the directory where the checkout command was run. The `trunk` directory is now your working copy. It contains copies of the versioned files located inside the `trunk` directory, as well as a directory named `.svn`, where Subversion stores metadata about the local working copy.

If you want to check out a working copy into a directory other than the directory where the `svn co` command is actually run (for instance, if you create a script to automate the checkout), you can pass a path to the checkout command, after the URL, which will tell Subversion where to place the checked out working copy. So, if you want to check out a repository into your home directory, you can run the following command from anywhere:

```
$ svn co http://svn.example.com/repos /home/bill/repos_wc
A repos_wc
A repos_wc/trunk
A repos_wc/trunk/foo.c
A repos_wc/branches
A repos_wc/branches/branch1/foo.c
A repos_wc/tags
```

Subversion also allows you to specify multiple URLs to check out on the same command line. If you do supply multiple URLs, Subversion will check out each of the repositories (or subsets of a repository) given, and place them either in the local directory or the directory given as a path after all of the URLs.

```
$ svn co http://svn.example.com/repos/trunk http://svn.mycomain.com/ ¬
  repos/branches
A trunk
A trunk/foo.c
A branches
A branches/branch1/foo.c
```

If for one reason or another you don't want to check out the subdirectories of a repository, you can also pass svn co the argument --non-recursive (-N) to tell it to only check out the directory given, without checking out the contents of any directories it contains. If you do this though, the working copy will remember that you didn't check out any of the subdirectories, and it won't get them when you do an update either. If you do want to get a subdirectory that wasn't checked out originally, you can get it by running svn update with the name of the directory you'd like to get.

```
$ svn co --non-recursive http://svn.example.com/repos
Checked out revision 21657
$ cd repos/
$ ls -a
.  ..  .svn
$ svn update trunk
A  trunk
A  trunk/test.c
$ ls -a
.  ..  .svn  trunk
```

There may also be times when you want to check out a revision of the repository other than the HEAD revision. You can do this by passing --revision (-r) with the revision that you want to check out. The revision can either be an explicit revision number, or it can be a date (which needs to be enclosed in brackets). For example, if you want to check out the last revision committed before July 20th, 2004 at noon, you could check out with the following command.

```
$ svn co --revision "{2004-07-20 12:00}" http://svn.example.com/repos
```

5.2.1 Keeping Up-to-Date

After you have a repository checked out, you will want to keep it up-to-date with changes made by other developers. The basic command for doing this is svn update (or svn up). When it is run without any options, the differences between the current revision of files in your working copy and the HEAD revision of the repository are downloaded from the server and applied to your working copy. As it updates, Subversion will show you which files were updated, and what sort of update occurred.

```
$ svn update
A   trunk/vid/wildflowers.mpg
U   trunk/src/anim.c
D   trunk/src/works.c
G   trunk/src/Makefile
C   trunk/README
Updated to revision 1450.
```

As you can see here, there were five files modified by the update, and each one has a different letter in front of its name. Each of those letters tells you what Subversion did when it updated the file in your working copy. Only files that were in some way updated are shown in the output.

- The A tells you that a file named trunk/vid/wildflowers.mpg has been added to the repository since your last update, so Subversion downloaded a copy of it and added it to your working copy.

- The U tells you that the file trunk/src/anim was updated with changes from the repository.

- The D tells you that file was deleted from your working copy, because it no longer exists in the repository.

- The G tells you that Subversion merged the changes received from the repository with the locally modified file trunk/src/Makefile.

- The C indicates that Subversion was not able to merge the changes to the file trunk/README, and has instead declared a conflict.

If the update command is run with no path supplied, it operates on the current directory and recursively updates that directory and all of its contents. If a path is supplied, it updates the directory or file that is given, as well as anything contained within if the path points to a directory. If recursive updating is not what you want (for instance, if you want to update the properties associated with a directory without updating its contents), you can use the --non-recursive option. The following command, for example, will update the trunk directory, but leave its contents untouched.

```
$ svn update --non-recursive /home/bill/repos/trunk
U   trunk
Updated to revision 1478.
```

It is important to note that svn update operates on files and directories known to the repository, regardless of whether those files have been locally removed from your working copy. The advantage of this is best illustrated by the following snippet.

```
$ ls
foo.c       bar.c
$ rm bar.c
```

```
$ svn update bar.c
U  bar.c
Updated to revision 503.
$ ls
foo.c         bar.c
```

As you can see, Subversion makes it easy to recover files that were locally deleted, eliminating any worry about causing real harm to data within the working copy. Recovering a file by deleting and updating can also be handy if a file in the working copy somehow gets corrupted. In most cases, if Subversion is misbehaving on a versioned file, you can get things back to a sane state by just deleting (or moving) it and performing an `svn update`.

Another command that is useful for restoring a working copy to a known state is `svn revert`. This command works similarly to `svn update`, but instead of updating to a different revision in the repository, the revert command restores locally modified files to a pristine version of the file, corresponding to the most recent checkout, update, or commit.

Reversions that are done with `svn revert` are very fast, because Subversion always keeps a pristine copy of every versioned file in the working copy.[1] This allows the revert to occur without contacting the remote repository, saving not just time but also bandwidth.

As a safety feature though (because the command can destroy local changes), `svn revert` does not recurse into subdirectories like `svn checkout` and `svn update`, nor will it do anything if you run it without explicitly identifying the files to revert. If you want recursion, you have to explicitly request it with the `--recursive` (`-R`) option. Subversion also can't revert directories that were locally deleted. To do that, you have to use `svn update`.

5.3 Modifying and Committing Data

The meat of Subversion is its usefulness for tracking changes in files over time. That makes getting those changes into the system a very important part of the system. The primary tool that you will use to get data into the system is the commit command, `svn commit`. In general, the basic committing process will go something like this.

```
$ svn update
At revision 3215.
$ svn status
M      light.c
$ svn commit --message "Added a status variable."
Sending        light.c
Transmitting file data .
Committed revision 3216.
```

It's a good idea to run the `svn update` command first, so that you can get any changes that others have made to the repository and make sure they will be compatible with your change. If there are any other changes merged into your working copy when you run update,

---

1. Subversion stores pristine copies for every file in a working copy directory inside the corresponding `.svn` directory.

it's also a good idea to recompile and run a test suite if one is available, to ensure that everything still works as you expect. Subversion won't let you commit changes that will result in a merge conflict without first making you resolve those changes by hand. However, it doesn't have any context for your source, and will not in any way prevent changes that cause logical conflicts in the project. The only conflicts that it catches are instances where either two people edited the exact same lines of a file or two people edited the same binary file.

It is also a good idea to run the `svn status` command before you commit, in order to get an idea of what it is that you'll be committing. That way, you help avoid getting a stray change in an unrelated file mixed in with your commit just because you forgot that you made the change. You can also make use of the `svn diff` command if you don't remember exactly what changes you made to individual files. To find out more information about `svn status` and `svn diff`, take a look at Section 5.4, "Getting Information About the Repository."

As soon as you feel that you have a good understanding of what you are committing, it's time to perform the actual commit. In the preceding example, the command was run with no path and with a log message on the command line. When `svn commit` is run with no path telling it what to commit, it recursively commits all modified files in the current directory. Recursion can be turned off with `--no-recursion` if you need to commit a directory without committing its contents.

When the commit command runs, it sends the local modifications to the files being committed to the remote repository. Only the differences are sent, so no bandwidth is wasted by sending redundant information. If no paths are specified by `svn commit`, it recursively commits all of the modified files in the current directory. If you don't want to commit all of the locally modified files, you can instead specify one or more files on the command line, and it will instead commit only those files. Or, you can specify directories on the command line, and Subversion will commit that directory and any changed files or directories it contains (unless you specifically turned off recursion).

In addition to files to commit, `svn commit` also requires a log message to associate with the commit. The log message can be supplied on the command line by giving the `--message` (-m) option. If you supply the log this way, the log message should follow the `--message` (separated by a space), and be enclosed in quotes.

```
$ svn commit -m "A little inline log message. How cute."
```

Entering log messages on the command line can quickly become unwieldy—especially if they are long messages. To make entering long messages easier, you can leave off the `--message` option, and Subversion will automatically open an editor for you to enter a log message (as you can see in Figure 5.1). Subversion will then block until you quit the editor. If you have entered a log message and saved the file, Subversion will use the contents of that file as the log message for the commit. If you quit without changing the file, Subversion will instead ask you if you want to use a blank log message or abort the commit. This abort

Figure 5.1. Adding a log with a text editor.

capability can come in handy when you realize that you were a little too quick to commit and either forgot to add a file to the those that are being committed, or are accidentally committing too many files. As an aid to helping you figure out what is being committed Subversion will put a section in the commit log file, when it opens the editor, that tells you exactly which files are being committed. That section will then be removed from the file before Subversion sets the commit log.

A third method for entering log messages is to put them in a file and have Subversion read the file by using the option `--file` (`-F`)—which takes a single argument specifying the file to read. When specifying a file for the log message though, Subversion will not, by default, allow you to use a file that is already under version control. If you do want to use a file that is under version control for your log message, you can override Subversion's limitation by passing `--force-log` to `svn commit`.

5.3.1 Adding New Files

New files added to the working copy need to be explicitly put under version control before they can be committed to the repository. Adding files is a two-step process. The first step is to schedule the file for addition, with the `svn add` command, which adds the file in the working copy, but doesn't contact the remote repository. The actual transfer of data to the repository doesn't occur until `svn commit` is run on the newly added file. If you decide not to add the file, before performing the commit, you can unschedule the file by running `svn revert` on it.

```
$ svn add memory.*
A          memory.c
A          memory.o
$ svn revert memory.o
Reverted 'memory.o'
```

```
$ svn status
A       memory.c
?       memory.o
$ svn commit --message "Added a file for managing memory."
Adding          memory.c
Transmitting file data .
Committed revision 1492.
```

If svn add is called on a directory, it will recursively add all of the files in that directory, unless you call svn add with --non-recursive.

```
$ svn add my_project
A         my_project
A         my_project/file_1.c
A         my_project/file_2.c

$ svn add --non-recursive my_project
A         my_project
```

5.3.2   Removing Files

Occasionally, it is also necessary to remove files from the repository. Subversion handles this with the svn delete command, which removes a file from the local working copy and schedules it to be removed in the next revision of the repository when a commit is executed. When files are removed though, Subversion only removes them for subsequent revisions. The file will always be there in any past revisions.[2]

```
$ svn delete image.cpp
D         image.cpp
$ ls image.cpp
ls: image.cpp: No such file or directory
$ svn status
D         image.cpp
```

As you can see, when svn delete was run, it did indeed delete the file image.cpp and an svn status shows that the file is scheduled to be deleted. As with svn add, if you later decide (before committing the deletion to the repository) that you really didn't want to delete the file, you can undelete it by running svn revert with the name of the file you want to get back. After you have committed a remove operation, you will have to use the command svn copy to get the file back into the HEAD revision.

When performing an svn delete, you need to be cautious about local modifications that have not yet been committed. After a file has been removed, you can use revert to get back a pristine version of the file from the last update, but all uncommitted local modifications will be irretrievably lost. Fortunately, Subversion has a safeguard that will prevent

---

2.   There is talk of a feature that would allow files to be retroactively removed, but as of this writing, no such feature exists.

you from doing this accidentally. If `svn delete` detects local changes, it will fail, with a message telling you that you need to explicitly force it to delete the file, which you can do with the `--force` option.

```
$ svn delete mobius.pl
svn: Use --force to override this restriction
svn: 'movius.pl' has local modifications
$ svn delete --force mobius.pl
D        mobius.pl
```

In addition to removing files via your working copy, it is also possible with Subversion to directly remove files in a repository by specifying the file with a URL. Unlike removing a file in your working copy, when you use a URL you do not need to perform an explicit commit to cause the deletion to take effect in the repository. Instead, `svn rm` performs an implicit commit automatically when it is operating on a URL. Just as it does when you do an `svn commit`, the implicitly triggered commit will bring up an editor to allow you to input a log message, if you haven't supplied one with a `--message`.

```
$ svn delete --message "Removed build.xml" http://svn.example.com/repos ¬
  /trunk/build.xml
Committed revision 702.
```

5.3.3 Moving Things Around

One of the biggest strengths of Subversion is the ease and efficiency with which it allows you to copy and move files under revision control. With relative impunity, you can shuffle files around with few worries about running into difficulties down the road as a result. All repository-side copies and moves are also done without physically copying the data. Instead, the repository simply makes a note of the new file's location and makes it point back to the original data. Then, if a copy is changed down the road, Subversion stores those changes along with the entry for the copy. In that way, a copy can "branch" from the original file, retaining the original file's history (precopy), but continuing on its own path from that point on. To help illustrate how this works, Figure 5.2 shows an example of the different versions of a file that has been copied. As you can see, the copy, `Bar.cpp` has diverged from the original, but continues to maintain a linkage back to its history at the time it was created.

The two primary commands that you will use for dealing with moving and copying files are (shockingly) `svn move` and `svn copy`, which can be shortened to `svn mv` and `svn cp`, respectively. For the most part, both commands work the same—except for the obvious difference. Like the `svn delete` command, they operate immediately on a working copy, but only schedule the operation to be sent to the repository on the next commit. Similarly, if you give a repository URL instead of a working copy path, the operations will be performed immediately on the repository with an implicit commit.

Be careful though. When you are working within a working copy, you should always make sure that you use the Subversion copy and move commands for any versioned files,

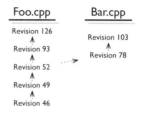

Figure 5.2. Two copies of a file, stored in the repository.

instead of the operating system equivalents. If you copy or move a file using a non-Subversion command, Subversion will not be aware of the change, and will continue to expect to find the file at its old location. The copy or moved version will be unversioned, and Subversion may complain that it can't find the old copy (or it might just quietly put it back during an update).

```
$ svn copy foo.s bar.s
A         bar.s
$ svn move foo.s foo.s.old
A         foo.s.old
D         foo.s
$ svn status
A  +   foo.s.old
D      foo.s
A  +   bar.s
```

You may have noticed, after the copy and move in the preceding example, the status output has a new addition. Instead of just saying that foo.s.old and bar.s are scheduled to be added, it also puts a + in the fourth column of the output. This plus sign, which is always located in the fourth column of a status line, indicates that a file being added already has history associated with it, which will of course be carried over to the copied file.

You'll also notice that the svn move command shows the old file as deleted and the new file as added. In fact, svn move is identical to running svn copy, followed by an svn remove on the original file. This is due to the process that Subversion uses internally when moving versioned files around. When a file is copied, Subversion creates the new file and points it back to the original file that it came from. That way, the file's history is preserved in the copy without any extra space requirements. Similarly, when a file is moved, Subversion does the same thing, but then removes the original file from the new revision. Hence, the result is identical to running svn copy followed by svn remove.

Using copy to Undelete Files

The svn copy command allows the source of a copy to come not only from the current revisions of either a working copy or the repository, but also from different revisions. This can be a handy way of "undeleting" a file that accidentally (or otherwise) was deleted in a previous revision. Revisions are entered just as they are with any other command that takes a revision, by using the command option `--revision`.

```
$ svn copy --revision 921 http://example.com/repos/html/index.html http ¬
  ://example.com/repos/html/index.html
```

5.4   Getting Information about the Repository

Subversion has a number of different commands that allow you to query the repository and working copy for a wealth of information about their current states, as well as their history. As your development in a working copy progresses, these commands will become invaluable tools, letting you quickly find out things like "what files have I changed since the last commit?" or "which branch of this directory am I currently working on?"

5.4.1   Getting Information on the Current State

The current state of the repository is easily queried with the `svn status` command, which outputs the current state of all files in your working copy that have been in some way modified from their pristine repository state.

```
$ svn status
A  +   pie.txt
D      cake.txt
_M     custard.txt
```

The output for `svn status` consists of a list of files, one per line. By default, each line is made up of five columns of status information, followed by a filename. Each of the five columns uses single character symbols to convey the current status of the file. This is shown in Table 5.1.

Table 5.1. Status Command Ouput Symbols

First column					Shows whether a file was added, removed, or modified.
					The file has not been modified.
A					The file is scheduled for addition to the repository.
D					The file is scheduled for deletion.
M					The contents of a file have been modified locally in the working copy.
C					A conflict occurred during a merge or update.
G					Reserved for showing merged files, but not yet used. (Non-conflicted, merged files will be marked with an M.)

(Continues)

Table 5.1. Status Command Output Symbols *(continued)*

First column (cont.)					
?					The file has never been under version control.
!					The file was under version control, but was removed from the working copy using a tool other than Subversion.
~					Subversion tried to add a file of this name (e.g., during an update), but an unversioned file of the same name already exists.
X					An unversioned file used by an externals definition. (See Section 6.3.1, "File Properties," for more information on externals.)
R					A versioned file that has replaced another versioned file of the same name.
I					An ignored file. Only shown when both the `--verbose` and `--no-ignore` options are given.
Second Column					Shows whether a file's properties have been modified.
					No properties have been modified on the file.
	M				A property has been modified locally on the file.
	C				A conflict occurred when merging or updating one or more of the file's properties.
Third Column					Indicates whether a file or directory has been locked in the working copy, due to another in-progress operation.
					The file or directory is not locked.
		L			The directory has been locked in the working copy. If there is no in-progress operation, you may need to run `svn cleanup` to remove the locked state. (This can happen if a command is interrupted.)
Fourth Column					This column indicates files scheduled for either addition or modification that are bringing previous history with them from another file.
					No history is being brought from another file.
			+		The file is contained within a directory that is scheduled for addition with history.
A			+		This file is scheduled for addition, and brings history from another file with it, probably as a result of an `svn move` or `svn copy`.
M			+		The file is contained within a directory that is scheduled for addition with history, and has also been locally modified.
Fifth Column					Indicates whether a file's path has been switched.
					The file's base URL is the same as its parent directory.
				S	The file has been switched (using `svn switch`) to a URL different from the URL of the file's parent directory.

Normally, `svn status` doesn't contact the repository. Instead, it determines which files have been modified by comparing them with pristine copies of the files, which Subversion keeps in the working copy's .svn directory. Sometimes, though, you are interested in seeing which files have also changed in the repository (and thus will be merged at the next `svn update`). To get this information out of Subversion, you need to run `svn status` with the --show-updates (-u) option.

```
$ svn status --show-updates address.cpp
```

The --show-updates option tells Subversion to output three pieces of extra information. The first is an * in the eighth column of output of each file that has been modified in the repository. Additionally, Subversoon will output the current revision of each file in the repository, as well as the HEAD revision of the repository, which the comparison is being made against.

```
$ svn status --show-updates
M             34   run.sh
       *      56   stop.sh
Status against revision:      92
```

If you want even more information, you can run `svn status` in verbose mode, using the --verbose (-v) option. In this mode, the status command will output all files, not just ones that have been modified (ignored files will still be ignored). Additionally, it will show the last revision in which each file was committed and who made the commit, as well as the current revision in the working copy, in the following order: current revision, last committed, last committed by.

```
$ svn status --show-updates --verbose
             29      29 bill       passwd
M            34      34 bill       run.sh
       *     56      56 bill       stop.sh
Status against revision:      92
```

If you would like to output all files, including those that have been ignored in the configuration files or the `svn:ignore` property, you can tell `svn status` to disregard ignores with --no-ignore.

Getting Detailed File Info

Sometimes you need detailed information about a particular file or directory. In this case, the command you want to use is `svn info`. The info command gives you a dump of all the information that Subversion has stored about a file or directory in the working copy.

```
$ svn info Table.m
Path: trunk/Table.m
Name: Table.m
```

```
URL: http://svn.example.com/repos/trunk/Table.m
Revision: 3276
Node Kind: file
Schedule: normal
Last Changed Author: bill
Last Changed Rev: 3271
Last Changed Date: 2004-07-23 10:25:19 -0660 (Fri, 23 Jul 2004)
Text Last Updated: 2004-07-23 10:25:19 -0660 (Fri, 23 Jul 2004)
Properties Last Updated: 2004-06-13 14:33:54 -0660 (Sun, 13 Jun 2004)
Checksum: fe1f3b5946fd8d68cd2879c38457f447
```

The first few lines of the info command's output identify the file that we're dealing with. The Path entry shows the location of the file relative to the base of the working copy, whereas the Name entry shows just the basename of the file. URL, on the other hand, shows the URL of the file in the repository.

After the identifiers, the next three items show the current state of the file in the working copy. The Revision entry shows the current revision of the file in the working copy, and the Node Kind entry indicates whether the entity being examined is a file or directory. Schedule shows whether the file is scheduled for any action on the next commit. An entry of normal (as in the preceding example) indicates that no specific action is scheduled.

Next, some information about the file's history is given. The Last Changed Author entry gives the username of the last person to commit a change for the file, and of course the Last Changed Rev and Last Changed Date give the revision number and date of the last commit. Additionally, there are entries that tell you when the files contents (Text) were last updated, and when the file's properties were last updated in the current working copy.

The final piece of information shown is a checksum. This is an MD5 sum of the pristine state of the file. This can be used to verify that the download from the repository wasn't corrupted, or to see if a file has changed in the working copy (of course, svn status is a much easier way to find that out).

Often you only want a particular piece of information about a file, not the entire info data dump. The svn info command doesn't have any way to explicitly specify a particular piece of data, but it is easy enough to get that information by combining svn info with the UNIX command grep. All you have to do is use a pipe (|) to pass the output of svn info to grep and search for a string that begins with the property name that you're looking for (the ^ before Checksum tells grep to only find lines that *begin* with the word "Checksum").

```
$ svn info Table.m | grep ^Checksum
Checksum: fe1f3b5946fd8d68cd2879c38457f447
```

By default, svn info is a non-recursive command. If you prefer that it recurse into directories, you can use the --recursive (-R) option. Of course, with multiple files it is even more likely that you will want to grep for just a single item in the output. However, if you just grab a single line, the output will be nearly useless, because in many cases you will have no idea which file each line is referring to. The easiest way to get useful, but not excessive, output (in this case) is to use the `grep` command to search for both the item of interest and either the `Name` or `Path` entries. That way, the name of each file is output, followed by the data entries you are interested in. For example, the following command finds the last changed date for every file in `trunk`.

```
$ svn info --recursive trunk/* | grep -E '^Path|^Last Changed Date'
Path: hello.c
Last Changed Date: 2004-12-04 01:03:39 -0500 (Sat, 04 Dec 2004)
Path: Makefile
Last Changed Date: 2004-12-06 11:12:47 -0500 (Sat, 06 Dec 2004)
```

Examining File Changes

After you get in the habit of using it regularly, the `svn diff` command will easily become one of your most used and most trusted tools in the Subversion toolbox. The basic function of `svn diff` is to output the differences between two revisions, showing additions and deletions inline with each other.

By default, `svn diff` shows the differences between a file in your working copy and the pristine version of the current revision of that file. So, for example, if you have made changes to the file `rabbit.c` in your working copy, the diff command will show you exactly what those changes were.

```
$ svn diff rabbit.c
Index: rabbit.c
===================================================================
--- rabbit.c     (revision 8)
+++ rabbit.c     (working copy)
@@ -5,5 +5,5 @@
        if(item == CARROT)
                eat(item);
        else if(item == CAT)
-               run_away(FAST, item);
+               hop_away(FAST, item);
 }
```

The `svn diff` command doesn't stop at showing local modifications, though. By using the `--revision` (`-r`) option, you can make `svn diff` output the differences between arbitrary revisions of files. All you need to do is pass the `--revision` option with two revision numbers separated by a colon. The command then returns the differences between the first revision and the second revision.

```
$ svn diff --revision 32:48 cat.html
Index: cat.html
===================================================================
```

```
--- cat.html    (revision 32)
+++ cat.html    (revision 48)
 ---- output snipped ----
```

You can even get svn diff to give you the differences between two completely different files, from two completely different revisions. To do so, first you give svn diff two different paths to files in your working copy or URLs to a repository. Then, if you want to specify the revisions for each file, you enter a --revision REV1:REV2, just as with a single file.

```
$ svn diff --revision 736:103 http://svn.example.com/repos/hen.h http ¬
  ://svn.example.com/repos/fox.py
Index: hen.h
======================================================================
--- hen.h        (revision 736)
+++ fox.ph       (revision 103)
 ---- output snipped ----
```

There is also another subtly different method that you can use for identifying which revision of a file to use, which is the peg revision method. Say, for example, that in revision 12 you had deleted a file named cat.html. Then, later, you renamed the file kitty.html to cat.html. If you do a diff on cat.html and compare revisions 10 and 32 using -r 10:32, Subversion will follow the history of the current cat.html file to compare it at the given revisions (which, at revision 10 was the file kitty.html). If you really want to compare the file cat.html that existed at revision 10 with the current cat.html, you need a way to specifically tell Subversion. This is done by appending the revision numbers after each filename with an @, instead of using the --revision option.

```
$ svn diff http://svn.example.com/repos/cat.html@10 http://svn.example. ¬
  com/repos/cat.html@32
```

5.4.2   Getting the Repository's History

Subversion provides a couple of commands for examining the history of a file or directory in the repository.

Checking the Logs

You can easily see the entire log history of a file (or collection of files) by using the svn log command. When svn log is run with no options, it outputs the logs for the current directory, which includes the change histories for all of the files that are contained in the directory.

```
$ svn log
----------------------------------------------------------------------
r9 | bill | 2004-08-05 22:44:48 -0500 (Thu, 05 Aug 2004) | 26 lines
```

```
Added a check to test porridge temperature.
Temperatures are represented with an enumeration, using
  values of TOO_HOT, TOO_COLD, and JUST_RIGHT


------------------------------------------------------------------
r8 | bill | 2004-08-05 22:21:48 -0500 (Thu, 05 Aug 2004) | 52 lines

Initial commit of porridge.cpp


------------------------------------------------------------------
```

To specify individual files and directories that you would like the history for, you can list files on the command line that `svn log` should examine. These can either be a list of files in your working copy or a URL (which may be followed by a list of files relative to the URL to be used instead of the base URL).

```
$ svn log http://svn.example.com/repos/branch/foo_branch foo.cpp foo.h
```

Subversion shows each log entry, in descending revision order, for every file involved. All of the log entries for the different files are mixed into a single listing, and each log is shown only once, even if it applies to multiple files. By default, `svn log` doesn't give a breakdown showing which files each log applies to, but if you pass the `--verbose` (-v) option it will show that information.

```
$ svn log --verbose
------------------------------------------------------------------
r10 | bill | 2003-06-14 19:44:06 -0500 (Sat, 14 Jun 2003) | 98 lines
Changed paths:
   A Bear.cpp
   A Bear.h
   M Makefile

 Added the class Animal::Bear
------------------------------------------------------------------
```

The default behavior of `svn log` is to output the logs for all of the revisions from the given file's BASE revision back to revision number one (or, in the case of a URL, from the repository HEAD back to revision one). If you don't want that much information, you can restrict the revisions that are looked at by passing the `--revision` (-r) option to `svn log`, with a range of revisions in the form `REV1:REV2` (you can also give just a single revision if that's all you want).

```
$ svn log --revision 45:82 test.c
```

There is one quirk that you should be aware of regarding how svn log works. Its default behavior, if no URL or path is given, is to show the log for . (i.e., the current working copy directory). When the files in a directory are committed, though, the BASE revision of the directory is not updated. So, if you check out a directory at revision 2859 and then perform three commits of changes to files inside the directory, the directory will still be at revision 2859, even though some of its contents are at later revisions. If you then perform an svn log in the directory with no path, the BASE will be taken from the directory (2859), and none of the changes that were committed will be shown (which is probably not what you really wanted). To get a complete log output, with the BASE revision of the most recently committed file in your directory, a better way to run svn log is with a wildcard, instead of an empty path.

```
$ svn log *
```

Who's to Blame?

Another useful tool for examining a file's history is the svn blame command. The blame command causes Subversion to output an entire file, with information about which user committed each line, and what revision that commit occurred in.

```
$ svn blame rabbit.c
    20      bill #include "rabbit.h"
    20      bill
    32      bill int examine_item(int item)
    32      bill {
    53      ted     if(item == CARROT)
    53      ted         eat(item);
    53      ted     else if(item == CAT)
    86      drew        hop_away(FAST, item);
    53      ted     return 0;
    32      bill }
```

You should be a little careful when trusting the output from svn blame, though. The blame entry for a line shows the last revision where *any* change was made, including whitespace. So, if a developer adjusts the spacing on a line, and then commits, that developer will be shown as the author, even though someone else may have actually made the last substantive modification.

Examining Files in the Repository

Often, you will find yourself wanting to know what files are in a particular directory in the repository. One option, of course, is to check out a working copy of that directory, but if all you want to know is the contents of the directory, checking out the whole thing wastes time and bandwidth, and is just generally an all-around clunky way of dealing with the problem. Fortunately, Subversion comes to your rescue with the svn list command.

When you run `svn list`, it contacts the repository and downloads just a list of the files in the given directory, which are then output to the terminal. The directory to list needs to be supplied as a URL to a directory or file in a repository, or as a path to a directory in a working copy (in which case Subversion will use that file's associated URL to contact the repository). If no directory is given, `svn list` uses the current working copy directory.

```
$ svn list http://svn.example.com/repos/branches
test_harness-branch_bill/
web_site-dev_branch/
application-version_2_0_beta/
```

The default behavior of `svn list` is to non-recursively display only the files that are in the HEAD revision of the given directory. If you would rather see a different revision, you can specify one with the `--revision` option, in which case Subversion will list the files that existed in that particular version. If you would like to see a recursive tree of the files in the given directory, you can request that with the `--recursive` option.

```
$ svn list --revision 7 --recursive http://svn.example.com/repos
branches/
tags/
trunk/
trunk/Makefile
trunk/app.c
```

If you need more information than just the names of the files in a directory, you can use the `--verbose` option. In verbose mode, `svn list` will show (in addition to each file's name) the last revision the files were committed in, the user who made that commit, the date of the commit, and the size of the file, in bytes.

```
$ svn list --verbose http://svn.example.com/repos/trunk
      7 bill            9 Aug 03 22:16 bar.c
      6 bill            0 Aug 03 22:12 foo.c
     10 bill            0 Aug 06 00:37 test.py
      2 bill              Jul 31 13:47 trunk/
```

Getting a Single File

Sometimes, you need to look at just one single file from the repository. Unfortunately, `svn checkout` doesn't allow you to specify just a single file, only directories. Getting single files is where the `svn cat` command comes in handy. When run, `svn cat` contacts the repository and downloads just a single file, which it outputs to the terminal. In many cases, you will then want to redirect (using a >) `svn cat`'s output into a file.

```
$ svn cat http://svn.example.com/repos/trunk/foo.c > foo.c
```

5.5   Changing the Working Copy Target

Inside a working copy, Subversion makes it fairly simple to move files and directories between different revisions, and even different repositories. For the most part, movement between revisions is done using the svn update command. Running svn update, by default, updates a file or directory in a working copy to the latest revision in the repository. However, if you supply a --revision (-r) option when the command is run, Subversion instead updates the file in the working copy to that revision, even if it is prior to the current revision in the repository.

```
$ svn update --revision 1773 foo.c
U foo.c
```

In addition to moving between revisions with svn update, you can also use the svn switch command to change a working copy's URL. This allows you, for instance, to switch a directory to a branch. As an example, the following svn switch command switches the trunk directory in the working copy to instead represent the mybranch branch in the branches directory.

```
$ svn switch http://svn.example.com/repos/branches/mybranch trunk/
U foo.c
A foo.h
U bar.c
U Makefile
D README.txt
```

The preceding use of svn switch requires that the given URL be in the same repository as the working copy. You can, however, also use svn switch to completely change the repository that a working copy looks to. This is done by running the command with the --relocate option, which goes through a working copy and changes the base URL of every file or directory that matches the given original base (think find and replace). For example, the following example shows a URL relocation of the working copy trunk directory (and its contents) from example.com to example.net.

```
$ svn switch --relocate http://svn.example.com/repos http://svn.example ¬
  .net/repos trunk/
```

5.6   Resolving Conflicts

Whenever Subversion encounters changes from two different sources, it attempts to perform an automatic merge. If Subversion fails to successfully merge, a conflict occurs. This can happen in a couple of cases. The first is the instance where the changes occur in the same location in the two versions of the file. Because Subversion doesn't know anything about the context of a file, it has no way to merge colliding changes, and must declare a conflict. The other case where a conflict occurs is the case where a binary file is being merged. Binary files are usually very intolerant to minor changes performed by something that doesn't understand the file, which means that using Subversion's textual merge on a binary file would more often than not result in a file that was unreadable. Because Subversion doesn't have any means to merge a binary file, it always declares a conflict when changes from two different sources must be merged.

When a conflict does occur, Subversion creates several different copies of the original file in your home directory. Each copy of the file is a different version of the file from one of several different revisions. The files are all named with an extension telling where the file came from, appended onto the original name of the file. For example, if the file comes from revision 52 of the file `foo.h`, it will be named `foo.h.r52`. If the version of the file is the local working copy version, it will have `.mine` appended. If the conflict occurs as the result of a merge, the righthand and lefthand files from the merge will be named with `.right` and `.left`, respectively. In total, the versions of the file that Subversion will create in the case of a conflict consist of the local working copy version of the file with all local modifications, a pristine copy of the local version with no local modifications, and any remote versions of the file that are involved in the conflict.

If the conflicted file is a text file (i.e., not binary), Subversion also modifies the original version of the file (in the working copy) so that it contains both versions of any conflicted sections inline. The conflicted sections are placed, one after the other, with a separator between them (consisting of = signs). Each version is also labeled with its source. The top version shows its source at the beginning of the section, and the bottom source ends with a source label. The labels are denoted with <s and >s respectively, as you can see in the following example.

```
The Fox: A poem

The quick brown fox
<<<<<<< .mine
with a javelin, leaped
=======
jumped over
>>>>>>> .r378
the lazy dog
```

The work of resolving the conflict is left to you to perform by hand. When you are done, the final, resolved version of the file should reside in your working copy under the original name of the file being resolved (if the file is `bar.txt`, the resolved version should be `bar.txt`). You can accomplish this either by editing the original file or by overwriting it with another file—such as one of the versions of the file that Subversion generated in response to the conflict.

While a file is in a conflicted state, Subversion doesn't allow you to commit the file. If you try, it throws an error and the commit fails. To be able to commit again, you need to tell Subversion when you have finished resolving a conflict. This is done with the svn `resolved` command, which removes all of the extra files created by Subversion when the conflict was declared (leaving only the originally named version of the file) and removes the block on committing the file. It does not in any way modify the originally named file. As an example, the following shows the complete process you might go through when resolving a conflict during an update. In this case, the version of the file in revision 75 is the correct one to use; it's moved to replace `bar.c`.

```
$ svn update
C bar.c
$ ls
bar.c  bar.c.mine  bar.c.r75
$ mv bar.c.r75 bar.c
$ svn resolved
Resolved conflicted state of 'bar.c'
$ ls
bar.c
```

5.7   Branching, Tagging, and Merging

As I explained in earlier chapters, most version control systems allow you to create branches and tags from the main trunk of your repository. Tags allow you to mark specific points in your development (such as releases) for later referral, and branches allow you to split the development of your repository and continue development in parallel on a secondary path. Unlike many other version control systems, Subversion doesn't actually have a built-in concept of branches or tags. Instead, it just uses cheap server-side copies that preserve history, while not taking up any additional space. Subversion just marks the location of the copied file or directory and notes where it came from. It then allows you to merge the changes from a "branch" back into the main trunk of the repository at a later date. Although the current implementation of Subversion's copy-merge system does pose the occasional problem—for instance, you can quickly lose track of a file's full merge/branch history if it becomes more than trivially complex—the flexibility of the paradigm more than makes up for its shortcomings in most cases.

5.7.1   Creating a Branch or Tag

Creating a branch or tag in Subversion is trivially easy. All you need to do is run `svn copy` on the file or directory that you want to branch/tag. Generally, your repository will be set up with one or more directories named `branches` and `tags`, which will be where you want to place copies that are conceptually branches or tags. This is a convention, however, and is in no way enforced by Subversion. As far as Subversion is concerned, directories named `branches` or `tags` are identical to any other directories.

A typical repository layout is to have three top-level directories in the repository, named `trunk`, `branches`, and `tags`. The `trunk` directory contains the main development branch of the repository, and all branches and tags are created by putting copies in their respective directories. By separating the three directories at the top level, you can then check out only the `trunk` directory, and deal with `branches` and `tags` only in the repository most of the time. When you need to use or edit parts of the repository that are in branches, you can use `svn switch` to swap them into your working copy of the `trunk` directory.

Creating a Branch/Tag in the Repository

The most efficient way to branch or tag a part of the repository is usually to perform the copy entirely in the remote repository. When Subversion performs a copy in the repository, it doesn't make a copy of the data, but instead just points the copy back to the data from the original. This allows copies of any sized file to occur in a constant amount of time, be it five kilobytes or five hundred megabytes. On the other hand, if the copy is performed in the local working copy, the repository-side copy still occurs in constant time, but you also make a copy of the data in the working copy, which is proportional to the amount of data to be copied.

A repository-only copy is performed using `svn copy` with repository URLs for both source and destination. When the command is run, Subversion performs an immediate commit, which means that it opens an editor to allow you to enter a log message if you don't supply one on the command line. As an example, the following command shows how you might create a branch of your entire trunk in a typical repository.

```
$ svn cp --message "Created a new branch" http://svn.example.com/repos/ ¬
  trunk http://svn.example.com/repos/branches/mybranch
Committed revision 2353.
```

Creating a Branch/Tag from the Working Copy

Sometimes, creating a branch or tag entirely on the repository is impractical. For example, you might want to create a tag or branch that includes uncommitted local modifications, or consists of multiple mixed revisions. In such cases, you need to pass `svn copy` a working copy path as a source. You can also pass a working copy path as the destination of the copy, but that is generally not what you want, because that would result in the data being copied on your local copy. Instead, if you make sure the destination is still a URL, Subversion only sends the local changes to the repository and all other copies are done as the usual cheap repository-side copies.

```
$ svn cp --message "Tagging a snapshot of the local working copy" ~/ ¬
  repos/trunk http://svn.example.com/repos/tags/mytag
Committed revision 2193.
```

Switching to the Branch/Tag

Regardless of how you create a branch or tag, the best way to edit it locally is usually to use `svn switch` to change the URL that all or part of your working copy points to. If you have a working copy of your trunk already checked out, you will generally save a lot of bandwidth by using the switch command, because it only downloads the differences necessary to switch the URL. The other advantage of svn switch is that it allows you to branch only a portion of your trunk, and then switch that portion in your working copy to the branch without invalidating any relative paths to the rest of your working copy.

5.7.2 Merging a Branch

As you work with a branch, you may periodically want to update it with changes from the main trunk, in order to get changes made by others. You will also usually want to merge the changes that you make in the branch back into the main trunk after they have reached a stable point. Both of these situations are handled with the svn merge command.

The svn merge command is conceptually the hardest Subversion command to deal with, but after you understand how it works, using it is not that complicated. The most basic usage of svn merge is to run it with two revision numbers and a source, as in this example:

```
$ svn merge --revision 100:150 http://svn.example.com/repos/branches/ ¬
  mybranch
U goodbye.cpp
A hello.cpp
```

In this example, svn merge takes the differences between revisions 100 and 150 in the mybranch branch and applies them to the current working copy. The application of the changes occurs just as if you had done an svn update, and any conflicts are handled accordingly.

Another way to run svn merge is to give it two URLs or working copy paths, with revision numbers, and perform a merge of their differences.

```
$ svn merge branches/mybranch@1426 branches/myotherbranch@253
D goodbye.cpp
U hello.cpp
```

As you can see, in the preceding example, there is no requirement that the first revision number should be lower than the second. In fact, regardless of which revision is lower, Subversion will always merge the differences calculated by subtracting the lefthand revision from the righthand revision. So, if a file exists in the righthand revision and not in the lefthand revision, it will be added by the merge. Conversely, if it exists in the lefthand revision but not the righthand, it will be removed.

You will also notice in the last example that I used peg revisions to identify which revisions should be used to identify the files. Peg revisions in a merge work the same as they did for svn diff (see Section 5.4.1, "Getting Information on the Current State").

Keeping Track of Merges

One of the things that Subversion handles poorly is a file or directory's merge history. Subversion does not keep a record of what has been or hasn't been merged. Because of this, it is important for you to keep your own merge history, in order to avoid merging a change twice (which could cause that change to be undone). The easiest way to keep track of your merge history is to record in the commit log what files/revisions were merged.

```
$ svn merge --revision 305:356 branches/mybranch
U Makefile
$ svn commit --message "Merged in revisions 305 to 356 of mybranch"
Committed revision 1398.
```

Then, the next time you want to merge the changes from `mybranch` into `trunk`, you can use `svn log` with `grep` to quickly see which revisions have already been merged in.

```
$ svn log | grep 'Merged'
Merged in revisions 305 to 356 of mybranch
Merged in revisions 284 to 305 of mybranch
Merged in revisions 246 to 320 of myotherbranch
$ svn merge --revision 356:423 branches/mybranch
```

Reverting Changes with Merge

Another use for the merge command is to revert changes that were applied in a previous revision. Say, for instance, that you removed a couple of functions (named `doFoo()` and `getBar()`) from your source file, but now realize that you actually need them. Assuming that they were both removed in discrete commits (i.e., nothing else was changed in the source file at the same time those functions were removed), merging them back into the HEAD revision is quite simple.

First, you'll want to check the logs to find out which revisions the function removals actually took place in. If the file is an active one, with a long log, you might want to use the `grep` command to pare the output down to something a little more manageable. As an example, the following command will search for any lines containing the word "removed" as well as lines that begin with "r" and a number (most likely log entry headers).

```
$ svn log | grep -E 'removed|^r[0-9]'
r15 | bill | 2004-06-14 19:44:06 -0500 (Sat, 14 Jun 2004) | 98 lines
r76 | bill | 2004-07-17 12:35:24 -0500 (Sat, 17 Jul 2004) | 32 lines
removed doFoo()
r85 | bill | 2004-07-23 10:23:19 -0500 (Fri, 23 Jul 2004) | 15 lines
r97 | bill | 2003-08-07 15:54:29 -0500 (Thu, 05 Aug 2004) | 145 lines
removed getBar()
```

After you know which revisions the functions were removed in, you can revert the removals by performing a merge with a range that goes backwards, from the revision where the removal took place, to the revision immediately preceding the removal. This will merge the removed sections back into your current working copy, where you can make any necessary modifications and then commit.

```
$ svn merge --revision 76:75 foobar.c
U foobar.c
$ svn merge --revision 97:96 foobar.c
U foobar.c
$ svn status
M       foobar.c
$ svn commit --message "Reverted changes from revs 76 & 97 to foobar.c"
Sending         foobar.c
Transmitting file data .
Committed revision 245.
```

Looking before You Merge

Merges can cause a lot of changes to be applied to the files in your working copy, and undoing those changes can be difficult if there are a lot of local changes. It can be helpful, then, to find out exactly which files Subversion will change (as well as what conflicts will occur) before actually performing the merge. Subversion allows you to do just that with the `--dry-run` option. When `svn merge` is invoked with `--dry-run`, Subversion will perform all of the necessary calculations for the merge and output a list of files that will be modified (as well as how those files will be modified), but it will not actually change any of your local files.

5.8   Troubleshooting the Working Copy

Subversion is a robust, stable system, but occasionally problems do occur—usually as a result of an interrupted command or unstable network connection. If such an interruption does occur, Subversion may leave active lock files in your working copy, which could block subsequent commands from being able to execute. If this happens, you may have to explicitly force Subversion to clean up after itself.

You can tell Subversion to clean up all extraneous working copy lock files by running the `svn cleanup` command. When the cleanup command is run, it will go through the working copy (or part of a working copy) specified on the command line, completing all unfinished actions and removing all lock files.

```
$ svn cleanup repos/trunk
```

If the `svn cleanup` command doesn't solve your problems, you may need to clean things up on the repository side (or have your repository administrator do it). The commands and techniques for doing repository troubleshooting are explained in Chapter 10, "Administrating the Repository."

In a worst-case scenario, your working copy could get irretrievably corrupted (most likely through disk error or a bug in Subversion). If this happens, you may have to delete and recheck out a working copy. In general, this is not a tragic solution, but you may have to take a few extra steps to avoid data loss if you have any uncommitted local modifications.

The best way to approach a delete-checkout solution is to first use the `svn status` command (if possible) to figure out which files have been locally modified. Then, make sure those are backed up somewhere outside the working copy (by copying them). When all of your local data has been saved, remove the working directory and run `svn checkout` to get a fresh working copy. Then, you can copy the backed up files into your new working copy and be ready to commit again.

5.9 Summary

In this chapter, you learned the commands that a day-to-day client user of Subversion needs to know when dealing with her working copy. You saw how to get data out of a repository, using commands such as `svn checkout` and `svn update`, as well as how to get data into the repository using `svn add`, `svn import`, and `svn commit`. Additionally, you learned how to query the repository for information, using such commands as `svn log` and `svn status`, and learned more advanced techniques such as branching, tagging, and merging. Finally, you saw how to recover a working copy that has become corrupted or blocked.

In the next chapter, you will learn about storing file metadata, using properties. The chapter will show you the mechanics of using the Subversion commands for manipulating properties, and will give an overview of the built-in properties that Subversion uses for special features.

Chapter 6

Using Properties

One of Subversion's most powerful features is its property system. In addition to storing the history of a file, Subversion also allows you to associate arbitrary metadata with each file, directory, or revision. Properties are keyed with a user-defined name, and can contain any data that you would like to associate. Additionally, Subversion provides several special properties that Subversion clients use in order to provide added functionality to versioned files.

Properties in Subversion come in two forms. Conceptually, both forms of properties are the same, and both are dealt with using nearly identical syntax. The key difference between the two forms lies in how they are versioned, and how those versions are accessed and modified.

The first form is a versioned property, which is applied to a file or directory. These sorts of properties are the most common, dealt with directly on a day-to-day basis, and tend to just be referred to as *properties*. Changes to versioned properties are stored with new revisions, when a file is committed, just as changes to the contents of a file are.

The second form of property is an unversioned property that is attached to a specific revision, instead of a file in the repository. These properties, which are called *revision properties* because they are attached to a revision, can be modified, but their history is not stored. If a revision property is modified, its previous state is irretrievably lost. Internally, Subversion uses revision properties to store information such as commit dates and log messages, but users can also store their own properties as revision properties.

6.1 Storing Metadata

Properties are associated with a file or directory by using the svn propset command. The simplest way to set a property is by passing to the svn propset command the property key and value, along with the file to set the property on.

```
$ svn propset property_key "property value" repos/trunk/foo.h
```

The property key is a string of your choosing, which will be used later for retrieving the associated data from the file. Property keys are handled internally by Subversion as XML, and therefore the property keys themselves are restricted by valid XML NAMES, which is basically any string that contains letters, digits, ., -, and _. For a more formal definition, see the XML standard, available from the World Wide Web Consortium (www.w3.org).

When choosing property names, it is a good idea to use some sort of naming convention. The naming scheme used by the built-in Subversion properties is to begin each property key with svn:. This might seem like a good convention to adopt for your own property names, but alas, the colon isn't really a valid character in property names. It can only be used reliably in the svn: prefix. It is, however, a sound idea to use prefixes to categorize your properties. You just can't categorize them with a colon. Instead, I suggest using a period to separate a category prefix from a property name. This allows you to assign properties to different categories, and name them accordingly, making it easy to quickly identify broad purposes for the properties, which makes specific meaning easier to discern and remember. You are also able to selectively search for all of the properties in a given category, using the svn proplist command, as I will discuss later in Section 6.2.1, "Listing Properties."

As an example, let's say that you use Subversion properties to store automated tests and file ownership information. You can then standardize on two property categories, named test and ownership. A property containing a unit-testing script could be named test.unit, and properties containing the file's author and copyright could be named ownership.author and ownership.copyright.

Subversion property values can be of any form, either text or binary. If the property is short, it is easy to provide it as a parameter on the command line (remember to enclose it with quotation marks if it has spaces though). If the property is long, or if it is a binary file, entering the property value on the command line is impractical. In that case, you can direct svn propset to read the property from a file using the --file (-F) option, which directs Subversion to read the property's value from a file, as in the following example.

```
$ svn propset property_key --file ~/property_val.txt repos/trunk/foo.h
```

6.1.1   Editing Properties

Sometimes, you don't want to change an entire property, but would rather make a small change to an existing one. In these cases, Subversion provides you with the svn propedit command, which opens the current property in the current editor.[1] After you have finished editing the property's value, you can save the file and quit. As soon as you quit, Subversion will apply the modified property value to the file or directory's property.

Subversion does not require that a property must exist prior to calling svn propedit. If you have a long property to add to a file or directory, it is often easier to call svn propedit instead of svn propset to add the initial property value to the file. All you need to do is just run the propedit command and type in the property to the new document that is opened in the editor. When you're done, save and quit.

6.1.2   Automatically Setting Properties

If you have a property that needs to be set for every file of a certain type that's added, it's almost a guarantee that you will forget at least once if you need to set the property

---

1.   See Section 7.2.1, "The config File."

manually every time. Fortunately, if the value of the property is static for every file of a certain filename pattern, you can tell Subversion to set the value automatically. All you have to do is set up the Subversion configuration file with the appropriate patterns and values (see Section 7.2.1).

6.1.3 Committing Properties

When you run `svn propset` or `svn propedit`, Subversion sets the new property value in the working copy, but does not contact the repository. Instead, the property changes are scheduled to be committed to the repository on the next `svn commit`. You can tell which files and directories will have properties committed on the next `svn commit` by running `svn status`. The status command will show all files with modified properties by placing an M in the second column of its output.

When you commit a file or directory property to the repository, it is handled just like file data. It is applied to the new revision, but doesn't affect any previous revisions.

6.1.4 Storing Revision Properties

Revision properties are stored using the `--revprop` option to either `svn propset` or `svn propedit`. They must be set on a particular revision, so you also need to use the `--revision (-r)` option when setting or editing a revision property. Be careful when using `svn propset`, because changes are applied immediately and are not undoable. Any previous data in the revision property will be irretrievably lost. It is almost always better to use `svn propedit` when working with revision properties, as it is much harder to accidentally delete important data that way.

As an example, the following command will invoke an editor to edit a property that stores which issue-tracking issue is fixed in the last revision that you committed.

```
$ svn status --show-updates
Status against revision:   2225
$ svn propedit --revprop --revision 2225 issues.fixes
```

You'll notice that I didn't run `svn propedit` with the HEAD revision label, but instead used `svn status -show-updates` to get the number of the HEAD revision. I do that to ensure that I am setting the revision property on the revision that I think I am. If another user were to commit a new revision while I was editing the property, the HEAD would be changed to point to the new head of the repository, which is likely not the revision that I want to edit. It's always safer to get the revision number and then use that explicitly.

6.2 Retrieving Metadata

Properties are retrieved via the `svn propget` command, which gets a keyed property from a file or directory and outputs it. The command takes a property key, and a file to retrieve the property from (which can either be a file in a working copy or a repository URL). It outputs the property's value, as in the following example.

```
$ svn propget ownership.author hello_world.c
William Nagel
```

Subversion also allows you to pass multiple files to `svn propget`, in which case it will output the supplied property for each of the given files. To make it easier to differentiate the property values for the multiple files, Subversion will also prepend the name of each file in front of each value.

```
$ svn propget author *.txt
Cathedral_and_Bazaar.txt - Eric S. Raymond
GPL.txt - Richard M. Stallman
```

When outputting a property value, Subversion adds a newline at the end of the property in order to prettify the output a bit. That and `svn propget`'s filename prepending on multiple files, however, is undesirable behavior when the property is a binary file that you want to output. In those cases, you can use the `--strict` option to turn off both additions. With strict output, the `svn propget` output is suitable for redirecting into a file.

```
$ svn propget --strict advertising.poster MyFlick.mov > poster.jpg
```

6.2.1   Listing Properties

To retrieve property values, it's sometimes necessary to first check to see what properties are available. With Subversion, you can list available properties using the `svn proplist` command. When you run `svn proplist`, the command will take a list of versioned files and/or directories and output all of the properties that are set for them.

```
$ svn proplist svc.tex
Properties on 'svc.tex':
  copyright.author
  copyright.date
  copyright.publisher
```

If you would also like to get the values of all properties associated with a file, you can run `svn proplist` in verbose mode with `--verbose` (-v). To save you from accidentally dumping the entire contents of a binary file to standard out, `svn proplist` will not output a binary property value. Instead, it will output ???? to let you know that the value is nonASCII.

```
$ svn proplist --verbose svc.tex
Properties on 'svc.tex':
  copyright.author : William Nagel
  copyright.publisher : Prentice Hall
  img.cover : ????
```

The default `svn proplist` behavior is to work non-recursively. If you would like to see the properties that are set on all of the files inside a directory though, you can turn on recursive listing with the `--recursive` (-R) option.

```
$ svn proplist --recursive trunk/book
Properties on 'trunk/book/svc.tex':
  copyright.author
  copyright.date
  img.cover
Properties on 'trunk/book/chapter1.tex':
  copyright.author
  copyright.date
```

Sometimes, you need to get the values of several properties from a collection of files. Although Subversion has no built in mechanism for finding such information directly, you can easily get the information you want by using the `grep` command to filter `svn proplist`'s output. For example, say you have a directory full of image files, each with copyright information attached as a set of properties with names starting `copyright`. If you would like to output all of the copyright information on all of those files, you could run a command similar to the following.

```
$ svn proplist --recursive --verbose trunk/images | grep -E '^ ¬
  Properties on|^  copyright' > copyrights.txt
```

6.2.2 Outputting Multiple Binary Properties

Occasionally, you will need to retrieve the contents of multiple binary properties and put them into distinct files. If there are only a couple of files, it's easy enough to just run multiple `svn propget`'s, and redirect them into their own files. On the other hand, if the number of files is large, individually retrieving them can be impractical. However, by using a looping construct, such as the `for` loop in the Bourne Again Shell (BASH), you can easily get multiple files. As an example, the following command will take a list of C files and output the Python testing scripts that are embedded in each file as a property named `test.script`.

```
$ for FILE in *.c;
> do svn propget test.script $FILE > ${$FILE/%.c/-test.py};
> done
$ ls
bar.c  bar-test.py  foo.c  foo-test.py
```

In this example, the `for FILE in *.c;` tells BASH that it should loop through every file that ends in a `.c` and place its name in the variable `FILE`. It will then run the `svn propget` command for that file and redirect the output into a file that has the same base name as the file containing the property, but with the `.c` suffix replaced by `-test.py`. As you can see, after the command has run, both of the C files have had a test script extracted.

6.2.3 Getting Revision Properties

Revision properties are retrieved in pretty much the same manner as regular versioned properties. The only difference is that you must explicitly refer to a revision when getting a revision property, using the `--revision` (`-r`) option. As with the property setting commands, you also need to tell Subversion that you are referring to a revision property by using the `--revprop` option, like in the following example.

```
$ svn propget --revprop --revision 4356 svn:log
```

6.3   Built-in Properties

Subversion provides a number of built-in properties that have special meaning to a Subversion repository or client. The built-in properties are split into two categories: the file properties and the revision properties. The file properties are assigned to specific files or directories and are generally only assigned explicitly by a user—with the exception of the `svn:mime-type` property, and the `svn:executable` property, which can be set automatically when a file is added. The revision properties, on the other hand, are all set automatically when a revision is committed to the repository, but can be changed later if the need arises. All of the built-in Subversion properties are named with a naming scheme that starts with `svn:`.

6.3.1   File Properties

Subversion provides several file properties that you can set for individual files or directories. Internally, these properties are handled the same as every other property, but each has added meaning and is used by Subversion clients to add functionality to the files.

svn:eol-style

Subversion uses the `svn:eol-style` property to determine how it should handle line-ending characters when a file is checked out or committed. By default, Subversion doesn't do any processing of line-endings and instead just leaves them in the same form as when they were committed. If your repository is being used by users on Windows and UNIX, though, line endings can become a problem. Because Windows uses both a carriage return (CR) and a line feed (LF) character to denote a line ending, whereas UNIX uses just the line feed, dealing with files on both platforms can be difficult—especially if the tools being used on the different platforms don't understand how to deal with files from another system. If you need to change this behavior, you can use the `svn:eol-style` property to tell the Subversion client how it should handle files.

The most common case is a user wanting files to include the line-ending character that is appropriate for his own system. In other words, Windows users will want text files that they check out to use CR/LF to end lines, whereas UNIX users will want just an LF. To ensure that this is exactly what each user sees, you can set `svn:eol-style` for a file to `native`. Then, when clients check out a file they will check to see if the `svn:eol-style` property is set, and if it is `native` they will transform all of the line-ending characters in the file to match the platform on which the client resides.

Transforming characters on checkout is not always desirable though. If the `svn:eol-style` property is set to a specific line-ending type, instead of the word `native`, the Subversion client will explicitly transform each line ending in all text files that are checked out to the supplied type. The supported line-ending types are CRLF, CR, and LF.

svn:executable

On UNIX-based systems, executable files are defined by the "executable" permission bit. It would be nice if files that were checked out of a repository retained information about whether that executable bit should be set. Not all platforms that Subversion runs on use the same format for storing permissions though, so it doesn't make sense for Subversion to directly store those permission bits when they are committed. To work around this limitation, Subversion uses the `svn:executable` property. Files that have the executable property set (to any value) will be automatically set to executable when checked out on any platform that supports the UNIX-style executable permissions. Files that are set to be executable will automatically have the `svn:executable` property set when they are added to a repository (via `svn add` or `svn import`). On filesystems that don't have an executable permission bit (e.g., Win32 with NTFS or FAT32), this property will have no effect.

svn:externals

The `svn:externals` property allows you to attach a property to a directory, which will tell the Subversion client to check out another part of the repository, or even another repository altogether, and place it in a subdirectory. This can be handy if you have multiple projects that have complex interdependencies, or even if you have a dependency on an external project that is also available from a Subversion repository.

As an example, let's say you have two repositories. One contains a code library, and the other contains a project that uses the library. When developers check out the project, they need to have access to the library in order to compile it. To further complicate things, the project expects the library to be located in a particular subdirectory relative to the base of the project.

One option, of course, would be to instruct each developer in the need to check out both repositories, as well as where the second repository needs to be checked out in relation to the first. At best, this is unwieldy. However, by using the `svn:externals` property, you can direct the Subversion client to perform the second checkout automatically.

In our example, all you would need to do to set `svn:externals` properly would be to add a line to the property (on the project's base directory) that contains the relative path to where the library should be checked out, followed by whitespace and then the repository URL that should be checked out. So, depending on the layout, it might look something like this:

```
$ svn propget svn:externals trunk
libraries/mylib        http://svn.example.com/library_repos/trunk/mylib
```

If you have multiple dependencies, you can declare them using multiple lines in the `svn:externals` property.

```
$ svn propget svn:externals trunk
libraries/mylib        http://svn.example.com/library_repos/trunk/mylib
libraries/otherlib       http://svn.example.net/repos/tags/ ¬
  otherlib_rel_1_0
```

You can also set up an externals link to grab a particular revision of a repository.

```
$ svn propget svn:externals trunk
libraries/mylib     -r 1256    http://svn.example.com/repos/trunk/mylib
```

svn:ignore

Working copies have a tendency to get cluttered with files that you need, but don't want to be committed to the repository, such as object files, compiled executables, editor swap files, and other temporary files. Unfortunately, these unversioned files tend to get in the way of Subversion. Because Subversion shows these files in svn status with a ?, they can quickly clutter up its output, making it hard to see files with legitimate output information (for example, I tend to use Subversion commands while the Vi editor is running, and it's not uncommon for me to have twenty to thirty files open in the same directory—that leaves twenty to thirty .swp files that swamp all other svn output). It can also be easy to accidentally add files that you didn't mean to, especially if you recursively add a directory.

The svn:ignore property lets you set unversioned files that will be ignored by all Subversion commands, except svn status when it is run with the --no-ignore, or svn add and svn import when they are explicitly directed to add the ignored file. Elements to be ignored are listed in the svn:ignore property, one per line. Ignored elements can either be an exact filename match or a pattern that contains wildcards (*).

The following example shows an svn:ignore property that is directing Subversion to ignore all files that end in .o, all files that start with a dot (.), and the file named debug.out.

```
$ svn propget svn:ignore trunk/src
*.o
.*
debug.out
```

It should be noted that svn:ignore is not recursive. It applies only to the directory that you set it for. If you want to set ignores for an entire repository, you either have to use svn propset with the --recursive option or set up a user-level ignore (which is discussed in Section 7.2.1).

svn:keywords

It's all well and good to be able to use Subversion commands to find out information like the last time a file was modified, but sometimes it's useful to actually store that information in the file itself—especially if you are planning on distributing that file to someone via a means other than the Subversion repository. In those cases, Subversion has the capability to perform inline replacements on certain keywords, whenever a file is checked out or updated.

By default, Subversion will not perform any keyword replacements. If you want to turn keyword replacement on, you need to do it by setting the svn:keywords property, which should contain a list of the keywords that you want Subversion to perform substitution on, separated by whitespace. So, if you want Subversion to substitute the keywords HeadURL and LastChangedRevision, your svn:keywords property would look like this:

```
$ svn propget svn:keywords foo.c
LastChangedRevision HeadURL
```

The set of keywords that Subversion will replace is actually fairly small, and mostly revolve around the last time the file was changed. In fact, three of the five keywords are information about the last file change. Those keywords are LastChangedBy, LastChangedDate, and LastChangedRevision. If you would like to save yourself a few keystrokes, these keywords can be abbreviated with Author, Date, and Revision (or even Rev), respectively. The content of each substitution should be fairly self-explanatory.

Subversion also provides a keyword for embedding a URL to the file in the HEAD revision of the repository, called HeadURL. It can also be abbreviated as URL.

The fifth and final keyword is Id. The Id keyword is a summary keyword that includes data from several other keywords. Its content is made up of the name of the file, the last revision number of a commit for the file, a date showing when the file was last modified, and the username of the person who committed the last modification.

Keywords are placed into a file surrounded by dollar signs ($). When a substitution is performed, Subversion will add the value of the substitution after the keyword, separated by a colon. It is important that the keyword itself be left in the file; otherwise, Subversion wouldn't know that it was substituted text when you next commit the file, and wouldn't keep the keyword.

The following example shows an (admittedly contrived) file with keywords, followed by that file after it has been checked out and the keywords have been substituted.

```
original file:
This file was last changed on $Date$,
by $Author$, in revision $Rev$.
It can be found at $HeadURL$
$Id$

substituted file:
This file was last changed on $Date: 2004-08-12 01:56:13 -0500 (Thur ¬
  , 12 Aug 2004) $
by $Author: bill $, in revision $Rev: 1276 $.
It can be found at $HeadURL: http://svn.example.com/repos/trunk/ ¬
  keywords.txt $
$Id keywords.txt 1276 2004-08-12 01:56:13 bill $
```

svn:mime-type

The de facto cross-platform standard for identifying file types is the Multipurpose Internet Mail Exchange (MIME)-type, which consists of a general type and a specific type, separated by a slash. MIME-types are used by many programs (especially Internet-based ones, like Web browsers and e-mail clients) to determine how they should handle a file. Because the MIME-type is a useful piece of information to have, Subversion provides the svn:mime-type property as a standard place to store the MIME-type for a versioned file.

In addition to using svn:mime-type as a standard location, Subversion also uses a file's MIME-type for its own purposes. Primarily, Subversion uses the MIME-type to determine when a file is binary and should not be textually merged. It determines which files are binary by looking at the general type of a file's MIME-type. If the general type is anything other than text (i.e., the MIME-type doesn't begin with text/[2]), Subversion will assume that the file is binary. Additionally, Subversion will send the svn:mime-type through the Apache server whenever a client requests a file's type.

The svn:mime-type property can be set manually, just like any other property, using svn propset or svn propedit. However, to make life a little easier on you, Subversion will also try to guess which files are binary when they are added to the repository. If it decides that a file appears to be binary, it will automatically set the svn:mime-type property equal to application/octet-stream. If you don't like what Subversion decides, you can always change it later.

If you are using a UNIX-like system, you can use the file program to determine the type of a file. If file is run with the -i option, it will output a file's MIME-type. You can combine this with svn propset to set a file's MIME-type in a single step, as in the following example (the -b tells file not to output the name of the file it processed).

```
$ svn propset svn:mime-type "`file -i -b foo.txt`" foo.txt
$ svn propget svn:mime-type foo.txt
text/plain; charset=us-ascii
```

svn:special

This property is new in version 1.1 of Subversion, and is used to identify special types of files. It is not meant to be edited directly by a user. Instead, the Subversion client uses it internally to recognize files that it should interpret in some special way, based on the file's contents. Currently, this is only used to implement symbolic links. When a symbolic link file is checked out on a system that supports symbolic links, the file will be read to determine how the symbolic link should be created. If the operating system does not support symbolic links (e.g. Windows), the file will not be interpreted, but rather will be checked out as a normal file.

---

2.   Subversion also treats image/x-bitmap and image/x-pixmap as text.

6.3.2 Revision Properties

When new revisions are committed to a repository, Subversion automatically sets three revision properties. Each of these properties can be changed if necessary, but remember that revision properties are unversioned and a change results in the loss of the property's previous value. Also, modification of revision properties is disabled by default. To allow revision properties to be modified, you must have a hook script set up to process revision property changes. Hook scripts are discussed in Section 11.1, "An Introduction to Hooks."

svn:author

The svn:author property contains the username of the user who committed the revision. Changing this can be useful if the username listed on the commit was not the actual user who logically performed the commit (if, for instance, you borrowed a colleague's computer to make a quick change).

svn:date

Subversion stores the date and time that a revision was committed in the svn:date property. In general, this is the revision property that you are least likely to need to change. Usually, the need to change it will only come about because of an incorrect clock at the time of the commit.

If you do need to change the svn:date property, Subversion stores the dates in UTC (Coordinated Universal Time), using the ISO-8601 format, which looks similar to the following.

```
$ svn propget --revprop -r 1262 svn:date
2004-07-30T05:28:19.312099Z
```

The details of the ISO-8601 format are beyond the scope of this book, but if you simply need to slightly modify a time it should be relatively easy to figure out what you need to do. Remember, though, that UTC time is time-zone independent and not likely to be the same as your time zone (unless you live near Greenwich in England). If you modify svn:date, you will need to manually compensate for the time zone. For example, if you live in the Eastern time zone of the United States, you will need to add five hours to your local time in order to get UTC.

Now that I've given you a lecture on how you *can* change the svn:date property, let me stress that I strongly suggest you *don't* change it unless you absolutely have to. The change will not be undoable, and a messed up date can really throw things off in your repository.

svn:log

The automatically generated revision property that you are most likely to need to change is the svn:log property. Subversion stores the log entry for each revision in this property. If you make a commit and then realize that you forgot to put something into the log, or realize that something you put in was incorrect, you can modify this property. Do so with caution though, as a slip could erase valuable information. As a precaution, I suggest always editing log files using the `svn propedit` command, which will open the log entry in an editor for you to edit. If you use `svn propset`, it is much easier to accidentally wipe out information that you didn't want to lose. (Imagine your horror when you realize that you just overwrote the log for revision 21 instead of revision 12.)

6.4   Summary

In this chapter, you learned how to make use of Subversion's property metadata to enhance the information stored in your repository. The first section explained how to get and set properties on files, directories, and revisions—as well as a variety of best practices to help you get the most out of your properties (such as categorizing property names). Then, in the second section, you learned about the numerous built-in properties that Subversion uses to provide added functionality to the Subversion client.

Chapter 7

Configuring the Client

When using a Subversion client, either from the command line or a graphical tool, there are a variety of things that you may want to configure to be true *every* time you run a Subversion command. To allow you to configure these options, Subversion maintains a few configuration files.

7.1   Finding the Configuration Files

Configuration options can be set either on a per-user basis or as system-wide defaults (which will be used by every user on the system who hasn't overridden them). Options are stored in configuration files—or in the case of Microsoft Windows, configuration files *or* registry entries.

On UNIX-based systems, such as Solaris, Linux, or Mac OS X, per-user configuration files are stored in the `.subversion` directory in each user's home directory. System-wide configurations, on the other hand, are stored in `/etc/subversion`.

If you are running a Microsoft Windows variant instead, the per-user directory will be named `Subversion`. As to where it will be located on the filesystem, that's not such an easy question to answer. Every version of Windows handles things a little bit differently, and thus ends up with the directory in a different place. In many cases, it is even hidden. Your best bet is probably to search for it on your particular system, although it will often be in the directory pointed to by the `%APPDATA%` environment variable. Similarly, the system-wide configurations are also stored in a directory named `Subversion`, which should be located wherever your version of Windows stores system-wide application data.

When a Subversion client is run for the first time by a user, the client will automatically create default configuration files for that user in the appropriate places (depending on the OS that you're using). It won't create system-wide configuration files though. For those, you (or your administrator) will need to create the files by hand.

7.2   Editing the Configuration Files

Inside the configuration directory (e.g., `.subversion`), you will find two configuration files that you can edit: `config` and `servers`. These are both plain text files with options that you can change. (Subversion sets them up with reasonable defaults when they are

created.) You will also find a file named README.txt, which explains the format of the
configuration files. In many cases, there will also be a directory named auth, which contains repository authentication information. Unless you *really* know what you're doing,
there is very little in the auth directory that can be edited by hand.

7.2.1   The config File

The configuration file config is used to set a variety of options that control how a Subversion client will act by default. The file itself is broken down into four sections, each
of which contains several different options. The sections (in the order they appear in the
automatically generated default config file) are: [auth], [helpers], [tunnels], and
[miscellany].[1]

Setting the Authorization Retention

The first configuration section, [auth], has two options (one of which was added in version 1.1). The first controls whether Subversion saves your passwords to repositories (in
the .subversin/auth directory), whereas the second allows you to turn off *all* caching
of authentication credentials to disk. By default, Subversion does save your authorization
information, but for security purposes that may not be what you want. This is especially
useful if a working copy is shared by multiple people who have their own repository accounts, but share a shell account on the machine where the working copy resides (on a test
server, for instance). In such a case, it would be much better if Subversion demanded a
username and password every time the repository was accessed, which is what you will get
if you set Subversion to not store passwords.

The option to set for turning off password caching is called store-password, and
should be set to either yes or no, as in this example, which shows a complete [auth]
section:

```
[auth]
store-password = yes
```

If you want to go a step further and disable all authentication caching, you can instead
set the store-auth-creds to no. If you use store-auth-creds, there is no need to also
use store-passwords, because password storing is disabled by this option, along with
the caching of any other credentials, including usernames and SSL or SSH certificates.

```
[auth]
store-auth-creds = no
```

Setting Your Helper Programs

Subversion has the capability to make use of several external utility programs (although
it has its own internal default version for most of them). If you need to change which
programs Subversion uses, you can set those in the [helpers] section of the config file.

---

1. This is accurate through version 1.1 of Subversion. Subsequent versions may introduce new options or
sections.

One of the helpers that you may want to modify is the text editor that Subversion uses to obtain log entries from users when they run commands that modify the repository. By default, Subversion looks at the environment variables $SVN_EDITOR, $VISUAL, and then $EDITOR to determine which program to run. If you would rather specify that command in the configuration file, though, you can override Subversion's environment variable checking by setting the editor-cmd option, like in the following example entry.

```
editor-cmd = /usr/bin/emacs
```

The other set of programs that you may need to set are the diff programs that Subversion uses to compare files. Subversion has its own diffing algorithms built into the system, but you may find that a third-party diff tool, such as GNU diff, better serves your needs. For instance, if you need the output of a Subversion diff command to be in a format other than the unified diff format that Subversion uses, you would need to use an external diff tool.

Subversion uses two different diff commands, each of which you can independently set a command for. The first is the standard diff program, used for finding the differences between two files, and is set by the diff-cmd option. The other diff program that Subversion uses is a three-way diff, which it uses when performing merges. You can set the three-way diff program with diff3-cmd. You can also tell Subversion whether it should pass a --diff-program option to the three-way diff command to tell it which two-way diff program to use, using the diff3-has-program-arg option. If you do change the default diff command, there is one word of caution: Subversion assumes that your command takes GNU-style diff/diff3 options, so you may have to write a wrapper script to do a conversion.

The following example shows how you might set up the diff commands in the config file.

```
diff-cmd = /usr/bin/diff
diff3-cmd = /usr/bin/diff3
diff3-has-program-arg = false
```

Setting Up Tunnels

Subversion has the capability to access a remote repository by tunneling through another program to a remote server. When it connects to the remote server, it will run svnserve on the remote server to connect to the repository. Normally, the scheme used for tunneling is SSH (which Subversion supports by default), but you can set up other tunneling schemes through your config file.

Entries for different tunneling schemes are entered in the [tunnels] section of the config file. Each entry defines a different scheme (and the program that Subversion should use for the tunneling). The basic form for the entries is the name of the scheme, followed by an equals sign, and then the name of the program that Subversion should run (along with any options that should be fed to the program). So, to set up Subversion to be able to tunnel through rsh, using the username bill, you could set up your config file with an entry like the following example.

```
rsh = /usr/bin/rsh -l bill
```

To invoke this scheme, you would then run your Subversion client with a repository URL such as `svn+rsh://svn.example.com/var/svn/myrepos`, which would cause Subversion to run the command

```
rsh -l bill svn.example.com svnserve -t
```

You can add as many tunneling schemes as you want, and can use whatever names you would like to identify them. This means that you could set up multiple schemes in the `config` file to use the same program with different options, such as these entries, which set up two SSH schemes for connecting with different usernames.

```
ssh_bill = ssh -l bill
ssh_drew = ssh -l drew
```

Setting Global Ignores

Often, you will end up with files in your working copy that you have no intention of ever adding to the repository. For example, object files that are generated when you compile a program are not something that you usually want to store in the repository, instead preferring to have them regenerated in each individual working copy. The problem with files you don't want to ever add to the repository is that they can easily clutter the output of the Subversion status command, and can often get accidentally committed if you are not careful.

The solution is to use global ignores in your `config` file, to give Subversion file patterns that it should ignore when running Subversion commands. So, if you don't want to see object files, you could tell Subversion to ignore all files that end in `.o`. Ignore patterns are entered under the `[miscellany]` section, with the option `global-ignores`. As an example, the following entry would tell Subversion to ignore all files that end in `.o` or `.exe`.

```
global-ignores = *.o *.exe
```

Setting the Log File Encoding

Subversion always stores log messages in UTF8, using your local system's locale. In some cases, though, your editor may be providing log messages to Subversion in a different encoding. If that is the case, you need to tell Subversion what encoding to expect so that it can perform the proper conversions. To do that, you can set the `log-encoding` option under the `[miscellany]` section, like in this entry, which tells Subversion to use ASCII encoding.

```
log-encoding = ascii
```

Controlling File Timestamps

When you check out or update a file in a working copy, the timestamps on files will normally reflect the date and time when the checkout or update created the current version of the file in your working copy. If you would instead like to have the timestamps reflect the last time those files were changed in the repository, you can tell Subversion to set them appropriately by setting the `use-commit-times` option (in the `[miscellany]` section) to `yes`, so that your entry will look like this:

```
use-commit-times = yes
```

Automatically Setting Properties

Subversion has the capability to automatically assign property values to files, based on their names, using rules that are set up in the `config` file. To turn auto properties on, you need to set the `enable-auto-props` option to `yes` in the `[miscellany]` section (or enable it on the command line with `--auto-props` when a command is run). Then, you can add an `[auto-props]` section to your config file and set up as many automatic property entries as you need. Each entry consists of a filename pattern (which can use wildcards to match multiple files), followed by an equals sign, followed by a semicolon-separated list of property/value pairs. For example, the following snippet shows a sample `[auto-props]` section.

```
[auto-props]
*.c = svn:keywords=Id
*.h = svn:keywords=Id
*.bat = svn:eol-style=CRLF;svn:executable
```

7.2.2 The servers File

In most cases, connecting to Subversion repositories will require no special intervention. You will just give the URL to your Subversion client and everything will work. Occasionally, though, some repositories will require extra information to connect properly. For instance, you may need to set up parameters for using an HTTP proxy to deal with a firewall, or fine-tune the way the Subversion client handles SSL certificates for a secure connection.

Subversion allows you to set these special server-specific connection options in the `servers` configuration file, which is located in the same place as the `config` file from the previous section. In it, you can set up a variety of options for connecting to specific servers, or groups of servers.

Setting Up Server Groups

The `servers` file is split into three types of sections.

- One or more sections that define the server options for individual groups

- A section that defines the groups (and the servers they are associated with)

- A section that defines global server options

You define groups in the [groups] section. Each entry defines a group, along with the server or servers that the group applies to. Servers can either be entered as a single server name (such as svn.example.com) or with wildcards to match an entire domain (such as *.example.com). You can also add more than one specific server or server pattern by entering multiple servers, separated by commas. As an example, the following sample [groups] section sets up two groups of servers.

```
[groups]
mygroup = svn.example.com
myothergroup = svn.example.org,*.example.net
```

You can have as many groups as you would like, and can give each group a name that makes sense to you. The names that you use will then be used later in the document as the section headings to identify which group a set of options applies to.

Configuring HTTP Proxies

HTTP proxies are used for a wide-ranging variety of reasons, from security to traffic management to preventing access to certain sites or domains (and a lot of things in between). Proxies act as an intermediary for HTTP requests. They receive requests from clients, and then forward the request to the real server. Therefore, a client needs to be configured to send requests to the proxy, instead of trying to contact the server directly. In Subversion, the place to configure proxies is in the servers configuration file. For each group, you can specify all of the information necessary to direct your requests through a proxy, as well as specify certain servers that won't need the proxy. The following example shows how you might set up a group of servers to use a proxy.

```
[mygroup]
http-proxy-host = proxy.example.com
http-proxy-port = 8880
http-proxy-username = bill
http-proxy-password = mypasswd
http-proxy-exceptions = internal-1.example.com *.internal-example.com
```

This sets up Subversion to send all requests to the server in mygroup through the proxy.example.com proxy server, which is listening on port 8880. When it connects to the proxy, it will use the username and password that you have supplied. If you don't supply a username or password, Subversion will have to ask you for them on every request, which can get very annoying (imagine typing your username and password 50 to 60 times per day). Because the password is stored in plain text, though, you need to be careful and make sure that the servers file is not readable by anyone but yourself. Finally, the http-proxy-exceptions option allows you to specify certain servers or domains that Subversion should contact directly, instead of through the proxy.

Configuring Other HTTP Stuff

Subversion has a couple of other HTTP-related options that are unrelated to proxies, but are worth mentioning. They are `http-timeout` and `http-compression`. In most cases, you will not have to change either option. However, if you have an especially slow-to-respond repository server, you may need to set `http-timeout` to a high number to avoid premature connection failures due to timeouts. Additionally, if you are experiencing unknown failures, you may find it useful to set `http-compression` to `no` in order to allow you to look at the network packets that are being sent, in the hopes of debugging the problem. By default, Subversion *does* use HTTP compression, if the server supports it.

Dealing with SSL Certificates

Often, the data that is in a repository is not something that you want everyone to get their hands on—or if it is something you want everyone to get their hands on, the odds are that you don't want everyone to be able to directly modify the repository. For this reason, many repositories are accessible only through a secure HTTP link, which is encrypted using the Secure Socket Layer (SSL). If a repository that you are connecting to is set up thus, it may be necessary for you to configure Subversion to recognize the certificate that identifies the server and the keys for connecting to it.

The first thing that you may need to do is to tell Subversion which certificate authorities it should use to validate a server certificate. A certificate authority (CA) is a trusted source, which is capable of validating the authenticity of a certificate you receive. Without the certificate authority, you have no way to ensure that a certificate received from a server is valid and authentic. To tell Subversion which certificate authority it should use, you need to get a certificate identifying the CA and then point Subversion to the file containing it. You do so through the `ssl-authority-files` option in your `servers` file, which is a list of authority files, separated by colons. If you set the `ssl-trust-default-ca` option to `yes`, Subversion will also look to a set of built-in default CAs.

Some servers will require you to have a client certificate to prove your own identity. In this case, you will want to tell Subversion where to find that file, too. Subversion looks for the client certificate in the location pointed to by the `ssl-client-cert-file` option (if there is no such option listed, it will ask you for the certificate when you run the client). Additionally, you may need to tell Subversion which type of certificate you are providing it, using the `ssl-client-cert-type` option, which takes `pem` or `pkcs12` as valid values. If your client key isn't stored in the same file as your client certificate, you may also need to tell Subversion where to find it, using the `ssl-client-key-file` option. If your certificate requires a passphrase, you may also want to place that in your `servers` file, using the option `ssl-client-cert-password` option. Be careful though. As with the HTTP-proxy password, this will be stored in plain text, so you need to take steps to secure the `servers` file itself.

Security is always a good idea, and in general it's a bad idea to turn off the built-in security safeguards that Subversion provides when authenticating a certificate—especially because Subversion can be directed to allow unknown certificates on a case-by-case basis, after prompting for your approval. That said, we're all adults here, and sometimes, even with the best intentions of having a secure environment, the practical reality of things means that you need to cut some security to improve usability. To that end, Subversion provides you with a few options that you can use to relax your communications to an SSL-enabled server. If a server has a certificate that is self-signed (or otherwise signed with a certificate authority you can't check), you can direct Subversion to ignore the unknown certificate authority by setting the `ssl-ignore-unknown-ca` option to `yes`. Similarly, if you are accessing a machine that has an incorrectly dated certificate, you can set the `ssl-ignore-invalid-date` option to `yes` in order to direct Subversion to accept the certificate anyway. And finally, if the host that a server is reporting as its location doesn't match the certificate for that server, you can direct Subversion to allow the mismatch using `ssl-ignore-host-mismatch` (again, set to `yes`).

To help tie all of this together, here is a sample `servers` file, showing a setup that you might use for setting up some sane global SSL options, along with a group that overrides those settings for a couple of local area network servers that have certificates that are not kept properly up-to-date.

```
[groups]
UnkemptServers = moe.localnet curly.localnet

[UnkemptServers]
ssl-ignore-unknown-ca = yes
ssl-ignore-invalid-date = yes

[global]
ssl-trust-default-ca = yes
ssl-authority-files = /home/bill/.ssl/localCA.pem
ssl-client-cert-file = /home/bill/.ssl/myCert.pem
ssl-client-cert-password = mI^paSs-42  # this is the password,
                                       # not an encrypted version
```

7.3 Summary

In this chapter, you've seen the configuration files that are available for configuring Subversion. Both of the configuration files, `config` and `servers`, were discussed, along with the options that you can set in each file. You saw how to configure authentication and proxies, as well as several other Subversion options, such as the default editor and diff command.

In the next chapter, you will see how to make interacting with Subversion easier by using a number of different external tools to integrate Subversion with the GUI and the development environment.

Chapter 8

Integrating with Other Tools

As a client user, the Subversion command-line svn program provides you with all of the tools that you need to interact with a Subversion repository. The command line is not always the most effective way to use Subversion though. If you program in an integrated development environment (IDE), for example, it is helpful to be able to perform all of your updates, commits, and other SVN commands from within the framework of the IDE. A GUI can also be useful if you use SVN too infrequently to learn the command-line tools effectively (or if you just don't have the time necessary to learn). Sometimes, other tools are also necessary because you don't have access to the command-line tool.

Subversion has a library of functions that programmers can use to develop new tools to interact with repositories, which makes the creation of tools beyond the svn command much easier than it is with many other version control systems. Accordingly, many very good integration tools have already been developed. In fact, so many have been developed that discussing them all here would be impossible. Instead, this chapter will give you an overview of several of the tools that are out there, which will give you a basis for finding and learning about the use of other tools.

8.1   Accessing SVN through a GUI Client

Most modern desktop or workstation operating systems depend heavily on the use of a graphical user interface (GUI) for interaction with the system—so much so that in many cases, the command line is a dying art. With such heavy dependence on a GUI, it only makes sense that it will often be easier to interact with Subversion through the use of a GUI-based tool. Fortunately, there are a number of GUI clients for Subversion, available for Windows, Mac OS X, and other more traditional UNIX-based systems.

8.1.1   RapidSVN

Whatever your platform of choice, the odds are that you can use the RapidSVN GUI client for Subversion. Although RapidSVN is a natively compiled application (and thus runs with the speed you would expect from a native application), it was written in a very portable manner, which allows it to compile and run on most major platforms.

RapidSVN works as a complete standalone client for Subversion, and presents the user with a straightforward, easy-to-use interface, which users of WinCVS will find familiar. It can be downloaded from the project's Web site, at `rapidsvn.tigris.org`. Compiled binary installations are available as packages for some Linux distributions, and there is an installer for Windows. RapidSVN will run on a number of other platforms (such as Mac OS X and Solaris), but you may have to compile the program from source code.

Features

RapidSVN is a full-featured Subversion client interface, with access to most of the Subversion client commands. Repositories and working copies are presented in a three-paned interface, as you can see in Figure 8.1. The top-left pane shows a tree view of all of the repositories and working copies that you currently have "bookmarked" in RapidSVN. In the top-right pane, you can see details about each of the files in the directory that is selected in the tree view. Finally, the bottom pane is used for status output from the running of commands.

RapidSVN shows the status of individual files through both the icon that is used to display the file and a textual representation in the "Status" column. For example, modified files are shown with a red file icon (with an M).

To perform a command on a file, you generally just have to select it and then select the command you would like to perform, either from the toolbar or a menu. If other options are required (such as a revision number), RapidSVN displays a dialog box for you to enter

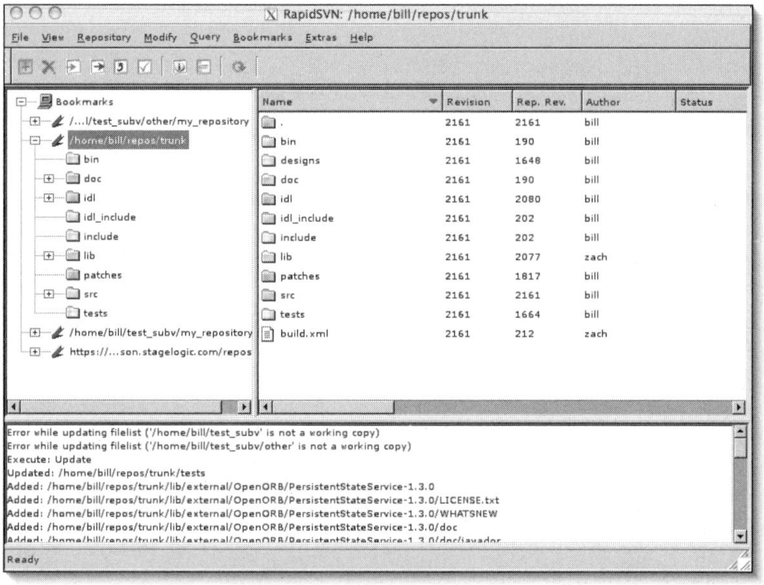

Figure 8.1. The RapidSVN interface.

them. So, as an example, if you have a modified file that you would like to commit, you can select it in the file detail pane and click on the Commit Selected button on the toolbar. RapidSVN pops up a dialog for you to enter the log message, and away you go.

When you use RapidSVN to run Subversion commands, you do not always have access to all of the options available from the command line, such as the merge command, which does not give you the option of performing a dry run that shows which files will change without changing them, as you can do with `svn merge`. Furthermore, RapidSVN makes some complex operations more difficult, or even impossible. Log messages, for instance, cannot be queried recursively—nor is there a way for binary files to be added to a file as properties. With many commands, it is also not possible to run the command simultaneously on a group of files.

When Should I Use It?

RapidSVN is a great tool for casual or less technically adept users of a Subversion repository. It has a low learning curve and a reasonably intuitive interface. Command options are presented to the user as either checkboxes or text boxes, and generally default to the most commonly used options. Uncommon options are often eliminated entirely, which will frustrate power users, but makes the interface cleaner and much simpler for the novice to understand. If your Subversion needs aren't too demanding, and you would like to trade a little flexibility for more ease of use, RapidSVN is a good choice.

8.1.2 TortoiseSVN

If you use Windows, TortoiseSVN is a very nice alternative to a standalone GUI client like RapidSVN. TortoiseSVN takes advantage of the extendibility of Windows Explorer to integrate interaction with the repository directly into the Explorer GUI. TortoiseSVN is widely used by many Windows-based Subversion users—in fact, after the command line, it is probably the most widely used Subversion client available. If you are using Subversion from Windows, this is probably your best choice for a Subversion client (beyond even the command-line tools).

TortoiseSVN is free software (GPL license), and can be obtained from the TortoiseSVN Web site: `tortoisesvn.tigris.org`. Installing the software is trivial, as the program comes with an installer program. All you need to do is run it and follow the instructions. You should be able to install TortoiseSVN on any version of Windows from Win95 or later, although '95 and NT 4 may require you to upgrade your version of Internet Explorer.

Features

TortoiseSVN provides you with access to all of the Subversion client commands through context menus in Explorer. You are able to easily update, commit, switch, copy, merge, and so on. As you can see in Figure 8.2, each command is easily accessible, although TortoiseSVN has chosen to use different names for some of the commands. For example, instead of `svn diff`, you have the *Create Patch...* menu item, and instead of `svn copy`, you have the *Branch/Tag...* item.

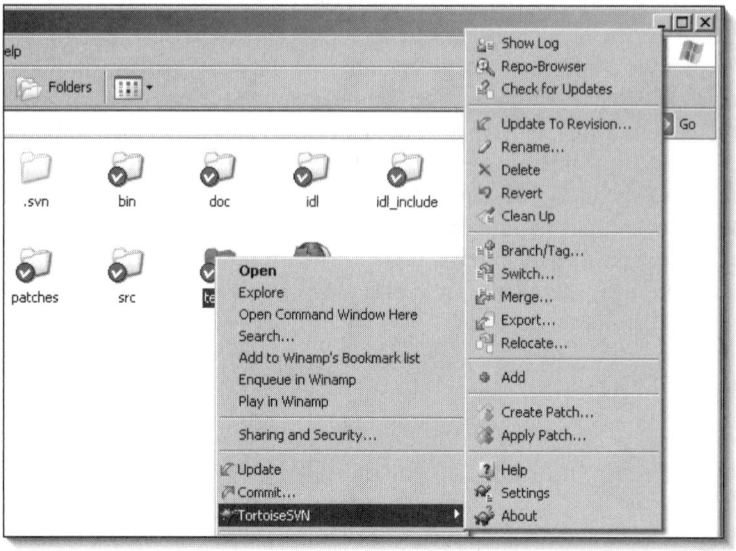

Figure 8.2. The TortoiseSVN interface.

TortoiseSVN also makes it easy to quickly see the status of versioned files, by placing an overlay icon on each versioned file. For example, in Figure 8.2, you can see that each folder has a circle with a checkmark over the lower-left corner of the icon. If the picture were in color, you would be able to see that the icon is green in color. This indicates that each of those directories has no uncommitted modifications.

8.1.3   ViewCVS

ViewCVS has for quite some time been the top choice for providing a Web-based interface to the CVS version control system. Recently, the ViewCVS project has expanded its support to include Subversion, although Subversion support is not yet available in an official release. To get ViewCVS with Subversion support, you will need to check out the ViewCVS CVS repository. Slow down and take a few deep breaths. Unfortunately, ViewCVS hasn't seen the light and moved to Subversion for its repository yet. The ViewCVS project can be found at `viewcvs.sf.net`.

Features

ViewCVS allows users to easily browse through a Subversion repository. Its view is similar to the view that you get when accessing the WebDAV share of a repository through a Web browser. The top level of the repository is listed, with links to each directory or file at that level. You can then view files by clicking on them, or descend into subdirectories. As you can see in the screenshot in Figure 8.3 though, the ViewCVS screen is much more advanced than the simple page provided by Apache/WebDAV. In addition to letting you browse the HEAD revision of the repository, ViewCVS gives you a number of other options.

- You can move to specific revisions and view all of the repository at that revision.

- When you select a specific revision, you can look at the log message for that revision, as well as the files that changed in that revision. For each changed file, you can also ask to see a diff of the changes made to it.

- For individual files, you can view the contents of the file, or the complete log for that file.

- You can obtain diffs of arbitrary revisions for a file, in a number of different formats, such as a color-coded side-by-side view, or a unified diff suitable for use with `patch`.

Because ViewCVS Subversion support is still in development, there may very well be more features supported by the time you read this. There may even be a version 1.0 release. In the meantime, there are some stable CVS snapshots available. I would suggest that you look at the ViewCVS package maintained by Christopher Baus, at his Web site (`www.baus.net/archives/000069.html`), which has a stable snapshot of ViewCVS. He also has an excellent set of installation instructions.

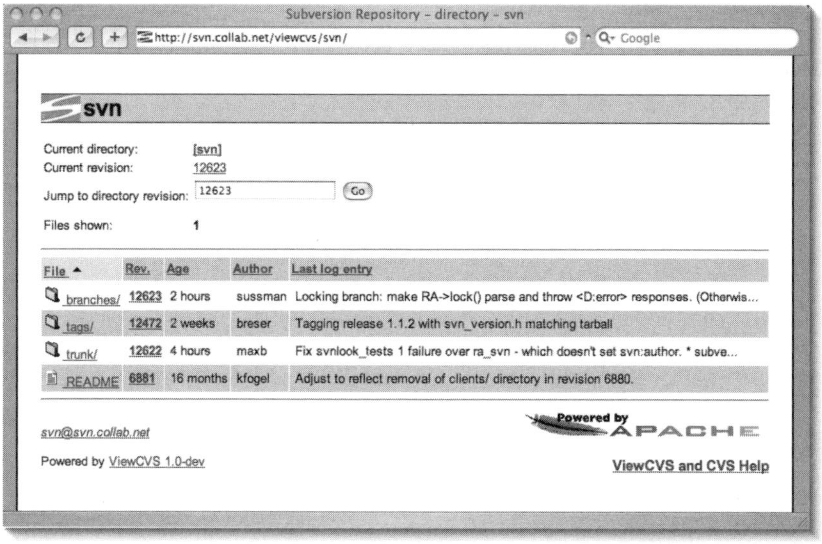

Figure 8.3. The Subversion project's ViewCVS page.

When Should I Use It?

ViewCVS is a great tool if you have users who need to access the Subversion repository, but might not need or want the overhead of installing a Subversion client. If your repository contains files that users would be likely to download individually, it can be an easy way to facilitate that, too. It can also be useful for developers who do have and use a Subversion client to check out and commit, but would like a quick way to see files from specific revisions or diffs of different revisions of a file.

ViewCVS is stable enough that you should be able to use it in a production environment. Because it doesn't modify the repository, there is little reason to worry about it corrupting your repository if a bug is encountered.

8.1.4   WebSVN

Another good choice for Web-based repository browsing is WebSVN. WebSVN is similar to ViewCVS and supports many of its features, along with some new ones that ViewCVS doesn't support. Because it was designed from the ground up to support Subversion, it also feels more at home with Subversion. The project itself is located at the WebSVN Web site (`http://websvn.tigris.org`), and installs very easily. In fact, installation is as simple as putting the WebSVN source in a Web-accessible directory and editing the `include/config.inc` file (which you need to create by copying the template file `include/distconfig.inc`).

Features

In addition to repository browsing features similar to ViewCVS, WebSVN offers a number of other ways to get information about the repository.

- Support for the Subversion blame command, which shows an annotated view of the selected file, with columns showing the user who last committed each line, along with the revision where the commit was made.

- RSS feeds that allow you to track changes to the repository.

- Comparisons of two directories, which show the differences between each file in the chosen directories. This makes it easy to compare the differences between the trunk and a branch or tag (or between two branches, and so on).

When Should I Use It?

WebSVN is useful in the same instances as ViewCVS, and the choice between the two is mostly a matter of taste. ViewCVS is a bit more mature than WebSVN (even though Subversion support hasn't been officially released), but WebSVN has more Subversion-friendly features. If you are planning on using one for your repository, I suggest that you try both (they're both reasonably easy to install) and see which one suits your needs best.

8.2   Accessing Directly from an IDE

When using an integrated development environment (IDE), it is usually easiest to be able to deal with Subversion directly inside the IDE interface. Fortunately, many popular IDEs are starting to add support for Subversion and others have plug-ins available that provide integrated support. As an example of what's available, here are a couple of plug-ins that will allow you to access Subversion directly from Microsoft's Visual Studio.Net and Eclipse.

As a general side note when dealing with integrated clients: many don't have support for unknown SSL certificates. If you need to use them to access a repository with an unknown certificate, you may have to first access that repository using the command-line client. When the command-line client asks you for permission to accept the unknown certificate, you should then tell it to accept permanently. After that, you should be able to use the integrated tool to access your repository with no troubles.

8.2.1   Visual Studio.Net

If your development environment of choice (or necessity) is Microsoft's Visual Studio.Net, you can use the AnkhSVN (`ankhsvn.tigris.org`) project to integrate the VS.net work environment with Subversion (see Figure 8.4). AnkhSVN is still in a beta release state, and doesn't yet support every Subversion feature (most notably, it has no properties support), but it is quite usable for most daily development work, and any missing features can still be accessed from the command line.

Figure 8.4. A commit from Visual Studio.Net, with AnkhSVN.

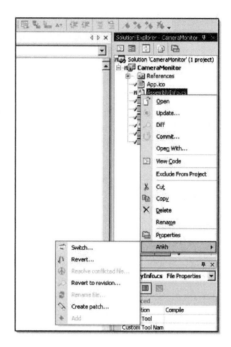

Figure 8.5. The AnkhSVN context menu.

Features

Like many of the other Subversion integration tools, Subversion commands are accessed
via AnkhSVN through menu items added to a pop-up menu. In this case, the items are
added to the VS.net Solution Explorer, where you can right-click on files and select Ankh-
SVN commands (see Figure 8.5). Additionally, the Solution Explorer also shows file status
by placing small icons on each file, such as a red *M* for modified files, and a green checkmark for files that are up-to-date. In addition to the critical basic features like committing
and updating, AnkhSVN also supports graphical views of diffs, switching a file to a branch
or tag, and creation of patches.

8.2.2 Eclipse

If you're a Java developer, the chances are that you are familiar with the open source
Eclipse IDE. It has quickly become one of the most popular integrated development environments for anyone working with Java, and for good reason. One of its most powerful
features is its excellent plug-in system, which allows third parties to easily develop plug-
ins that integrate seamlessly with the core Eclipse system. One such plug-in is Subclipse
(http://subclipse.tigris.org), which integrates the capability to work with a Subversion repository into Eclipse (see Figure 8.6).

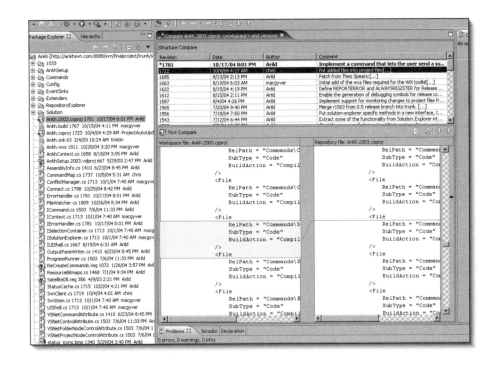

Figure 8.6. Subclipse, showing a graphical diff of two versions of a file.

Features

With Subclipse, you can check out new working copies from a repository and import them into Eclipse, bring an already checked-out working copy under Eclipse control, or create a brand new project that will be automatically imported into a Subversion repository.

Subclipse adds three new submenus to the pop-up menu that appears when you right-click on files or folders in the Eclipse file list, which give you control over a working copy. Figure 8.7 shows all three submenus in action.

- The *Team* submenu gives access to a number of common Subversion commands, which allow you to easily update, commit, and manipulate properties.

- The *Compare With* submenu gives you the ability to graphically compare files in your working copy with different versions of the file in the repository.

- The *Replace With* submenu allows you to exchange the version of a file in your working copy with another revision (i.e., `svn update -r`).

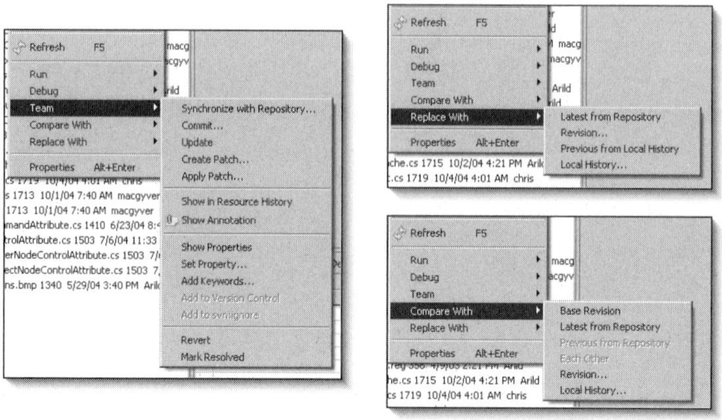

Figure 8.7. The three Subclipse context menus.

8.3   Using Autoversioning with WebDAV

The graphical file browsers on many operating systems allow you to mount WebDAV shares as remote directories that can be accessed the same as local files. This includes (but is not necessarily limited to) the following GUI file managers:

- Microsoft Windows Explorer (although older versions of the OS might need software installed)

- Macintosh OS X (albeit without any SSL support)

- The Nautilus file manager, available on Linux and most UNIX varieties

Because the Apache/WebDAV repository shares support standard WebDAV commands, this means that you can often mount a repository as a remote directory. Of course, in such a situation, the file managers don't know anything about Subversion, and can't support any Subversion-specific manipulation (like commits, updates, or properties). However, when a repository is accessed this way, Subversion does support a limited form of file modification, known as autoversioning.

Autoversioning allows users to open repository files directly from a mounted filesystem directory, edit the file, and then save it back to the repository (although some WebDAV clients might require you to copy the file to the local filesystem before you edit it, then copy it back after the edit). When the modified file is saved or copied back to the share, it automatically performs a commit, with a generic log message. In this way, users with little or no understanding of version control are able to edit files in the repository without the steep learning curve of the Subversion client. It also allows you to access and modify Subversion repositories from client machines that don't (or can't) have a full Subversion client installed.

Unfortunately, opening and saving repository files via a WebDAV share can be a problem if there are multiple people modifying the repository in parallel. If you open a file on your local system and another developer commits changes before you save your modified version back, that other developer's changes will be overwritten, not merged. Fortunately, this problem should be fixed in the upcoming 1.2 release of Subversion, which will support file locking that should work with autoversioning.

Enabling Autoversioning

By default, autoversioning is not allowed. The server will just reject changes to files that it receives through standard WebDAV means. To enable autoversioning, you need to add the SVNAutoversioning directive to your repository's Location section, which would give you a location that looks something like the following example.

```
<Location /repos>
    DAV svn
    SVNPath /var/svnrepos
    SVNAutoversioning on
</Location>
```

Autoversioning on OS X

Autoversioning with the Macintosh OS X Finder is a bit more difficult than with MS Windows or Nautilus, because OS X tries to get a lock on each file before writing to it (which Subversion WebDAV doesn't support). There is a workaround, though. The Apache module mod_dav_lock allows you to add support for file locking to Apache, so that the lock requests aren't rejected.

Warning: Apache is the only thing locking the file here. Subversion doesn't understand locks, so a Subversion client can make a change to the file. If you are using mod_dav_lock, make sure that no one is going to be using a Subversion client at the same time. This problem should go away with version 1.2 of Subversion, though, because it will support locking.

To enable mod_dav_lock support for your Subversion repository, you need to first tell Apache to load mod_dav_lock (the specifics of this are very specific to an Apache install). Then, you just need to tell your Subversion repository location what file to use for its locks, as in this example <Location>.

```
<Location /repos>
    DAV svn
    SVNPath /var/svnrepos
    SVNAutoversioning on
    DAVGenericLockDB /var/svnrepos/dav_locks
</Location>
```

8.4   Summary

In this chapter, you've gotten a taste for the tools that are out there for integrating Subversion and other tools. An in-depth discussion of each of these tools would be a book in itself, so I've only touched on them here. The amount of documentation that is available from each of these projects varies from project to project, but each is documented well enough that you should have few problems getting them installed. Most are reasonably self-explanatory in their use. To find more information about available Subversion clients and other Subversion-related projects, you can visit the Subversion project links Web page at `subversion.tigris.org/project_links.html`.

Part III

Subversion from an Administrator's Perspective

Chapter 9

Organizing Your Repository

In Part III, you will learn the ins and outs of administering a Subversion repository. Mostly that means repository setup, because Subversion rarely requires much maintenance after the repository is up and running. In the simplest cases, even the front-end administration is trivial—simply create a new repository and add a few lines to your Apache config files to point them to the repository's location. Conversely, for large, complex repositories, or repositories with many users, setup can get fairly involved. If you put in the effort to use hook scripts to automate integration and policy support, setup can provide a full-time job to one or more people for a decent period of time.

The ease of moving files and directories around in a Subversion repository means that it's no longer necessary to spend countless hours arguing over exactly how the repository should be set up (knowing that changing it down the road will be practically impossible). Just because changing things is easy, though, doesn't mean that you shouldn't take the time to devise a good repository layout that will help support your project's workflow. In fact, with Subversion's flexible layout, you have a large number of options when laying out the repository, and a little thought into how to do so can go a long way. In this chapter, you will learn about many of the issues that you should consider when laying out your repository to support your overall workflow and to ease your project's growth over time. You will also learn how to migrate an existing repository from a CVS or Visual SourceSafe repository.

9.1 Laying Out the Repository

Subversion gives you a lot of options for laying out a repository—or more to the point, it puts up very few roadblocks when you are laying out your repository. Your layout options are basically as unlimited as your options when laying out a regular filesystem. Additionally, because branches and tags are handled as copies, you are free to organize your repository layout to reflect the types of branches and tags that you expect to make (for example, a `releases` directory for release tags).

9.1.1 The Two Basic Layouts

There are two basic Subversion layouts. If you are putting together a simple Subversion repository, or don't know exactly what the project structure and workflow is going to look

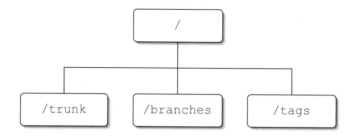

Figure 9.1. A simple monolithic repository layout.

like, your best bet may be to just use one of these simple repository layouts. Of course, as the project grows, you can always move things around to improve the layout at a later date.

Monolithic Layout

The first layout is the basic monolithic project layout. In this layout, you have a single project in each repository, with a top-level directory for the trunk, as well as directories for branches and tags (see Figure 9.1). This is the better layout to choose if you have multiple projects that are unrelated (or only loosely related), in which case you can place each project in its own repository with a monolithic layout structure. It's also the obvious choice if you are only tracking a single project.

The main project trunk will go into the `trunk` directory, whereas branches and tags will be copied into the `branches` and `tags` directories, respectively. This allows a user to easily check out just the `trunk` directory, and use `svn cp` with URLs to create branches and tags. Then, when the user wants to work on a branch (or use a tag), it is easy to use `svn switch` to move the branch in to the checked out working copy of `trunk`.

By keeping multiple projects separated in their own monolithically organized repositories, you maintain the ability to relocate or back up individual repositories. That would, for example, allow you to maintain two heavily accessed repositories on different servers, or to archive the repository for a cancelled project off onto an offline storage medium to free up space on your active servers. Individual projects in separate projects also allow those projects to have their own revision numbers. If a modification is committed to project `foo`, project `bar`'s head revision won't increase by one.

If your projects are closely related, or are likely to share a lot of code, having each project in its own repository can be constraining. You lose the ability to copy or merge source from one project to another (while maintaining the history of the file in both projects), and you lose the ability to branch or tag both projects together. Also, because each project has its own independent revision numbers, it is hard to compare the state of two projects at an arbitrary point. However, if the projects are not closely related, but do reference each other, externals may allow you to share some commonalities between repositories without sacrificing the advantages of separate repositories.

Multiproject Layout

The second basic layout scheme is better for projects with lots of closely connected projects. In this scheme, instead of putting each project in a separate repository, with `trunk`, `branches`, and `tags` directories at the top level of the repository, you will create a top-level directory for each project in the repository. Then, at the top level of each project directory, you will put `trunk`, `branches`, and `tags` directories specific to that project, as in Figure 9.2.

With this layout, you can easily copy source from between projects or create tags and branches that encompass multiple projects. All of the projects will also share revision numbers, so you always know what state other projects were in at a given revision number for the project you are working on.

Of course, you lose the separation of multiple repositories and gain little advantage if the projects are not closely related. If two projects are unrelated or only reference each other with no (or at least very little) possibility that code will be copied from one to the other, you may be better off with a monolithic layout.

9.1.2 Organizing the Trunk

The trunk is the main branch of a project. As far as Subversion is concerned, it is no different from any other directory, because Subversion has no concept of special directories.

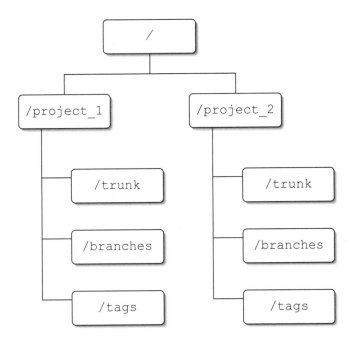

Figure 9.2. A repository layout with multiple projects.

Conceptually, though, it is the directory where the primary version of the project resides. Branches and tags are usually created from a revision of the trunk, and work done on a branch is often merged back into the trunk when they are complete.

The trunk is usually stored in a directory named `trunk`, but could be named something else (like `main_branch`) if there were a compelling reason to do so. Generally, there is either a single trunk for the entire repository, or individual trunks for each project. This allows each project to have a clear place for the most current new development (also called the head development).

Although most projects have only a single trunk, in theory you could have multiple "trunks" for a single project, but you should carefully consider the way you will be using the repository first. In most cases, you will find that things are better organized as multiple projects, or as branches of a project. For instance, if you maintain separate development paths for a consumer version and professional version (or versions for different platforms), the different development paths might be cleaner if they were different projects in the same repository. Similarly, if you have multiple versions of the same project, those might be more cleanly handled as branches, instead of multiple trunk directories.

In many cases, the trunk will be the only part of the repository that users will check out into their working copy (using `svn switch` to get at the other parts). This means that you need to be sure that your trunk is a complete entity, containing all of the parts of the repository necessary for working with the project (if the repository is split into a scheme with one trunk for each project, it's acceptable—and usually desireable—to make each product so it needs to be checked out separately). What you want to avoid, though, is source that uses a relative path that points to parts of the repository outside the current project's `trunk` directory.

9.1.3   Organizing Branches

Branches are just that, branches of the main path of development that may or may not be merged back in at a later point. Typically, they are used for working on sections of development that may break the main trunk, or that may be tangential to the main trunk of development. Often, branches are long-running, but they may also be used for quick forays that only take a revision or two before they're merged back into the trunk and deleted.

Branches are usually stored in a directory named `branches`, under a descriptive name that describes what part of the trunk the branch was created from, as well as purpose of the branch. For example, if your project has a graphics engine that is stored in a directory named `graphics_engine` and you want to add real-time processing to it, you might create a branch named `graphics_engine-real_time_proc`.

The ease with which branches are created means that you can very easily end up with a lot of them. Furthermore, it is likely that many (if not most) of the branches will end up with semi-cryptic names that mean little to anyone except their creator. End result: The `branches` directory quickly becomes cluttered with a huge number of hard-to-sort-through branches. This "branch clutter" can easily get out of hand in a long-running project, and although it's unlikely to be a major drain on anyone's productivity, it can lead to developer frustration (which tends to result in less reliance on branches,) as well as improper use of branches (which will make the repository more difficult to deal with, as well as making its history harder to track properly).

One possible solution to the problem is to make sure branches are deleted as soon as they are no longer used. This can help to keep the clutter to a minimum, but it can also make older branches harder to find. It also doesn't help the problem much if most of your branches are long-running branches, where deletion makes no sense. A better solution is to keep the repository organized in a sane manner that makes branches easy to find and list.

The best structure for organizing branches depends a lot on your project's workflow, and the circumstances under which branches are typically generated. There are a wide number of uses under which developers will typically create branches, and it usually helps if you organize those branches categorically. Sometimes, you will want to categorize with subdirectories under your `branches` directory (or directories). For other branches, it may make more sense to place specific branch directories at the top level of the tree. The following examples illustrate some (but by no stretch all) of the possible ways you might organize different types of branches.

- If you generate a unique branch for the purpose of resolving each issue created in your issue tracking system, you may find that it is helpful to create a special sub-directory for issues. If you have your repository split into multiple projects, you will probably want this directory at the individual project branches level. You will also want to mandate a naming scheme that identifies the issue that each branch is aimed at, so that you may end up with `/branches/issues/issue-1587` and `/branches/issues/issue-1592` to fix issues #1587 and #1592 from the issue tracking system.

- It may be helpful to give each developer his own private branches directory, where he can create individual branches for specific tasks or features, without cluttering the list of branches that other developers see (if fine-grained authorizations are being used, these directories could even be made *truly* private by denying access to other users). To keep things clean, you'll probably also want to have a `public` branches directory, too, thus giving you a layout similar to the one shown in Figure 9.3.

- If you maintain a development version and several release versions of your project, you can set up top-level branches that correspond to those directories. When a new

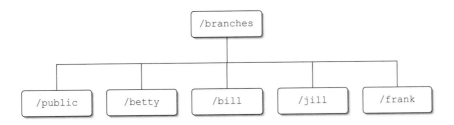

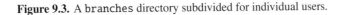

Figure 9.3. A `branches` directory subdivided for individual users.

release is made, the development branch can be copied to the new release, with the development branch continuing on with development on the next version. With this setup, the development branch essentially becomes your main trunk, although it's more clear if you name the directory something like `development`, instead of `trunk` (in this case, you might not have a directory named `trunk` at all).

In short, you are limited only by your imagination and desire to create a level of organization that fits your development teams (which for many projects may indeed mean a monolithic `branches` directory). If you would like more ideas for how you can organize your branches, check out the development process case studies in Chapter 14, "Case Studies in Development Processes."

9.1.4   Organizing Tags

In contrast to branches, which represent forks in the development line, tags are static benchmarks that preserve the state of the repository (or a particular working copy) at a specific point in time, for easy reference later. Even though tags are just copies, the same as branches, they never change over time like branches do (if they do change, they become a branch instead, by definition). The closest thing to change that a tag should see is if an existing tag is removed and replaced by a new tag of the same name, such as if a tag named `current_release` is used to always represent the current release of a project. When a new release of the project is made current, the old tag would be removed, and a new tag named `current_release` would be created (you could achieve the same effect by using a merge into the tag, but removing and recopying is usually easier, less likely to cause problems, and uses less disk space).

Keeping tags organized suffers from similar problems as the organization of branches. In general, if you have a lot of tags, it will quickly become difficult to wade through the tags to find the one you want if everything is stored in a monolithic `tags` directory. Instead, you are usually better off categorizing your tags into separate directories. In many cases, it can even be advantageous to move some of the tag-categorizing directories out of the `tags` directory and promote them to the top level of your repository. For example, if you tag your releases, it may be useful to create a top-level `releases` directory, where all of the release tags are created, such as in the layout shown in Figure 9.4.

Top-level special tag directories can be especially useful if your repository has individual `tags` directories for each project. A top-level `current` directory, for instance, could store the most current release of each project. Then, individual developers would be able to easily check out the full project suite contained within the release, into a single working copy, while maintaining the benefits of splitting different projects into individual subdirectories with their own branches and tags.

Remember, with Subversion's "cheap copies," tags take up essentially zero space in your repository, so there is no reason not to take advantage of them whenever possible.

- Tag internal and external releases. For example, if you have a quality assurance team, in addition to your development team, developers can tag revisions of the repository that are ready for testing by the QA team. Conversely, the QA team can tag specific

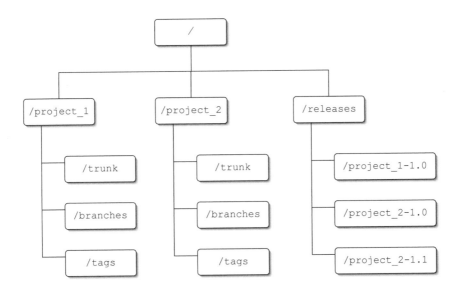

Figure 9.4. A `releases` directory can make project releases easy to find.

revisions when it finds a bug, and include that in the bug report that is filed. Then, when a developer begins to work on fixing that bug, the developer can create a branch from the tag to work on the bug.

- Track your merge history. One of Subversion's biggest weaknesses is its lack of adequate internal tracking for merges. The method that is usually recommended for merge tracking is to record merge points in the log history, when the merge is committed. Instead, though, you could make a tag of the directory that was merged, and use that to calculate the next merge. For example, follow these steps:

  1. You create a branch of your trunk, named `branch_1`. At the same time, create a parallel directory named `tags/branch_1_merges`, and also make a tag of the trunk in that directory, named `trunk_09-12-04_14-34` (where the numbers indicate the date and time when the tag was made).

  2. After working on `branch_1` for a while, let's say that there are changes from the trunk that you would like to merge in. Instead of looking up the revision number from the point where you made the branch, you can perform the merge by just taking the difference between the tag you made and the current HEAD of the trunk, like this:

     ```
     $ svn merge http://svn.mydomain.com/repos/tags/ ¬
       branch_1_merges/trunk_09-12-04_14-34 http://svn.mydomain. ¬
       com/repos/trunk
     ```

  3. After the merge is done, you can make a new tag of the trunk, with the new date, just as in the following:

```
$ svn cp http://svn.mydomain.com/repos/trunk http://svn. ¬
  mydomain.com/repos/tags/branch_1_merges/trunk_10-03-04_16 ¬
  -24
```

- Tag interesting revisions that you'd like to remember later. Sifting through long log files to figure out which revision it was where you finally got a new feature to work right, or started working on code refactoring, can be time-consuming and error-prone (for example, the log entry that indicates the feature was finished may be misleading if you added a critical file that had been forgotten, three revisions later). Instead, if you make tags at revisions you might be interested in later, you can much more easily get back to the state of the project at that moment in time.

9.2 Planning for Growth

Because Subversion repositories are so innately malleable, there is a tendency to ignore long-term repository growth and just plan a repository for what works best immediately. After all, you can always move things around later, right? To a certain extent, that's one of the great advantages of Subversion. In most cases, you can defer much of your long-term planning to the long term, and just do what works "right now." However, if you in fact do a bit of long-term planning up front, you may find that you save yourself a few headaches in the long run.

To make sure that you've planned well for future growth, make sure that you ask yourself the following questions before laying out a new Subversion repository.

- Is this one project or many?

  If your repository is made up of a single project, you have little to worry about. You can easily put everything at the top level, and then move it down into a subdirectory at a later date if you add more projects. Such a move should cause few problems for people, and will make the repository simpler until a second project is added. Of course, if you have definite plans for a second project in the near future, you may be better off starting off with everything in subdirectories, just to save everyone the small headache a change will cause.

  If you start off with multiple projects instead, it's easy to begin with each project in its own individual subdirectory, which will make adding new projects down the road much less painful (it will also make it simpler to delete projects, if the need ever arises).

- If the repository includes multiple projects, are those projects likely to share data?

  This is an important question to ask, mainly for the case where the answer is "no" — the reason being that if you plan to have many unrelated projects, you might want to consider creating multiple repositories, instead of putting all of your projects in a single repository. This has the advantage of helping you prevent a repository that gets too big (although Subversion has no fixed limit on repository size), as well as allowing you to move an individual project to a different server if you so desire.

The downside to multiple repositories is that Subversion currently has no way to perform a copy or merge that crosses from one repository to another. In other words, if you need to take data from one repository and replicate it in another, you will have to perform the copy by using a filesystem copy from one working copy to another, which will not preserve history for the copy. If a merge is necessary, it will have to be done by hand.

- Will individual projects be primarily worked on by one developer, or many?

  This question isn't quite as important as the previous one, but it is a good one to consider when laying out a repository. The answer helps to determine the scale at which you need to plan out the organization of the repository. If each project will exist on its own, with interaction only by one person (or a small group), there may be little need to impose a repository-wide standard on the way that particular project is laid out. On the other hand, if the repository will be accessed and modified by a large team of users, the project will almost certainly benefit from an up-front plan for laying out the directory structure, including how branches and tags will be organized.

9.2.1 Merging and Splitting a Repository

After you've decided on using a single repository or multiple repositories, it's usually best to stick with that choice. Sometimes needs change, though, and occasionally you will want to combine two repositories into one, or split a single repository in two. Fortunately, Subversion provides ways for you to do both.

Merging Two Repositories

If you have two repositories that you would like to combine into a single repository, your best solution is to dump one of the repositories (using `svnadmin dump`) and then load it into the other one (using `svnadmin load`). For example, let's say you have two repositories named `fooproj` and `barproj`, each laid out in a monolithic structure with the `trunk`, `branches`, and `tags` directories at the root of the repository. Now, let's say that as time has gone by, the two projects have converged to the point where you would like to be able to share code between them, so it would be nice to have them in a single repository. The following steps show how you could go about merging the two repositories by merging `barproj` into the `fooproj` repository.

1. To start, you want to rename the repository to reflect its new multiproject status (make absolutely certain no one can access the repository while you do this; if you can't do that, use `svnadmin hotcopy` instead).

   ```
   $ mv /srv/fooproj /srv/foobar_repos
   ```

2. Because you're combining two projects into a single repository, it would make sense to move from a monolithic repository structure to a multiproject layout. That means that you want to continue by creating new project directories.

```
$ svn mkdir file:///srv/foobar_repos/fooproj file:///srv/ ¬
foobar_repos/barproj
```

3. Next, you need to move the `fooproj` directories into the newly created `/fooproj` project directory.

```
$ svn mv file:///srv/foobar_repos/trunk file:///srv/foobar_repos/ ¬
fooproj/trunk
$ svn mv file:///srv/foobar_repos/branches file:///srv/ ¬
foobar_repos/fooproj/branches
$ svn mv file:///srv/foobar_repos/tags file:///srv/foobar_repos/ ¬
fooproj/tags
```

4. After everything is moved around in your first repository, it's time to dump and load the second one. Because the `svnadmin dump` and `svnadmin load` commands output and input (respectively) the dump files on `stdout` and `stdin`, you can perform the whole dump/load cycle in a single command. To load the project into our newly created `barproj` project directory, we can also give a location in the repository for Subversion to use as a root for the loaded files.

```
$ svnadmin dump file:///srv/barproj | svnadmin load file:///srv/ ¬
foobar_repos
```

When Subversion loads a repository dump into an existing (populated) repository, it preserves the dates when the loaded repository's revisions were committed, but not the revision numbers. Instead, it adds each revision as a new revision in the existing repository, with revision numbers being incremented from a starting point of the existing repository's HEAD revision. For example, say you have two repositories; the first repository has 15 revisions numbered 1–15 and the second has 12 revisions numbered 1–12. If you dump the first repository and load it into the second repository, the revisions 1–15 will be added as revisions 13–27 in the second repository.

Splitting a Single Repository

The converse to merging two repositories into one is to take a single repository and split it into two separate repositories. To illustrate, let's say that instead of two repositories named `fooproj` and `barproj`, you start with a single repository named `foobar_repos` that contains both projects (in root directories named `fooproj` and `barproj`, respectively). Now, let's say that those projects have grown extremely large, and your server no longer has the power to serve both projects. So, you decide that because the projects don't share much, it would be easiest to just split them into two different repositories and serve them from separate servers.

The best way to accomplish a repository split is by using the tool `svndumpfilter`. With `svndumpfilter`, you can dump a repository and either include only paths that begin with a set of prefixes or exclude paths that begin with a set of prefixes. In our case, we want to create two repositories from two different root directories, so we'll run the dump filter twice and include only the project we want each time, as in the following example steps.

1. Create two new (empty) repositories to hold each of the split repositories.

```
$ svnadmin create /srv/fooproj
$ svnadmin create /srv/barproj
```

2. Dump the original repository and run it through a filter that will only include the fooproj project directory. Then, load that into the newly created repository.

```
$ svnadmin dump /srv/foobar_repos | svndumpfilter include --drop-¬
  empty-revs --renumber-revs /fooproj | svnadmin load --ignore-¬
  uuid /srv/fooproj
```

   - Using the --drop-empty-revs and --renumber-revs options with svndumpfilter will cause the revisions of the newly created repository to be collapsed down, with any revisions that didn't include changes to the fooproj project removed. If the revision numbers are important to you, you can cause Subversion to leave them the same by leaving out those two options.

   - The --ignore-uuid option is important, because Subversion will set the repository UUID to the UUID from the dump file if you are loading into an empty repository. You don't want your two newly create repositories to end up with the same UUID though, so --ignore-uuid will tell Subversion not to change the UUID. Because the UUIDs of the repositories will change, users of the repository will have to check out new working copies from the appropriate new repository.

3. Repeat the dump and load to populate the barproj repository.

```
$ svnadmin dump /srv/foobar_repos | svndumpfilter include --drop-¬
  empty-revs --renumber-revs /barproj | svnadmin load --ignore-¬
  uuid /srv/barproj
```

9.3 Migrating an Existing Repository

Sometimes, a Subversion repository will be created as part of a brand new project. In those cases, getting initial data into the repository is easy—there is none. More often than not, though (especially because Subversion is so new), a new Subversion repository will be part of a migration away from another version control system. As part of that migration, there is a whole history of data that most people aren't going to want to lose. Therefore, the ideal solution is to be able to take the entire repository history from the old system and migrate it over to Subversion.

The two most common version control systems that people migrate to Subversion from are almost certainly CVS and Microsoft's Visual SourceSafe. This has led to the creation of migration tools that allow you to take repositories from both systems and create a Subversion repository that preserves the history of all of the files in the old repository.

9.3.1   The Basic Migration Process

Whatever the system that you are migrating from, there are a few things that you should always remember. Failure to heed these warnings will not harm pets or small children, but could result in loss of data, or even loss of a job.

- Always back up your existing repository before attempting any sort of migration. Just because the migration tool shouldn't mess with your old repository doesn't mean that, if something bad happens, it won't.

- Always back up your existing repository before attempting any sort of migration. Just because the migration tool shouldn't mess with your old repository doesn't mean that, if something bad happens, it won't. (Yes, I meant to say that twice.)

- Have a migration plan. Do you intend to move everyone over to Subversion immediately? If not, are some people going to continue using the previous system as their primary VCS while others migrate completely, or is everyone going to mirror all of their changes into both systems during a transition period?

- Keep the old repository around, just in case. Until you are positive that your new Subversion repository is going to work out, make sure that you can go back to the old system.

- Test everything in the new repository after the migration. Make certain that the HEAD revision of your repository is correct and working inside the Subversion repository. It might even be a good idea to run a diff on all of the files in a working copy of your Subversion repository, to make sure they match the files from your old VCS.

- Know what you're losing. Because the VCS that you're migrating from is not Subversion, it doesn't store exactly the same things that Subversion does. Invariably, some data (however minor) will be lost in the transition. Make sure you know what you are losing, and store it somewhere else if it's important to keep (properties may be a good place to store information that you want to save).

9.3.2   Migrating from CVS

If your existing project source is stored in a CVS repository, you are in luck. The cvs2svn utility provides excellent conversion tools for migrating a CVS repository to SVN, while preserving most (if not all) of your history data. You can even import data from a CVS repository into an existing Subversion repository that already contains other data, and can pick and choose exactly which data you want to import.

You can acquire cvs2svn from the project's Web site, cvs2svn.tigris.org. The program is a Python script, so it doesn't require any installation, and can run on either MS Windows or a UNIX-like system, as long as you have Python and a couple of other prerequisites installed. To find out exactly what you need to install, you can look at the official cvs2svn documentation on the project's Web site.

Full Repository Migration

A complete migration of an existing CVS repository to a brand new Subversion repository can be accomplished by running cvs2svn with the name of the Subversion repository and the CVS repository. If the Subversion repository referred to doesn't already exist, cvs2svn will create it for you (unless you pass --existing-svnrepos to tell it to only use a Subversion repository that already exists).

```
$ cvs2svn -s /var/svnrepos /var/cvsroot
```

If you would rather have cvs2svn create a Subversion dumpfile, instead of directly importing into a repository, you can pass --dump-only instead of -s repository.

```
$ cvs2svn --dump-only /var/cvsroot
```

Then, you can load the dumpfile into a Subversion repository later, using the svnadmin load command.

```
$ cat cvs2svn-dump | svnadmin load /var/svnrepos
```

Partial Repository Migration

If you don't want to migrate an entire CVS repository, cvs2svn allows you to only migrate part of the repository. For example, you can migrate just the trunk of a repository by running the conversion with the --trunk-only option.

```
$ cvs2svn --trunk-only -s /var/svnrepos /var/cvsroot
```

Or, you can convert a custom selection of branches and tags by using the --exclude option to tell cvs2svn what parts of the repository you *don't* want to be converted. The exclude option allows you to pass regular expressions that cvs2svn will use to determine which branches/tags to ignore during the conversion. For instance, the following example will convert an entire repository, except for the branches that were used for fixing issues in the issue-tracking system.

```
$ cvs2svn --exclude='issue-*' -s /var/svnrepos /var/cvsroot
```

Handling Data Differences

CVS and Subversion are very similar, but they don't store data in exactly the same way. The most obvious difference, of course, is the way the two handle branches and tags. Instead of using copies, like Subversion does, CVS deals with tags and branches differently than it deals with the repository trunk. That means that when cvs2svn converts the repository, it needs to convert the CVS branches and tags into copied directories inside the Subversion repository.

By default, cvs2svn creates top-level branches, tags, and trunk directories and places branches and tags correctly into their respective directories. If you want to create a repository that places branches, tags, and the trunk somewhere other than the default top-level directories, you can do so by passing the `--branches`, `--tags`, and `--trunk` options, respectively. For instance, the following example shows a conversion that will place the converted repository into a subdirectory specific to the CVS repository's project.

```
$ cvs2svn --trunk='myproject/trunk' --branches='myproject/branches' -- ¬
  tags='myproject/tags' -s /var/svnrepos /var/cvsroot
```

Another fairly major difference between Subversion and CVS is the handling of revision numbers. CVS keeps revision numbers for each file individually, whereas Subversion keeps a global repository revision number. In most cases, this change isn't a big deal, but sometimes developers will remember the revision numbers to use later. If you don't want to lose the file-specific CVS revision numbers when you perform the migration, you can pass `cvs2svn` the `--cvs-revnums` option. This tells it to create a property to store the CVS revision numbers for each file that is converted.

Handling end-of-line markers can be another sticky area of conversion. CVS's standard mode of operation is to convert line endings to the native line-ending format for the local operating system of the working copy when a file is checked out. Subversion, on the other hand, never makes any modifications to the file, by default. If you have a CVS repository, though, it is likely that some of your developers have come to rely on the default CVS line-ending modifications. To make the conversion a little bit easier, `cvs2svn` automatically sets the `svn:eol-style` property to `native` for all files that CVS hasn't been explicitly told not to do line-ending conversions for. If you don't want `cvs2svn` to set all of the files from your CVS repository to do line-ending conversions when they're checked out, you can pass the `--no-default-eol` option when it converts the repository.

CVS doesn't know anything about MIME types for files. Subversion, however, can use MIME types constructively in a number of situations, which would make it useful if the repository conversion could automatically set the `svn:mime-type` property for all of the files in your CVS repository. Well, as you may have guessed already, it can do just that. If you pass `cvs2svn` the `--mime-types=FILE` options, with `FILE` pointing to a `mime.types` file, it will attempt to assign the MIME type for every file it converts.

The `mime.types` file tells `cvs2svn` what MIME types it should match to files with given file extensions. Each entry in the file will contain a MIME type, followed by a list of the file extensions that should be matched with it. For example, you might have an entry in your `mime.types` file that told `cvs2svn` to give all files that ended in `.c`, `.cpp`, or `.h` the MIME type `text/x-c`, which would look something like the following.

```
text/x-c        c     cpp     h
```

If you have Apache installed on your system, you probably have a default `mime.types` file somewhere. You may want to find that file and use it as a starting point for writing your own `mime.types` file to use when converting your repository.

If you're using `--mime-types`, you may also want to have `cvs2svn` decide whether it should set the `svn:eol-style` based on the MIME type that it sets for each file. To do so, you need to pass the `--eol-from-mime-type` option to `cvs2svn`. However, this option will only have an effect if the `--mime-types` option is also used.

A final difference between CVS and Subversion that needs to be addressed is the way keywords are handled. CVS automatically performs keyword substitutions on all files that aren't explicitly identified as binary when the file is added to the repository. Conversely, Subversion doesn't perform keyword expansions on any files, unless it is explicitly told to. However, if you use a lot of keyword expansions in your CVS repository, the odds are that you would like to continue to use them in your new Subversion repository. Therefore, by default, `cvs2svn` will set the `svn:keywords` property on all of the files it converts to "`author id date`" (except ones marked as binary in CVS). If you *don't* want the property set, you can turn it off with `--keywords-off`.

9.3.3 Migrating from SourceSafe

Microsoft's Visual SourceSafe is not the darling of the version control market. In fact, it seems to be a common wisdom within Subversion circles that there are two kinds of VSS users in the world: those who have lost data to a corrupted database, and those who will. With such a charmless reputation, it's no wonder that migrations to VSS seem to be one of the most common types of migration performed. Fortunately, that means that if you find yourself clamoring to get away from VSS, there are a number of tools available to aid you in your plight.

The most full-featured tool available appears to be the `vss2svn.pl` conversion script, which is available from `vss2svn.tigris.org`. As I'm writing this book, the script is still listed as being in an alpha release, but it does have support for converting most of the information in a typical VSS repository. When you run the script, you will give it an existing VSS repository and an existing SVN repository (which can be a brand new one you just created). It then gets the data out of the VSS repository and inserts it into the Subversion.

The basic operation for the `vss2svn.pl` script is pretty simple. If you have VSS properly installed on your system, you can run the script from a Windows command prompt; just tell it which VSS project to migrate, and what Subversion repository to migrate it into. For example, if you want to migrate the project `foo` from your VSS repository into a newly created (empty) repository, you could run the following.

```
C:\vss2svn>vss2svn.pl --vssproject $/foo --svnrepo http://svn.example. ¬
  com/svnrepos/
```

The `vss2svn.pl` script also lets you do more complicated processing by allowing you to specify projects that should be excluded from the migration using `--vssexclude`, listing either absolute paths to exclude or paths relative to the project specified by the `--vssproject` option. You can also perform other processing on the migration, such as specifying messages that should be appended to every log message for migrated files (`--comment`), or you can tell `vss2svn.pl` to set the `svn:date` property for each migrated revision to reflect the original VSS commit date. If your VSS repository requires a login and password, you can specify that with the --vsslogin option, giving it a username and password, separated by colons.

If vss2svn.pl turns out to be insufficient for converting your repository, you may want to do a bit of searching online, as there are a few other VSS conversion tools being passed around. I can't vouch for how well or poorly any of them work, but as long as you have your database backed up, no harm should come to your data.

9.3.4   Migrating from Other VCSs

There are a number of other version control systems for which people have generated conversion scripts. The scripts appear to be in varying degrees of completion, and look to have often been created with just enough power and flexibility to convert the scriptwriter's own repository. However, that may just be enough for your repository too, and if it isn't, the modifications necessary to make it work may very well be easier than writing your own conversion tool from scratch.

Some of the version control system converters that I was able to find include a converter for a Perforce repository (this converter is linked to from Subversion's Web site), and a number of converters for a ClearCase repository.

9.3.5   What If There's No Migration Tool?

So, what if you don't use CVS or SourceSafe, but instead your entire code repository is in Bob's Discount VCS (or more likely, Bob's Mind-Bogglingly Expensive VCS)? In that case, you have a couple of options. The first step, of course, is to search online to see if someone else needed to migrate from your VCS to Subversion and wrote a conversion tool. You may also want to search the Subversion users' mailing list to see if someone out there did a similar conversion and is willing to share any tools that she created (or just some good advice about the problems she ran into). You also have the option of writing your own conversion tool if there is no sufficient tool already written. The source for existing conversion tools may be invaluable here. Or, you can just keep the old repository running as a reference and go from there.

If no tool exists (and creating one is impractical), your best bet is to check out a working copy of your current repository's HEAD, and then svn import that into a new Subversion repository. Then, you may want to go through and recreate important tags or long-running branches by hand. Simply check out the appropriate tags/branches and use svn import to add them to the new repository in the appropriate place. The new branches and tags won't have any history link to the files in the main trunk, but nothing else will have a history either, and Subversion won't care that there's no link down the road when you want to merge files from a branch or tag into the main trunk. If, for some reason, you decide that it is important for the branches and tags to be linked to the front, you can achieve that by creating the branch or tag inside the Subversion repository (using the newly imported trunk HEAD), and then copy over the versions of the files in the tag/branch from a working copy of the old repository.

After you have the new repository created, it's a good idea to keep the old repository up and running, in case someone finds that he needs some of the older repository information

(I suggest making it read-only). In most cases, though, you'll probably find that the old repository is rarely accessed. After a time, you may even find that you can mothball the old repository, and just keep a backup of the data that could be restored later if needed.

On the other hand, if your project's development process depends heavily on retrieving and comparing data from old revisions, separating your new and old data into different repositories may not seem like such a good idea. If there are no tools available (and creating them isn't an option), two separate repositories may be your only option. There are, however, a couple of things that you can do, which may make things a little bit easier to deal with.

- Keep working copies of both repositories handy. That way, if you need some information about a revision from the old repository, you can just hop over to that repository real quick and check what you need.

- Create wrapper scripts that will bind your new Subversion repository and your old repository together. If you have scripts for all of the common (read-only) repository history querying commands you perform (such as diffs and log checking), you will be able to compare information *almost* seamlessly between the two repositories. (I don't suggest trying to allow cross-VCS commands that write to both repositories, at least without an awful lot of testing, as this is likely to introduce subtle bugs that could result in data loss.)

  For instance, if you want to create a wrapper for the diff command that spanned two different repositories, you could write a script that took revision identifiers for either repository (perhaps with qualifiers, if the repository identifiers are ambiguous about the version control system they refer to). Then, if it got two revisions for the same repository, it could simply run the native diff command for that repository. If, instead, it was passed two revisions on different version control systems, it could retrieve those files from their respective system and run an external diff program to compare the two.

- After you have the new repository established, you very well may find points where you want to merge data that is in a revision from the old repository into a new revision in the new repository. If this happens, create a new tag in the Subversion repository that identifies the revision from the old repository you'll be merging from. (If it doesn't make sense to use the directory's name to identify the revision, use a property.) Then, import the revision to be merged into the new repository directory from the working copy of the old repository, just as if it were a set of unversioned files. After you have the new tag directory with the old repository revision, you can merge that directory into your Subversion repository trunk, using Subversion's standard merging tools.

  The downside to this method is that it causes your Subversion repository to grow, and if these sorts of merges occur often, they may grow the repository too much. If that is a concern, you can use external merging tools to perform the merge directly from your old repository's working copy into your Subversion repository. If you use this approach, it's best to use a property to keep track of where the merge occurred from, or at the very least make sure it's documented in the log for the merge commit.

- If you're really ambitious, you might want to modify a Web-based repository browsing tool (such as ViewCVS or WebSVN) to support both Subversion and your old version control system. Then, the Web site could serve as a frontend to both VCSs, making the transition between the two as seamless as possible.

9.4   Summary

In this section, you've learned many of the considerations that should go into laying out a new repository. You saw the basic `branches/tags/trunk` layout scheme, and saw a number of variations on that layout, along with some of the layout considerations that will help you support the different potential uses for the branch and tag concepts. Additionally, you learned about converting an existing repository from another version control system, with some discussion on the tools available to perform those conversions. In the case where no conversion tools are available, you learned some techniques for handling a migration to Subversion that doesn't include migrating the old repository.

Chapter 10

Administrating the Repository

Day-to-day, most Subversion repositories require little intervention on the part of an administrator. There are, however, a few essential skills that a good administrator needs to know to keep everything running smoothly, such as setting up user access, backing up the data in the repository, and recovering from crashes.

10.1   Controlling Access to the Repository

Subversion supplies you with a number of different repository access schemas that can be used from a Subversion client (as illustrated in Figure 10.1). Each schema represents not only a different access mechanism, but also a differing level of access control available to the administrator. The range of control varies from simply being able to use the operating system's file access controls to limit access to the whole repository using direct local repository access, to fine-grained per-directory access control via HTTP/HTTPS. Additionally, with all of the access methods (except direct local access), you can control whether users are allowed to access the repository through an insecure, unencrypted (albeit slightly faster) connection, or are required to access the repository through an encryption layer, such as SSH or SSL.

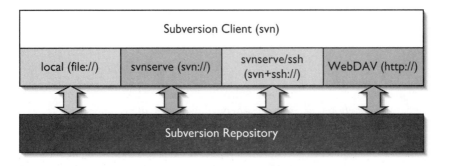

Figure 10.1. The respository access schema layer.

10.1.1   Direct Access Control

Subversion repositories on your local machine can be accessed directly by using a local access schema, through a `file://` URL. This is a handy way to access a repository that is only going to be used by one person, or even a couple of people using the same machine. However, this method doesn't scale up particularly well as the number of users grows. Subversion itself does not supply any sort of built-in access controls for direct repository access, so your ability to control access is limited to your operating system's capability to control read/write access to the repository itself. Also, there is no built-in way to provide access controls of a finer grain than whether a user has read or write access to the whole repository. You can use hook scripts (see Chapter 11, "The Joy of Automation") to provide better control, but because the user needs full filesystem access to the repository, those controls can be circumvented.

The security advantage gained from using direct access to access a repository is the lack of network access. Direct access doesn't require you to have any sort of server process running, and requires no network ports to be opened. Therefore, if you limit repository access to direct access, there is no way for anyone to access the repository without local access to the machine. (Remember, never access a Subversion repository from a network share if you're using Berkeley DB as your storage backend.)

10.1.2   svnserve Access Control

An alternate to direct access is the standalone Subversion server, `svnserve`. It allows you to make the repository available to remote users, while retaining access that is available only to certain users. Additionally, repository access can be performed using a custom Subversion protocol (easier) or through a tunneled SSH or RSH connection (more secure). Unfortunately, access through `svnserve` does have the same all-or-nothing limitations that direct access does, although hook scripts can still be used to limit access.

Unlike direct access, the Subversion protocol does not require you to allow filesystem access to every user, so hook script access controls are a little more secure when using the Subversion protocol—but passwords are transferred in plaintext. If you use tunneled SSH/RSH, you don't have to worry about plaintext passwords, but you do need to provide filesystem-level access to the repository, so hook script access controls could theoretically be circumvented. In general, `svnserve` is not a good choice if security is a concern.

If `svnserve` is started with either the `-i` or `-d` options, it will handle requests on a dedicated port, communicating over the custom Subversion access protocol. Access is provided to all users that are found in a Subversion-specific password file, pointed to by the `svnserve` configuration file. The `svnserve` configuration file is named `svnserve.conf`, and is located in the `conf` directory of the repository that the file refers to (each repository has its own `svnserve.conf` file).

The `svnserve.conf` file

The `svnserve.conf` file tells `svnserve` how it should handle user authentication. It is set up similar to the Subversion user configuration files (see Chapter 7, "Configuring the

Client"), and has a single section named [general]. In that section, there are a number of options that you can set.

If you would like to allow anonymous access to the repository, you can set up the anon-access option. If you want to allow anonymous users to get files from the repository, but not commit, you can set anon-access to read. Or, if you want to allow anonymous users full access to the repository, you can give them read/write access with the value write. On the other hand, if you don't want any sort of anonymous access, set anon-access to none.

Assuming you would like more than just anonymous access to the repository, you will need to set up some users with access. To tell Subversion where to find the file containing these users, you point it to the password file by setting the password-db file to the path to the password file. I'll describe the contents of the password file shortly.

Sometimes, you will have multiple repositories that should all share the same set of users. If you would like users to be able to authenticate with all of the repositories as a single group (i.e., cached authentication with one repository allows access to the other repositories), you can set up a realm. The realm is set with the svnserve.conf option realm, and should be the name you would like to use for the realm (users will see this when they log in). As a word of caution, make sure you have each repository in the realm point to the same password file. Otherwise, a user's ability to log into the realm may be dependent on which repository the user accesses first.

A complete svnserve.conf file may look something like this:

```
[general]
anon-access = read
password-db = /srv/svnrepos/conf/passwd
realm = Very Snazzy Repositories
```

The Passwords Database File

The passwords database for a repository (identified by the svnserve.conf file) contains a list of username/password pairs that identify the valid users for that repository. Each entry will be of the form username = password, with the passwords stored in their plaintext form (so make sure that only authorized people have access to the password file). The collection of username/password pairs will then all fall under the [users] section, as you can see in the following sample password database.

```
[users]
bill = ABadPassword
bob = K@tZ7&D()g$5
```

Secure Communication over SSH

Another option that is available for securing svnserve is tunneling it over SSH, by using an svn+ssh:// URL (or svn+rsh:// to tunnel over RSH). If you are tunneling svnserve, the svnserve program will be run locally on the server machine, using the -t option. It will also be run as the OS-level user who invoked the SSH tunnel session. That means two things.

- Instead of listing the users in a Subversion-specific password database file, each user will need to be a full user on the server system, with access to log in via SSH.

- Each user with access to the repository will need either read or read/write access to the actual repository, just as with direct access.

With SSH tunneling, the `svnserve.conf` file is not needed. After the user has authenticated, access is essentially identical to direct repository access.

10.1.3 HTTP/HTTPS Access Control

By far, your most flexible security options come from using the Apache HTTP/HTTPS repository server. In addition to allowing similar authentication options to `svnserve`, the Apache server allows you to define per-directory security constraints. This allows you to give individual users access to only some of the directories in a repository, instead of being forced to use all-or-nothing authentication.

Setting Up Password Protection

After you have Apache set up and serving a repository (see Chapter 3, "Installing Subversion"), you're probably going to want to protect it from unauthorized access (even open source projects don't usually allow unfettered write access to their repositories—it helps keep references to petrified movie stars out of the code). To add password authentication to your repository, you need to add a couple of lines to the `<Location>` section that points to your Subversion repository. These entries will tell Apache that it should require a username and password from all who try to connect, as well as where to find the file that lists the users and their passwords.

Apache supports two types of authentication: basic password protection and digest password protection. Basic authentication has wider support among Web browsers, but it sends passwords in what is essentially plaintext form. Digest authentication offers much better password security by using a challenge/response mechanism that avoids the transmission of the password itself. Although it is not quite as well supported, unless you need to have your users access the repository via an ancient browser, you are much better off using digest (the `svn` client program supports digest authentication). A password protected repository location entry with digest authentication will end up looking something like the following example.

```
<Location /myrepos>
  DAV svn
  SVNPath /srv/svnrepos
  AuthType Digest
  AuthName "My Subversion Realm"
  AuthDigestDomain /myrepos/
```

```
AuthDigestFile /srv/svnrepos/svn-auth-file
Require valid-user
</Location>
```

In this case, the five options of real interest are the four that begin with `Auth` and `Require`.

- The `AuthType` entry tells Apache that it should use digest authentication for challenging the client.

- The `AuthName` entry gives a realm name, which is displayed to the user when logging in. This realm is also used to match the username/password that the user gives when authenticating.

- The `AuthDigestDomain` entry gives a domain for the authentication. All paths underneath the given domain are included in an authenticated domain (for example, `/myrepos/trunk/` or `/myrepos/branches`).

- The `AuthDigestFile` entry defines the file where the digest passwords are stored.

- `Require` informs Apache that it should require users to enter a valid username/password before allowing access.

The digest password file should be a file created with `htdigest`, containing the usernames, realms, and encrypted passwords of every user that is allowed access to the repository. The file originally is created by running `htdigest` with the `-c` option, which tells it to create a new file. The following example shows how you might create a new password file containing the user `fredj`. Notice that the realm matches the `AuthName` given in your `<Location>` description earlier. This is necessary for the given username/password pair to work for that location. As you can see, `htdigest` prompts you for the password to use before creating the file.

```
$ htdigest -c /srv/svnrepos/svn-auth-file "My Subversion Realm" fredj
Adding password for fredj in realm My Subversion Realm.
New password:
Re-type new password:
Adding password for user fredj
```

After you have an existing digest file, you can use `htdigest` to add to that file by leaving off the `-c` argument.

Further Securing with SSL

The problem with password authentication under Apache is that it only keeps unauthorized users from accessing the repository, but does nothing to protect the data as it travels between the server and client. The casual user is prevented from going through your repository, but determined attackers will have no problems capturing data in transit. Therefore, in order to tack on an added layer of security, it is a good idea to also use the Secure Socket Layer (SSL) to encrypt all data that travels over the network.

The first thing you need to do when enabling SSL for Apache is to make sure that the `mod_ssl.so` module is loaded into Apache when it starts. This is accomplished in Apache by calling `LoadModule ssl_module mod_ssl.so` somewhere in the Apache configuration files. In many cases, this will already exist in your base Apache install, but may need to have something defined in order to turn it on, such as by running Apache with a `-D SSL` option.

After you have SSL enabled in Apache, you need to set your repository share to require the use of SSL for communications. This is done simply by adding the a `SSLRequireSSL` statement to your repository `<Location>`. So, the repository location from earlier would become.

```
<Location /myrepos>
  DAV svn
  SVNPath /srv/svnrepos
  AuthType Digest
  AuthName "My Subversion Realm"
  AuthDigestDomain /myrepos/
  AuthDigestFile /srv/svnrepos/svn-auth-file
  Require valid-user
  SSLRequireSSL
</Location>
```

Creating an SSL Certificate

SSL works on a trust-by-association mechanism for securely ensuring a site's identity. Any site that uses SSL will have a certificate that identifies the site (name, IP address, domain, and so on). That certificate will then be digitally signed by a certificate authority that vouches for the certificate's authenticity. That way, if someone attempts to intercept communications to your server by pretending to be you, he won't have the proper signed certificate and the Web browser or Subversion client will warn the user that something is amiss.

Certificate authorities (CAs) come in two flavors. The first variety is the large commercial CA, such as Verisign or Thawte, which gives your certificate a wide trust base (for a hefty annual cost, in most cases). Then, there are locally created certificate authorities, usually generated for intranets, where trust can more easily be established. Additionally, you can also self-sign a certificate, which is by far the easiest approach to getting an SSL-protected server up and going, but it is also the most vulnerable to attacks that intercept data from clients and pretend to be your server (this is known as a man in the middle attack).

If you want to set up SSL on your Web server, you need to set up some sort of SSL certificate. Dealing with a commercial CA and creating your own intranet CA are beyond the scope of this book. The steps toward creating a self-signed certificate are fairly simple though. If the number of developers accessing your repository is small (especially if they're all on an intranet), this is probably sufficient.

The first step toward creating a certificate is to generate a private key, which will be stored locally and not be accessible to anyone else. The key is generated by using the `openssl` program, with the `genrsa` command. In its simplest form, the command takes the name of the encryption cypher to use (`des3` in the following example), the number of bits to use (at least 1024), and a file to output the key into. To improve the security of your key, you should also provide a source of random data to be used when calculating the key. The best source to use is `/dev/random` (assuming you're on a UNIX-like machine that has a `/dev/random`); but if that is not available, you can also enter a file that has been otherwise populated with random data, or even a list of randomly chosen files from your system, separated by colons.

When `openssl genrsa` is run, it asks you for a passphrase, which protects your key from unauthorized users, even if the key itself is compromised. The downside to the passphrase is that it needs to be typed every time the Web server is started (which is likely undesireable). Therefore, you will probably want to remove the passphrase from the file and ensure that the resulting private key file is only readable by the root user, which you can do by running the `openssl rsa` command.

```
$ openssl genrsa -des3 -rand /dev/random -out svnsrv.key 1024
$ openssl rsa -in svnsrv.key -out svnsrv.pem
```

After you have your key generated, you need to generate a certificate request, which could then be sent to a certificate authority for signing, or you can self-sign it (as I'll show you how to do shortly). To generate the certificate request, you need to run the `openssl req` command, and give it your key. When the command runs, it asks you a number of questions about who you are, which are then included as a part of the signed certificate (and sent to clients that are trying to verify the certificate's authenticity). You can fill in as many or as few of the fields as you would like.

```
$ openssl req -new -key svnsrv.pem -out svnsrv.req
You are about to be asked to enter information that will be ¬
  incorporated
into your certificate request.
What you are about to enter is what is called a Distinguished Name ¬
  or a DN.
There are quite a few fields but you can leave some blank
For some fields there will be a default value,
If you enter '.', the field will be left blank.
-----
Country Name (2 letter code) [AU]:US
State or Province Name (full name) [Some-State]:Indiana
Locality Name (eg, city) []:Terre Haute
Organization Name (eg, company) [Internet Widgits Pty Ltd]:
Organizational Unit Name (eg, section) []:
Common Name (eg, YOUR name) []:William Nagel
Email Address []:
```

```
Please enter the following 'extra' attributes
to be sent with your certificate request
A challenge password []:
An optional company name []:
```

After you've created the certificate request, you can then use that to create a self-signed certificate.

```
$ openssl req -x509 -days 365 -in svnsrv.req -key svnsrv.pem -out ¬
  svnsrv.crt
```

Configuring Your SSL Certificate in Apache

The last thing you need to do to configure Apache to use SSL is to set it up to create a virtual host that is accessible on port 443 (the default SSL port). In your Apache configuration files, you need to add a `<VirtualHost>` directive similar to the following.

```
<VirtualHost _default_:443>
    DocumentRoot "/srv/www/localhost/htdocs"
    SSLEngine on
    SSLCertificateFile /etc/apache2/ssl/svnsrv.crt
    SSLCertificateKeyFile /etc/apache2/ssl/svnsrv.pem
  </VirtualHost>
```

Per-directory Access Control

One of the big advantages of using Apache as your repository server is the ability to control user access to the repository on a per-directory basis. For each subdirectory in the repository, you are able to specify read or read/write access (or *no* access) for individual users or groups of users.

To set up access on a per-directory basis, you need to load the `mod_authz_svn.so` module by placing a `LoadModule mod_authz_svn.so` entry after the `LoadModule` entry for `mod_dav_svn.so`. Then, configure your repository to use the Authz module, by pointing it to an access file, using the `AuthzSVNAccessFile` option. I'll explain shortly how to set up the access file. First, though, this is how you might build on the example `<Location>` section we've been using.

```
<Location /myrepos>
  DAV svn
  SVNPath /srv/svnrepos
  AuthzSVNAccessFile /srv/svnrepos/svn-authz-access
  AuthType Basic
  AuthName "My Subversion Repository"
  AuthUserFile /srv/svnrepos/svn-auth-file
  Require valid-user
  SSLRequireSSL
</Location>
```

The Authz access file itself can be placed anywhere, but needs to be readable by Apache. The repository directory is a good choice, because the repository already needs to be accessible by Subversion, and logically you then keep the authorization file near to the repository.

The access file itself contains a number of directory sections, followed by the users who are allowed (or disallowed) access to that directory (and its subdirectories). For example, you might want to give read access for the whole repository to all valid users, but only give write access to the users melinda and joe, which would give you an access file that looked like the following:

```
[/]
* = r
melinda = rw
joe = rw
```

Then, if you also want to give andrew write access to /branches, and deny access to /trunk/private_project to everyone except bob, you could add the following two entries to your file. Notice that the wildcard entry in the private project section has no permissions listed after the =. This tells Subversion to deny all access to the given users (in this case, everyone who isn't explicitly listed).

```
[/branches]
andrew = rw

[/trunk/private_project]
* =
bob = rw
```

Additionally, you can set up groups of users that can be used in place of individual users in the directory permission sections. For instance, you might create a group that would be used for all of the developers on the project foo, to give them all read/write access to that project's directory. The following example shows how you would set up that group, and then use it in the directory section for foo. The @ is used in front of the foodevs group name to indicate that you are specifying a group, and not an individual user.

```
[groups]
foodevs = joe, bob, janet, trisha

[/foo]
* = r
@foodevs = rw
```

If you are using the SVNParentPath directive instead of SVNPath (see Chapter 3 for more information), you can have all of your repositories share a single access file. To specify permissions for a specific repository, a section label should have both the repository name and the path separated by a colon, as in the following access entries that set different permissions for the trunk directories of two different repositories.

```
[repos_1:/trunk]
betty = rw

[repos_2:/trunk]
* = r
kate = rw
```

If you are using SVNParentPath and you *don't* specify a specific repository, the given entry will apply to that path in all of your repositories. This can be handy, for instance, to have a common set of permissions for every /tags directory.

If you use wildcards in your Authz access file, permission will be granted for all valid users, but anonymous access will still be denied. If you would like to allow anonymous access, you need to add the Satisfy Any directive to your <Location>, so that it would look like this:

```
<Location /myrepos>
  DAV svn
  SVNPath /srv/svnrepos
  AuthzSVNAccessFile /srv/svnrepos/svn-authz-access
  AuthType Basic
  AuthName "My Subversion Repository"
  AuthUserFile /srv/svnrepos/svn-auth-file
  Require valid-user
  Satisfy Any
  SSLRequireSSL
</Location>
```

10.1.4   Authenticating against a Windows Domain Controller

Using Samba and Apache, you can get a Subversion repository on a Linux server to use a Windows Domain Controller (WDC) as the source for its valid user list and authentication information. This can be very handy if you have an existing Windows Domain that you use for other server authentication, as it negates the necessity for you to keep multiple sets of usernames up to date.[1]

Configuring Apache

The first thing that you need to get working is the mod_auth_pam module for Apache. PAM (Pluggable Authentication Manager) will be used by Apache to authenticate with Samba (which will in turn talk to the domain controller). Most Apache installations don't

---

1.   The steps for authenticating with a WDC, described in this section, were graciously provided by Stuart Robinson and his employer, Absolute Systems (www.absolutesys.com).

have mod_auth_pam, so to get it you need to download it from the PAM project's Web site, pam.sourceforge.net/mod_auth_pam/. You should be able to build and install it by running make and make install in the mod_auth_pam source.

After you have mod_auth_pam installed, you need to enable it in Apache, by adding a LoadModule line to the Apache configuration file, which will look similar to the following example.

```
LoadModule auth_pam_module modules/mod_auth_pam.so
```

Additionally, you need to create a new file named /etc/pam.d/httpd (or edit if it already exists). This sets up PAM to grant access to users that have a Windows Domain account, but no local system account. To set this up, you will want your httpd file to look like the following.

```
#%PAM-1.0
auth      required      pam_nologin.so
auth      required      pam_stack.so service-system-auth
account required      pam_permit.so
```

After this is all done, Apache should be set up correctly. You can restart the Apache server and you'll be good to go. However, before Windows Domain accounts will work, you also need to set up Samba.

Configuring Samba

To configure Samba, you need to edit some of the options in the /etc/samba/smb.conf file. This file contains a large number of options, but the ones you need to edit are in the [global] section. When edited, the file will need to look something like the following.

```
[global]
   workgroup = MYWORKGRP
   server string = Subversion
   security = domain
   password server = 192.168.0.128
   wins server = 192.168.0.128
   winbind enum users = yes
   winbind enum groups = yes
   obey pam restrictions = yes
   realm = mydomain.com
```

The details of all the possible Samba options are well beyond the scope of this book. However, the important options to pay attention to when setting up Windows Domain accounts are the workgroup, password server, and wins server. The IP addresses point to the WINS server, and the workgroup option defines the Windows Domain that you would like your Subversion server to connect to.

Next, you need to set up the Kerberos configuration files to point to the Windows Domain. To the file /etc/krb.conf, you need to add the lines

```
myworkgrp
myworkgrp      192.168.0.128:88
myworkgrp      192.168.0.122:88 admin server
```

And to the /etc/krb5.conf file, you need to add a default_realm entry to the [libdefaults] section, so that it looks something like the following.

```
[libdefaults]
    default_realm = myworkgrp
    dns_lookup_realm = true
    dns_lookup_kdc = true
```

Also, to the same file, you need to add the following line to the [realms] section.

```
[realms]
    myworkgrp = {
      kdc = 192.168.0.128:88
      admin_server = 192.168.0.128:88
    }
```

Then, you need to set up /etc/nsswitch.conf to include references to winbind. (Note: These are not the only entries in the file, just the ones that should reference winbind.)

```
passwd:        files winbind
shadow:        files winbind
group:         files winbind
protocols:     files winbind
services:      files winbind
netgroup:      files winbind
automount:     files winbind
```

After /etc/nsswitch.conf is edited, you need to set up PAM to use winbind. To do this, edit the /etc/pam.d/system-auth file and add the following three lines:

```
auth           sufficient     /lib/security/$ISA/pam_winbind.so ¬
  use_first_pass
account        [default=bsd success=ok user_unknown=ignore] /lib/security/ ¬
  $ISA/pam_winbind.so
password       sufficient     /lib/security/$ISA/pam_winbind.so use_authtok
```

When all of these files are correctly configured, you can restart smb and winbind (likely by running /etc/init.d/samba restart and /etc/init.d/winbind restart). After things are restarted, you can tell Samba to join the Windows Domain by running

```
$ net join -w MYWORKGRP -U Administrator
```

10.2   Backing Up the Repository

I could tell you a story about a friend of mine losing vital data to a hard-drive crash, at the most inconvenient of times. I could tell you the story of a colleague losing weeks' worth of work because someone erased the wrong partition. Or, I could even tell you a story about the time I lost a college term paper because lightning struck my dorm. I won't, though, because you undoubtedly have your own stories of data loss and no desire to hear about someone else's misfortune. Because of your own personal experience, you almost certainly have no need for a lecture on the importance of regular backups. So, I won't give you one. Instead, I'll just show you how you can ensure that you don't lose your repository at a most inopportune moment.

10.2.1   Hotcopying the Repository

The best way to back up an entire Subversion repository is through use of the `svnadmin hotcopy` command. The hotcopy command ensures that the repository gets copied in a manner that is safe, even if other users are accessing the repository during the copy. If you are using a Berkeley DB (BDB) database backend, the `svnadmin hotcopy` command is critical (unless you can be absolutely certain the repository will not be accessed during the copy). If you just use a standard filesystem copy of the repository, even a simple read access could cause corruption in a BDB repository. If you are using a FSFS (filesystem-based backend) repository instead, the consequences of copying without using the `svnadmin hotcopy` command are not as dire, but you could have a bad revision file if the copy occurs in the middle of a commit. The safest choice in most instances is to always use `svnadmin hotcopy` to copy your repository.

Performing a hotcopy with `svnadmin hotcopy` is easy. All you need to do is run the command with the name of the repository and the final copy.

```
$ svnadmin hotcopy /srv/myrepos /mnt/backup/myrepos.backup
```

If you want Subversion to clean out unnecessary log files when it makes the copy, you can pass the `--clean-logs` option.

The Subversion source also includes a convenience Python script that you can use to perform hotcopies, named `hot-backup.py`. The `hot-backup.py` script takes the repository to back up, and a directory where the backup should be created. It then creates a new hotcopy named after the copied repository with the HEAD revision of that repository appended, so that multiple backups won't overwrite each other.

```
$ hot-backup.py /srv/myrepos /mnt/backup/
Beginning hot backup of '/srv/myrepos'.
Youngest revision is 265
Backing up repository to '/mnt/backup/myrepos-265'...
Done.
```

```
$ ls /mnt/backup/
myrepos-10
myrepos-146
myrepos-265
```

10.2.2   Dumping the Repository

Another way to back up a Subversion repository is through use of the `svnadmin dump` command, which dumps the contents of a repository into a text file that can later be used to populate another repository. Dumping the repository is not nearly as efficient as performing a hotcopy, but it does have its advantages. For instance, repositories can be dumped incrementally, so each dump doesn't need to contain the entire repository.

To perform a dump of your repository, say that you have a repository located at `/srv/svnrepos` that you want to back up. If you run the dump command with no options, except the name of the repository to dump, it will dump the entire contents of every revision of that repository to standard out (i.e., your console screen).

```
$ svnadmin dump /srv/svnrepos
--- Snipped Massive Amounts of Output ---
```

That's probably not what you want (unless you can read and memorize *really fast*). Instead, you want to add one more thing and redirect the output into a file, as with the following example. That way, the only thing output to the console will be the revisions that it has processed, as it progresses (which are sent to standard error, not standard out).

```
$ svnadmin dump /srv/svnrepos > svnrepos-091504.dump
* Dumped revision 0.
* Dumped revision 1.
* Dumped revision 2.
--- Snipped Output ---
* Dumped revision 1487.
* Dumped revision 1488.
```

Daily backups of your whole repository can get to be pretty big, pretty fast. Given that your old revisions will never change—unless you mess with revision properties—that may mean a lot of data is getting backed up with excessive redundancy. And even though storage space is cheap, that may mean a lot of wasted time and space, which does eventually add up. Subversion does have a solution, though, in the form of incremental dumps.

If you dump a repository with the `--incremental` option, and a range of revisions, it will only dump those revisions, such that multiple incremental backups can later be run consecutively to perform a full restore on the repository. In other words, if I dump the first 50 revisions of a repository and then later dump the next 75 into a different file, I can completely restore the first 125 by loading the first dump followed by the second dump.

```
$ svnadmin dump -r 3:5 --incremental /srv/svnrepos > svnrepos-r3-r5. ¬
  dump
* Dumped revision 3.
```

```
* Dumped revision 4.
* Dumped revision 5.
```

As I mentioned, though, there is a downside to doing all of your backups incrementally, because changes to revision properties in previously archived revisions won't be backed up. There are a number of ways that you can work around this issue, and still make use of incremental backups.

- Don't do anything. By default, revision properties are immutable. If you you never allow revision properties to be changed, you never have to worry about a revision property change being lost at a later date. If you do allow some revision properties to be changed by allowing them in a hook script, you can add specific logic to your `pre-commit` script that will only allow unarchived revision properties to be modified (see Chapter 11 for more information).

  This has the advantage of being the easiest solution to deal with, but it means you lose the ability to make backdated changes to things like log files if an error is found. If you use revision properties to store custom data that makes past revision properties volatile, this may also be impractical.

- Explicitly rearchive changed revisions. If a developer makes a change to a revision property in a revision that has been previously archived, make it that developer's responsibility to inform an administrator and trigger a re-archiving of that block of incremental revisions. For example, if the archive on June 15th contained revisions 38 through 75, and you make a change to the log for revision 46, you would then want to recreate the June 15th archive for revisions 38 through 75 and replace the old archive file.

  If changes to archived revision properties are rare, this may be the best solution. It allows you to take advantage of incremental dumps to save time and space, while providing a procedure for modifying archived revisions if necessary. The downside, though, is that it is the developer's responsibility to make sure everything stays in sync. If the developer forgets to note the change, it could easily cause problems in the future, long after everyone involved has forgotten what change was made.

- Make periodic full backups, in addition to more frequent incremental dumps. For instance, you might make incremental backups every night, but make a full repository backup every week or month. This reduces the chance of losing a change to archived revision properties, while still reducing your backup load significantly. Of course, you still run the risk of losing a change if a crash occurs before the next full backup, so you should weigh the risk carefully before using it.

10.2.3   Automating Your Backups

There is an innumerable variety of automated backup tools available to the discerning systems administrator, many very expensive, complex, or feature rich (some are even all three). For the administrator of a small and/or open source project, though, these heavyweight backup tools are often overkill. Therefore, in this section, I will show you how to do simple automated incremental backups of your Subversion repository, using just cron, and the Subversion dump command on a UNIX-like system. If you are using Windows instead, there are similar options available to you.

An Incremental Dumping Script

The first thing you need is a script that will create an incremental repository dump, starting with where your last incremental backup left off. Creating the incremental dump is easy, but retaining state from one dump to the next can be a little trickier. The following example script shows the solution that I used for my own company's Subversion repository backups. First, it mounts the backup server (via Samba) and performs a hotcopy of the repository. Then, it performs a dump of the revisions that have been committed since the last backup and sends the dump file to an offsite backup server.

```
#!/bin/sh
# Makes a backup of a subversion repository
# Usage: backup_subversion.sh REPOS

SAMBASHARE="//backupsvr/subversion"
SAMBAPASSWD="backupPasswd"
MOUNTPOINT="/mnt/backup_subversion"
REPOSBASE="/srv/repositories"
REPOS="${1}"

OFFSITE="backupusr@offsitebackup.example.org"

# Mount the samba shared backup server
/bin/mount -t smbfs -o password=${SAMBAPASSWD} "${SAMBASHARE}" "${ ¬
  MOUNTPOINT}"

# Remove the old "yesterday" backup (from two days ago)
/bin/rm -rf "${MOUNTPOINT}/${REPOS}.yesterday"

# Rename yesterday's backup
/bin/mv "${MOUNTPOINT}/${REPOS}" "${MOUNTPOINT}/${REPOS}.yesterday"

# Perform a hotcopy of the repository
/usr/bin/svnadmin hotcopy "${REPOSBASE}/${REPOS}" "${MOUNTPOINT}/${ ¬
  REPOS}"

# Unmount the samba share
/bin/umount "${MOUNTPOINT}"

# Get (and save) some information about the revisions for
#  the incremental backup
```

```
/usr/bin/svnlook youngest "${REPOSBASE}/${REPOS}" > "${REPOSBASE}/${ ¬
  REPOS}/end.rev"
BEGIN=`cat "${REPOSBASE}/${REPOS}/begin.rev"`
END=`cat "${REPOSBASE}/${REPOS}/end.rev"`

# If no new revisions have been created, there's nothing to send ¬
  offsite
if [ $BEGIN == $END ]; then exit 0; fi

# Make the incremental dump of the changes made to the
#  repository since the last backup.
/usr/bin/svnadmin dump --incremental -r ${BEGIN}:${END} \
       "${REPOSBASE}/${REPOS}" > "/tmp/${REPOS}-${BEGIN}-${END}.dump"

# If the dump was successful, use SCP to send the dumpfile to the ¬
  offsite
#  backup server
if [ $? == 0 ]
then
    /usr/bin/scp "/tmp/${REPOS}-${BEGIN}-${END}.dump" ${OFFSITE}:~
    echo $(((${END} + 1)) > "${REPOSBASE}/${REPOS}/begin.rev"
fi
```

Setting Up Cron

Now that you have your script for doing automatic incremental dumps, you need to set up the backups to happen automatically, using cron.

1. Run crontab for the user that owns the Subversion repository, with the -e option to indicate that you want to edit the file.

   ```
   $ crontab -u svnuser -e
   ```

2. Add a line to your crontab that will run the incremental backup every night (in this case, at 3:00 AM).

   ```
   0 3 * * *    /srv/svnrepos/backup.sh /srv/svnrepos
   ```

3. After you have your automated backup script set to run, you can send it to a long-term archive using whatever means best fits your server setup. For instance, you might copy it to a shared network drive on a backup server or archive it to a tape drive or CD-ROM.

10.2.4 Recovering

Near tragedy! Your server failed and you lost the entire Subversion repository! Fortunately, you've made regular backups, and can restore everything to the way it was last night at 4:00

AM (you have been making backups, right?).

If you are recovering from a backup made using `svnadmin hotcopy`, all you need to do to restore the backup is to copy the backup version back to your Subversion server and make sure all of the permissions/connection settings are set up properly.

If you are restoring from incremental dumps, the process is a little more involved, but still reasonably easy.

1. Get your server back online, with all of the necessary Subversion software set up and restored to the correct state (if you've backed up your configuration settings, this should be an easy step).

2. Create a new empty repository for storing the data, with `svnadmin create`.

   ```
   $ svnadmin create /srv/svnrepos
   ```

3. Start with your first incremental repository dump file (or your only one, if you haven't been using incremental backups) and load it back into the repository, using the `svnadmin load` command, with the newly created repository as an argument, and the contents of the dump file fed to it via `stdin`.

   ```
   $ cat svnrepos.dump | svnadmin load /srv/svnrepos
   ```

4. If you have more repository dump files, restore them by repeating step 3 for each of the dump files, in the correct order (it's very important that you load them in order, from oldest to newest).

That's it. Your restored repository should be back up and running.

10.3   Unwedging Your Repository

If you are using the Berkeley DB backend, you may occasionally find that the repository gets "wedged" after a system crash, failed transaction, or other nasty event. This can happen when the database (for one reason or another) fails to remove an internal lock, which causes every subsequent request to hang indefinitely. Fortunately, fixing the problem is *usually* easy. In most cases, if you run the `svnadmin recover` command, you'll be back up and running (although with a large repository, the command might take a while to run). Because this command may modify files in the repository, make sure you run it as the user who owns the repository. You should also make sure that nothing else is accessing the repository while you perform the recovery (i.e., shut down Apache or `svnserve`). Although the recover command obtains a lock on the database, you can still have problems if another process was already accessing the repository when you started the recovery. If possible, it's also a good idea to make a copy of your repository before you run a recovery, just in case.

```
$ svnadmin recover /srv/svnrepos
Please wait; recovering the repository may take some time...
```

```
Recovery completed.
The latest repos revision is 13729.
```

The svnadmin recover command is a wrapper for the most common use case of the Berkeley DB recovery command, db_recover. Unfortunately, the most common use case is sometimes not enough to recover a broken repository. So, if svnadmin recover fails, you may need to try a catastrophic recovery with db_recover itself. To perform a catastrophic recovery, you need to have an intact backup of your repository, plus all of the log files that have been generated since that backup was made (or just all of the log files that have ever been generated for your repository). Then, you need to follow these steps.

1. Shut down any Subversion servers to ensure that no one is accessing your repository.

2. Move the corrupted repository out of the way.

   ```
   $ mv /srv/svnrepos /srv/svnrepos.wedged
   ```

3. Restore a backup of the repository to the original repository location (for instance, /srv/svnrepos).

4. Copy any log files from your corrupted repository into the recovered backup version.

   ```
   $ cp /srv/svnrepos.wedged/db/log* /srv/svnrepos/db/
   ```

   If you have backups of log files that are stored elsewhere, you can copy them in, too. If you do copy log files from multiple places, make sure you copy from oldest backup to newest backup. Multiple backups may have different versions of the same log file, so copying from oldest to newest will ensure that you have the newest version of each log file.

5. Run db_recover with the -c option.

   ```
   $ db_recover -cv -h /srv/svnrepos/db
   ```

6. If the recovery was successful, you can safely remove the corrupted repository.

   ```
   $ rm -rf /srv/svnrepos.wedged
   ```

If you are recovering from a complete set of log files instead of a backup repository, you can skip steps 2 and 3. Instead, copy any necessary log file backups into the corrupted repository directory and run the recovery directly on it. You may need to remove the corrupted repository table files: nodes, revisions, representations, changes, strings, transactions, and uuids. Of course, you should still make a backup of the corrupted repository before you attempt the recovery.

10.4   Upgrading Subversion

Eventually, you are going to want to upgrade your Subversion installation. Presumably, you would like to do this without damaging your existing repository and its precious data. Fortunately, the Subversion developers thought about this, and have made upgrading Subversion a relatively easy task.

The exact effort that needs to be put into an upgrade depends on the version you are upgrading to.

- If you are upgrading to a patch release (e.g., from 1.1.0 to 1.1.1), you don't have to take any special action, other than upgrading the Subversion executables per the software upgrade process for your particular system. Additionally, you can rest assured that you will be able to undo the upgrade if the new version fails to work correctly for you. Subversion policy states that all patch releases will be forward and backward compatible, so if you perform the upgrade and have problems with the new version, you can always go back to the previous version.

- If you are upgrading a minor release (e.g., from 1.0 to 1.1), the upgrade process is identical to patch releases. Just upgrade the executables and go. Although minor releases will always be forward compatible, they won't necessarily be backward compatible. After you have performed an upgrade, you may not be able to take your repository back to an older version.

- If you are upgrading to a new major version release (e.g., from 1.0 to 2.0), it is possible that the database format has changed, and your current database won't work after the upgrade. This means that you need to create a dump of the database before the upgrade, upgrade Subversion, then use `svnadmin load` to reload the data into a new repository, just as if you were recovering after a crash (see Section 10.2.4, "Recovering").

  It's very important, though, to perform the dump before you upgrade Subversion, as the new version may not be able to dump the old repository.

I cannot stress enough, however, the importance of backing up your repository before even thinking about a Subversion upgrade, even if you are not going across a major version release. You never know what will happen during an upgrade, and a simple mistake *could* potentially destroy your repository.

10.5   Summary

In this chapter, you learned about Subversion repository access control. The discussion included security options for local repository access, `svnserve` access, and access via Apache. Additionally, you saw how to secure an HTTP connection with SSL and how to provide user authentication using a Windows Domain Controller.

You learned about creating backups of a Subversion repository, as well as how to automate those backups on a UNIX-like system. You also learned how to recover a database from backups, and how to revive a wedged Berkeley DB-based repository. Finally, you learned about some of the things to take into consideration when upgrading Subversion.

Chapter 11

The Joy of Automation

The whole point of computers is to make our lives easier and expand the possibilities of what can be done, yet most of us spend an inordinate amount of time in front of the computer making our lives more tedious and repetitive. Tedious and repetitive then lead to boring, and boring leads to mistakes (another area where computers are *supposed* to improve us).

Why do we torture ourselves with such mundane pursuits? Because we're *not lazy enough*. That's right, people pursue repetitive boredom (and the errors that result) because they don't get fed up with the work enough to find a way to avoid it. Does that sound like you? I didn't think so. That's why I know you're salivating over the prospect of learning how to craft Subversion into a tool that works for you, rather than letting it become a master that demands you to divide your time further than it already is.

In this chapter, you will learn all about the various tricks and tools available to you in Subversion to not only automate the mundane tasks specific to your development process that go along with organized use of a version control system, but also to automate the safeguards that help ensure everyone follows the rules that your process establishes.

The value of reducing repetition is obvious to everyone. No one wants to do the same thing over and over again. Repetition is also the place where computers most excel. The value of safeguards is also an easy one to recognize, but the extent of their value is often underappreciated. Sure, we all understand the need for security that protects against malicious attack, but in a development project, that is rarely the biggest danger to protect against. Much more insidious is the danger from an attack of inattention. All of us have done it. A moment's hurriedness or lack of thought leads to a forgotten procedure, which leads to any number of dozens of negative scenarios, from broken builds and hidden bugs to incomplete or incorrect documentation.

By taking the time, up front, to customize Subversion's automation tools to fit your development process, you will almost certainly end up with happier, more productive developers who are able to follow the development process with more consistency and fewer errors. This leads to less administrative work, and (with any luck) frees you up to pursue more automation that can start the cycle anew.

Subversion provides a number of hooks that give you a point where you can integrate automation tools into the Subversion client or server. It provides several execution points, where hook scripts can be run, to process or examine the data before or after Subversion places it into the repository. Additionally, it provides metadata in the form of properties and strictly formatted output (for ease of parsing) that allows you to examine Subversion with other tools in your development chain. Finally, if that's not enough automation for you, Subversion provides an API that you can use to interact with a Subversion repository using the same entry points as the Subversion client.

11.1   An Introduction to Hooks

Subversion provides for the capability to have scripts automatically run on the server at various repository access points. These scripts are able to examine the data that flows into the repository and make decisions about whether specific actions should be allowed, as well as trigger other side effects based on the data supplied (such as send an e-mail).

Each hook script is a program that is invoked on a particular trigger, to perform the necessary processing for that hook. Normally, hook scripts are shell scripts, but that is not a restriction. Hook scripts can be written in any interpreted or compiled language (for the rest of this discussion, I will refer to all forms as scripts). The only requirement is that they be some sort of executable that the Subversion server can run. When run, each hook script can either perform all of the necessary processing internally, or it can call one or more external programs and use their output.

Hook scripts are specific to a repository, and are stored in a directory named `hooks` inside the directory that the `svnadmin create` command created to store the repository database. The trigger action for each script is defined by its name (in Windows, they should also end in `.exe` or `.bat`). The different trigger actions available are the following.

- `start-commit`

- `pre-commit`

- `post-commit`

- `pre-revprop-change`

- `post-revprop-change`

When one of these actions occurs, Subversion invokes the appropriate script, and passes to it relevant information (which varies, depending on the action) via arguments. For all of the hook scripts except `post-commit` and `post-revprop-change`, if the script returns a non-zero value, Subversion will reject the data that was being processed (both `post-` actions occur after the processing, and can't cause an interruption).

11.1.1   Available Hook Scripts

Subversion supports several hook scripts, which are triggered on different events.

start-commit

The first thing Subversion does when it receives a repository commit is to invoke the `start-commit` script (if one exists), even before it creates a transaction for the commit.

This gives the hook script a chance to examine the target repository, and the user making the commit, and make a decision on whether that user is authorized to access that repository. One possible use for this script would be to prevent denial of service attacks against the repository from huge unauthorized commits.

The arguments passed to `start-commit` are

1. The path to the repository used for this commit

2. The name of the user attempting to make the commit

pre-commit

If a commit makes it past the `start-commit` script, Subversion creates a new transaction (which allows the repository to be returned to the state it was in before the commit attempt), in case the commit fails for any reason. After Subversion has created this transaction, it invokes `pre-commit`. The `pre-commit` script is able to examine the transaction, and make a decision on whether that data meets the requirements for a commit.

The arguments passed to `pre-commit` are

1. The path to the repository used for this commit

2. The name of the transaction for the commit

post-commit

This script is called after a commit has completed successfully. Because the commit has already happened, it has no power to affect the commit itself, but can perform logging or trigger other side effects.

The arguments passed to `post-commit` are

1. The path to the repository used for this commit

2. The revision number of the commit

pre-revprop-change

When a revision property is modified, Subversion invokes this script before actually performing the change. If you want to change revision properties, this script is *required*. If it isn't present, Subversion triggers a failure on every attempted revision property change. Because revision properties are unversioned, this script can be useful for disallowing dangerous (or otherwise undesired) revision property changes. It can also be useful for making a backup of modified revision properties before actually performing a commit, which can be very useful in avoiding accidental property data loss.

The arguments passed to `pre-revprop-change` are

1. The path to the repository used for this property change

2. The revision for which the property is being changed

3. The user attempting the property change

4. The name of the property being changed

In addition to the arguments sent to the script, Subversion also passes the revision property value itself on the script's standard input stream (`stdin`), instead of as an argument.

post-revprop-change

This script is called after a revision property change has successfully completed. Because the change has already occurred, the scripts can't affect the commit itself. It can, however, be useful for logging or generating some other side effect.

The arguments passed to `post-revprop-change` are

1. The path to the repository used for this property change

2. The revision for which the property is being changed

3. The user attempting the property change

4. The name of the property being changed

11.1.2   What a Hook Script Can Do

Hook scripts have a lot of latitude in what they're allowed to do when they run. There are really only a few restrictions (which I discuss in the next section), and everything else is fair game. However, there are a few actions that you will find most of your scripts needing to do, which deserve a little extra attention.

Examining the Repository

In a very few cases, the information provided in the arguments to the hook script is sufficient for the script to perform all of its required processing. The rest of the time, though, the script needs to examine the repository to get the information it needs. To perform its examinations, there are no enforced restrictions on what tools Subversion is allowed to use, but it is usually safest to use the `svnlook` program instead of `svn`, in order to avoid the potential of modifying the repository (which is strictly forbidden, but also not enforced). The specifics of what you can get out of `svnlook` are explained in detail, in Section 11.3.1, "The Subversion Commands."

The `svnlook` program is a tool for examining the repository. It has many of the same commands as `svn`, but without the capability to modify the repository in any way. Unlike `svn`, `svnlook` doesn't operate on working copies, nor can it communicate with a remote repository. Instead, `svnlook` must be used to examine a repository located on the local system.

Examining Transactions

The `pre-commit` hook script is provided with a unique argument, the name of a transaction. With this transaction name, `svnlook` can examine a transaction that is in-process, before the changes therein become a permanent part of the repository. To refer to a transaction, you have to run `svnlook` with the `--transaction` parameter, which takes the transaction's name, just as `--revision` would take the revision number (the only practical way to get a transaction name is when it is a parameter to a `pre-commit` script).

As a simple example, the following script gets the log message for the commit that is currently being processed, and appends it to an external log file that keeps track of all the commits attempted, regardless of whether they succeed.

```sh
#!/bin/sh

# Get the pre-commit script arguments
# $1 = The repository path
# $2 = The transaction name

RPS = "$1"
TXN = "$2"

# Append the log message to a log record.
/usr/bin/svnlook log --transaction "$TXN" "$RPS" > /var/log/txn.log

# Exit with zero, to allow the transaction processing to continue.
exit 0
```

Running External Programs

In addition to running Subversion commands from within hook scripts, you are free to run any other external programs that you need to in order to perform the desired processing in the script. This allows you to not only take advantage of already existing programs that perform the actions you need, but it also allows you to write your own external programs and scripts that can be shared among multiple hook scripts (either in the same repository or across multiple repositories). In fact, it is generally good practice to write all of your real hook script processing in one or more external scripts, and then call those from the actual hook script, in the correct order.

11.1.3   What a Hook Script Can't Do

Hook scripts are very flexible in their allowed actions, but there are a few restrictions that you need to be aware of. It is especially important for you to read this section carefully, because most of these restrictions are not enforced by Subversion. The results of trying to perform these forbidden actions can range from silent failure to potential repository corruption.

Don't Modify the Repository

You might be tempted to write a hook script that modifies a transaction. It would be handy to automatically modify code to fit a certain coding style, or encrypt certain files for added security. However, hook scripts should never modify the transaction they are operating on. Subversion has no mechanism for reporting back to the working copy if a transaction is modified, so the working copy and repository would become out of sync if you did modify the transaction.

Because none of the Subversion command-line tools have facilities that would allow you to modify the transaction, this is not a hard rule to follow. However, it is possible for a custom program using the Subversion libraries to modify a transaction, so consider yourself warned about not doing it.

Communication with Client Is Limited

Subversion will buffer anything that a hook script sends to standard error, and if the script fails, that output will be sent to the client and displayed along with the commit failure message. However, that is the extent of the direct capability a hook script has to communicate with the client. There is no way to give feedback to the user if the commit succeeds, nor is there a way to get any additional information from the user while the hook script is running.

If you need to get extra information to a user after a successful commit, you could get around the communication limitation by writing the output of the script to a log file that the user could access (possibly via a Web server), or by sending an e-mail. Getting extra information *from* the user is a more difficult limitation to work around, but you may be able to do it if you're creative. For instance, you could have the user place information in the log message that would be parsed by the hook script. Or, if you need to get information in the middle of hook script execution, you could find some alternate means of communication that works outside of the Subversion framework, such as an automated message sent to an instant messaging account that waits for a response to be sent back.

11.1.4   Tips for a Good Hook Script

There are a few things that you want to keep in mind when you are writing hook scripts. If you are an experienced script writer (or programmer of another sort), many of these things will be second nature to you, but if not, this is a good place to learn; and even if you are an experienced programmer, it is probably worthwhile to think about some of the points in this section in the context of writing good Subversion hook scripts.

You can also find some template scripts, which are automatically generated in the `hooks` subdirectory for your repository, when the repository is generated. These examples will give you a good idea what each hook script can do, and some ideas for what you might use that particular script for. You should note, though, that the scripts referred to in the templates are fictitious scripts that are merely there for illustration (although at least one — `commit-email.pl` — does exist in the utility scripts that Subversion supplies). Later on in the chapter, I will discuss how you might write some of the scripts alluded to in the templates.

Keep It Short

Hook scripts run whenever the action they are associated with is triggered. With the exception of the two revision property scripts, that means *every time a commit is performed.* Furthermore, every user has to wait for the execution of each relevant hook script (that's three on a successful commit) to execute, in its entirety, before being able to move on to other things. In an active development environment where commits are done frequently, that is a lot of time spent waiting for Subversion to finish running hook scripts.

Some time is expected, of course, but significant delays will quickly annoy your users, which will lead to fewer commits, which will make your repository less useful to you. Therefore, it is vital that all of your hook scripts run in as small an amount of time as possible. As a rule of thumb to figure out how short you should keep your hook script run times, I would suggest that you consider how often you think your average user will be committing changes to the repository. If you expect frequent commits (many per hour), you should keep the hook script runtimes under a few seconds each for the average case. If you expect less frequent commits (just a few per day, or less), it may be acceptable to have longer runtimes for your hook scripts; but remember that user feedback is minimal, so you want to make sure that things are kept short enough that users don't worry that the commit has locked up.

If you have a hook script with a long-running side effect, you might consider running it in the background, so that your hook script can finish and allow the commit to complete (thus returning control to the user) before the hook script itself has completed. Obviously, this is not practical for hook scripts that depend on the output of a program to decide whether the commit should succeed, but if the side effect is entirely independent (such as sending an e-mail or modifying a developer's Web site), it might be a good way to make commits to the repository feel faster without sacrificing functionality.

Do You Really Want It Every Time?

Subversion hook scripts will run every single time a commit is made, which for most people is a lot. Before you set up a hook script, put some thought into whether you really need it to run every time a commit is made. There are a lot of things that seem useful when you first think of them, but end up being nothing but annoying when they are put into practice. If a hook script has a side effect, like sending an e-mail or instant message that the user doesn't usually care about, it will quickly get ignored—it's just human nature to make repetitive actions a habit that doesn't require any conscious thought. Then, when the side effect is something important, it is likely to not be noticed.

For every hook, you need to carefully consider whether the script that you want to have run is really going to produce something that is of value to the receiver more often than not. If the answer is "no," you might want to consider adding a few checks to your hook script that will help determine when the information is actually useful, and refrain from sending it out at other times. Alternately, you can set up the hook script to perform the operation every n revisions (e.g., `if revnum % 10 == 0`). Not only will your users be happier, but they will also be more likely to notice and react to important side effects from the script.

Early On: Log What You Do

When you have developed a new hook script, it is a given that you will want to test it before making a deployment to the real repository. Pre-release testing can only go so far, though, and it is often the case that things that worked great in the lab will break under the pressure of real-world usage. In the case of Subversion hook scripts, this is especially ominous, due to the importance of a live repository, and the difficulty of noticing problems when there is no feedback to the user. Furthermore, if a commit is accepted that shouldn't have been, you can easily end up with broken data in your repository (not the kind that breaks the repository, but the kind that doesn't run as it's supposed to).

To avoid problems in the future, a new hook script that is introduced to a live repository should *always* (unless it's trivially simple) be run for a reasonable period with copious amounts of debugging output being sent to a log somewhere. This will save you many headaches and long hours in the future, not only by helping you pinpoint where any problems are occurring, but also by making it easier for you to correct any errors that occur, before they cause a chain reaction.

Remember the Edge Cases

Accounting for edge cases is an important tenet of software develpment, but one that is easy to forget in the context of writing small systems, such as hook scripts. When a hook script is run, you want to make sure that it can handle any sort of data that Subversion will allow the user to throw at it. For instance, if your `pre-commit` script expects a certain format of log message, make sure that it will properly handle not just wildly incorrect log messages, but also the log messages that are similar to the required format, but not quite correct (such as a keyword in the middle of data).

Reuse What You Can

Subversion comes from the culture of the UNIX world. In the UNIX world, there are many small, single-task programs that can be easily strung together to perform larger tasks. This makes development of complex scripts much easier, and allows programs to make use of well-tested components that can be shared among multiple applications. In other operating systems (Windows mostly), this sort of single-task application is not nearly so prevalent. This means that hook scripts don't have available to them the same rich set of default tools to use for processing the data they receive.

A first instinct may be to write all of the missing functionality into your hook script, but this can lead to bloated, slow scripts that are hard to debug. You are much better off if you take the UNIX approach and create individual component scripts that perform the individual tasks that you need performed. This makes it easier to share those tasks among multiple scripts and repositories, as well as making debugging of component functionality much easier.

Another option for Windows users, if you are looking for a rich set of UNIX-like tools for your hook scripts to take advantage of, is to install a Windows package (such as Cygwin, which provides a wealth of UNIX tools) that gives you a prebuilt set of com-

ponent programs that can be integrated into your scripts. This not only saves you the time
spent writing the functions themselves, but also the time spent debugging and testing the
components.

11.1.5 The Pre-made Subversion Scripts

To aid you in your quest to generate the perfect Subversion hook script, the developers of
Subversion provide you with a set of pre-made scripts that provide useful utilities commonly found in hook scripts. If you made an installation of Subversion from a binary
package, you will likely find them in a directory such as

/usr/share/svn/tools/hook-scripts

If they are not installed on your system, you can get them by downloading the Subversion
source and looking in the tools/hook-scripts subdirectory. The scripts that you find
should include (at the least) the following scripts.

- commit-access-control.pl

- svnperms.py

- commit-email.pl

- propchange-email.pl

- mailer.py

11.2 Making the Most of Hook Scripts

When working with your own Subversion repositories, you will invariably come up with
innumerable ideas for possible places where automation will make your life easier. In
fact, if you're anything like me, you'll find that the potential ways you can think of for
automating your troubles away are far greater in number than your time available. To help
you out a bit, in this section, I'll talk about some of the ways that you might add hook scripts
to Subversion to help with automation, along with some ideas on implementing them.

11.2.1 Automatically Send E-mails

If you have a mailing list set up that is dedicated to Subversion commit reports, you can
set up a commit script to e-mail that list every time someone makes a commit, either with
just the log or with a full diff of all the changes applied to the repository. Users who are
interested in keeping track of Subversion development can then subscribe to the e-mail to
see when changes are made, rather than needing to periodically check the Subversion logs
to see what has changed.

You can also check the section of the repository where the commit was made, and send
e-mails to different mailing lists in response. There are a couple of reasons why you might
want to do this.

- If you have multiple projects in your repository, you may want commit e-mails for each project to go to that project's own mailing list. This helps allow you to keep projects logically separated, even though they reside in the same physical repository (which gives you the advantage of allowing code to move between the two).

- You may find it useful to only send out notifications for changes made to the trunk of your project. This allows individual developers to perform a lot of small commits on a branch created for a given task without spamming the mailing list with huge numbers of e-mails. Then, when a change is merged into the trunk, all of those changes will be sent out in one compiled e-mail that shows the changes made during the merge.

Redundant Archival E-mails

A mailing list that receives commit messages can also be used as an emergency archive for restoring a lost repository. It is, of course, no substitute for nightly backups of the repository itself, but it could save you the loss of a single day's changes if a crash were to occur. If you have an archival mailing list where all repository commits (with full diffs, log messages, and other metadata) are sent, and your repository is lost in the middle of the day, you could go back to those archival e-mails and restore all of the changes that had been applied to the repository since the last repository backup.

To make a potential restoration even easier, you could set up your `post-commit` script to automatically run `svnadmin dump` to create an incremental backup file that could then be e-mailed to an archival e-mail drop. The following script shows how you might write such a script. The script itself is written in Python, but even if you don't know Python, it should be clear what is happening.

```
#!/usr/bin/python
# Subversion commit archival program.
# Takes a repository, a revision number, and an email address

import commands
import smtplib
from email.MIMEText import MIMEText

# Some variables that may need to be set for a specific repository
svnbinpath = '/usr/bin/'
svnadmin = svnbinpath + 'svnadmin'

fromaddr = 'svnrepos@mydomain.com'

# Runs 'svnadmin dump' and get its output
def dumpRevision(repos, revision):
```

```
  dump = getstatusoutput('%s dump --incremental -r %s %s'
                         % svnadmin, revision, repos)
  if dump[0] != 0:
    # svnadmin failed
    return None
  else:
    # return the dump
    return dump[1]

# Creates an email with the supplied revision dump
def createDumpMessage(address, revision, dump):
  msg = MIMEText(dump)
  msg['Subject'] = 'Dump of revision %s' % revision
  msg['From'] = fromaddr
  msg['To'] = address

# Sends the supplied email message
# Uses the local systems SMTP system
def sendDumpMessage(address, msg):
  s = smtplib.SMTP()
  s.connect()
  s.sendmail(fromaddr, [address], msg.as_string())
  s.close()


# Main execution point for the program
# This will use the other three functions to email a repository dump
if __name__ == '__main__':
  # Check to see that we have enough arguments
  if sys.argv.length() < 4: exit(1)

  # Parse the arguments
  repository = sys.argv[1]
  revision = sys.argv[2]
  address = sys.argv[3]

  # Get the repository dump and email it
  dump = dumpRevision(repository, revision)
  if dump == None: exit(2)

  msg = createDumpMessage(address, revision, dump)
  sendDumpMessage(address, msg)
```

Communicating with an Issue Tracker

Some issue-tracking systems can be controlled by sending them e-mails. For example, you may be able to create a new open issue, update an existing issue, or close an issue just be sending a properly formatted e-mail to the tracker. If you have your users format their log files properly, you can parse them automatically in a `post-commit` hook script and generate the messages to send to the issue tracker automatically.

Having the hook script automatically notify the issue tracker will remove one extra step from your user's commit process, which should reduce the chance for error. Of course, the downside is that the log message needs to be properly formatted for the issue tracker to be able to parse it properly. Ideally, the best way to help ensure proper formatting is to keep the formatting simple and distinct in a way that can be parsed even when mixed with unformatted text. For example, you might use a unique tag that would identify issue numbers or status changes. The parser could then search unformatted text for those tags and react appropriately. Additionally (or alternately), you could use a `pre-commit` hook script to check log messages for incorrect formatting and return an error if it doesn't parse correctly.

Subversion Supplied Scripts

Because automatically sending e-mails is such a commonly desired action, Subversion even provides three different example scripts that you can use for sending e-mails. They are robust enough to use "as is" for many purposes, and reasonably easy to modify if they don't quite fit your needs. Two of the scripts (`commit-email.pl` and `propchange-email.pl`) are written in Perl, and the third (`mailer.py`) is written in Python, so you have a choice of language to attack if you need to make modifications. All three can easily be run in your `post-commit` hook script to send e-mails.

commit-email.pl

The `commit-email.pl` script can be run by providing it with the repository, revision number, and an e-mail address, and it will send an e-mail with the author of the commit, the date, the log, and a list of the changes made. You can also set up multiple invocations of `commit-email.pl` to each match a specific subdirectory in the repository and only send an e-mail if a file in that subdirectory changed during the commit. In this way, you can configure different mailing addresses for different projects in the same repository.

The following example `post-commit` script shows how you might set up a hook script to run `commit-email.pl` with two different mailing addresses for the trunks of two projects in the repository (stored in `/project1/trunk` and `/project2/trunk`).

```
#!/bin/sh

# Get the post-commit script arguments
# $1 = The repository path
# $2 = The revision number
```

```
RPS = "$1"
REV = "$2"

# Send commit emails
COMMIT_EMAIL = /usr/local/share/tools/hook-scripts/commit-email.pl
$COMMIT_EMAIL "${RPS}" ${REV} -m "project1/trunk" "project1- ¬
  list@mydomain.com"
$COMMIT_EMAIL "${RPS}" ${REV} -m "project2/trunk" "project2- ¬
  list@mydomain.com"
```

propchange-email.pl

If you want to send out notification e-mails when revision properties change, you can use the propchange-email.pl script instead. It works almost identically to commit-email.pl, except it takes a property name and user in addition to the repository and revision number.

In this example post-revprop-change hook script, you can see how you might use propchange-email.pl to send a notice to an administrator every time someone made a change to a log file.

```
#!/bin/sh

# Get the post-revprop-change script arguments
# $1 = The repository path
# $2 = The revision number
# $3 = The user making the change
# $4 = The property being changed

RPS = "$1"
REV = "$2"
USER = "$3"
PROP = "$4"

# Send a property change email
PRPCHG_EMAIL= "/usr/local/share/tools/hook-scripts/propchange-email.pl"
ADDRESS = "repos-admin@mydomain.com"
if
   test ["$PROP"="svn:log"]
then
   $PRPCHG_EMAIL "$RPS" "$REV" "$USER" "$PROP" "$ADDRESS"
fi
```

mailer.py

Subversion also provides an example Python script that performs the same function as `commit-email.pl`. Additionally, `mailer.py` lets you set up complex sets of groups that determine which addresses to e-mail based on regular expressions that match the files that were changed. To find out more about the specifics of how this script works, see the script itself, and the sample configuration file that is included with it.

11.2.2   Send Notifications via RSS

RSS (Really Simple Syndication) has become a very popular means of getting notifications on changes to news sites, blogs, and other Web sites with rapidly changing content. It's not just limited to Web sites, though. In fact, it can easily handle any sort of frequently modified serial data, such as the record of commits made to a Subversion repository.[1]

RSS feeds are supplied to RSS readers as XML files, available through a Web browser. To get the latest RSS feed for a site, the reader simply redownloads the RSS feed XML file from a predetermined URL. So, if you set up a post-commit hook script to update the RSS feed every time a commit is made to the repository, you can have an up-to-date RSS feed of repository activity. This is especially handy in a rapid development environment, where short build/test cycles make it important for everyone to keep up with the activities of their coworkers.

Generating the RSS

To generate the RSS feed, you need a script, similar to the following one, that takes the repository and extracts the information about the last repository commit. The script itself is fairly long, but I'll go over what's happening shortly.

```bash
#!/bin/bash

# Main configuration variables
ReposName=$1
RepositoriesDir=/svnrepos/repositories
MaxItems=100

# Setup misc. variables
Repos=$RepositoriesDir/$ReposName
RssFile=/var/www/html/rss/$ReposName.xml
RssFileTmp=/var/www/html/rss/$ReposName.xml.tmp
RssHeader=$Repos/rss/header
RssFooter=$Repos/rss/footer
RssItemsDir=$Repos/rss/items
```

---

1.   The scripts and techniques in this section were graciously provided by Stuart Robinson and his employer, Absolute Systems (www.absolutesys.com).

```
#=======================================================
# Attempts to create a lock file so that this script isn't
# affected by other instances that might be started at the same time.
# If a lock-file already exists, this script is exited immediately.
AcquireLockFile ()
{
  LockFile=/svnrepos/locks/$ReposName.rssGen.lock
  if [ -a $LockFile ]; then
    # Another process is currently updating the RSS feed, so exit.
    echo "Lock-file $LockFile exists.  Exiting."
    echo ""
    exit 1
  fi
  # Create the lock file
  touch $LockFile
  echo "Lock-file $LockFile acquired."
}


#=======================================================
ReleaseLockFile ()
{
  rm -f $LockFile
  echo "Lock-file $LockFile released."
}


#=======================================================
ComputeFirstAndLastItemRevisions ()
{
  echo "Computing first and last item revisions:"
  SvnHeadRevision=`svnlook youngest $Repos`
  LastItemToInclude=$SvnHeadRevision
  FirstItemToInclude=$((LastItemToInclude-MaxItems+1))
  if [[ $FirstItemToInclude -lt 0 ]]; then
    FirstItemToInclude=1
  fi

  echo "  First revision to include: $FirstItemToInclude"
  echo "  Last revision to include : $LastItemToInclude"
  echo "  Max items                : $MaxItems"
}


#=======================================================
DeleteOldItemFiles ()
```

```
{
  echo "Deleting old item files"
  FirstMissingItem=$((LastItemToInclude+1))
  # Move all items we want to keep to tmp, and then delete all others.
  if [[ ! -a $RssItemsDir/tmp ]]; then
    mkdir $RssItemsDir/tmp
  fi
  for ((Rev=LastItemToInclude; Rev >= FirstItemToInclude; Rev--))
  do
    if [[ -a $RssItemsDir/Item.$Rev ]]; then
      #echo "  Moving $RssItemsDir/Item.$Rev to $RssItemsDir/tmp"
      mv $RssItemsDir/Item.$Rev $RssItemsDir/tmp
    else
      # We need items from FirstItemToInclude -> LastItemToInclude, but
      # the current item is missing, so record the revision number so
      # we can later access SVN to create the missing items.
      FirstMissingItem=$Rev
      #echo "  DEBUG: FirstMissingItem=$FirstMissingItem"
    fi
  done
  #echo "  Removing all other Item files in $RssItemsDir"
  rm -f $RssItemsDir/Item.*

  # Now move the items we want to keep back to $RssItemsDir
  #echo "  Moving the files we're keeping from $RssItemsDir/tmp back to ¬
  $RssItemsDir"
  mv -f $RssItemsDir/tmp/Item.* $RssItemsDir
  rmdir $RssItemsDir/tmp
}


#==================================================
# Creates new Items to represent each of the SVN revisions for
# which there are currently no item-files in $RssItemsDir (for revision
# numbers >= FirstItemToInclude, and <= LastItemToInclude).
CreateNewItemFilesFromSVN ()
{
  # Now access SVN to create RSS items for all revisions from $MaxRev ¬
  +1 -> $LatestRevision
  echo "Accessing SVN to create missing items"
  echo "  First missing item: Rev $FirstMissingItem"
  echo "  Last missing item: Rev $LastItemToInclude"
  for ((Rev=FirstMissingItem; Rev <= LastItemToInclude; Rev++))
  do
```

```
    echo "  Creating <Item> for SVN revision $Rev"
    RssItemFile=$RssItemsDir/Item.$Rev
    echo "    ItemFile=$RssItemFile"
    echo "    Computing vars..."

    AuthorId=`svnlook -r $Rev author $Repos 2>&1`
    Author=`getent passwd | grep $AuthorId | cut -d: -f 5`
    CommitMsg=`svnlook log -r $Rev $Repos 2>&1`
    CommitDate=`svnlook -r $Rev date $Repos 2>&1`
    CommitDateRss=`echo $CommitDate | sed -e "s/\([^ ]*\) \([^ ]*\) ¬
\([^ ]*\).*/\\1T\\2+02:00/"`
    # Sample valid date=<dc:date>2004-06-07T17:03:30+02:00</dc:date>
    URL="http://svnserver/viewcvs?rev=$Rev&root=$ReposName&view=rev"
    FirstModifiedPath=`svnlook -r $Rev changed $Repos | cut -b5 ¬
-1000 | sed -e "s{\([^/]*/[^/]*\).*{\1{" | uniq`
    Category=`echo $FirstModifiedPath | sed -e "s&\(.*\)/\(.*\) ¬
&\\2 (\\1)&"`
    echo "    Done computing vars"

    echo "  <item>" > $RssItemFile
    echo "    <title><![CDATA[$CommitMsg]]></title>" >> $RssItemFile
    echo "    <link><![CDATA[$URL]]></link>" >> $RssItemFile
    echo "    <description><![CDATA[$CommitMsg]]></description>" >> ¬
$RssItemFile
    echo "    <category>$Category</category>" >> $RssItemFile
    echo "    <dc:creator>$Author</dc:creator>" >> $RssItemFile
    echo "    <dc:date>$CommitDateRss</dc:date>" >> $RssItemFile
    echo "    <pubDate>$CommitDateRss</pubDate>" >> $RssItemFile
    echo "  </item>" >> $RssItemFile
    echo "CommitDateRss=$CommitDateRss"
  done
}


#=====================================================
# Echos the contents of RssHeader, followed by each of the Rss Item ¬
  files
# in revision-number-order, followed by RssFooter to the Rss file being ¬
  generated.
AssembleThePieces ()
{
  echo "Assembling the pieces"
  cat $RssHeader > $RssFileTmp

  local PubDate=`date +"%a, %d %b %Y %T %Z"`
```

```
echo "    <dc:date>$PubDate</dc:date>" >> $RssFileTmp
echo "    <pubDate>$PubDate</pubDate>" >> $RssFileTmp
echo "    <lastBuildDate>$PubDate</lastBuildDate>" >> $RssFileTmp

# Add all RSS items to the RSS file
for ((Rev=LastItemToInclude; Rev >= FirstItemToInclude; Rev--))
do
  cat $RssItemsDir/Item.$Rev >> $RssFileTmp
done

# Add the RSS footer
cat $RssFooter >> $RssFileTmp
mv -f $RssFileTmp $RssFile
}


#=================================================
# Generates a new RSS file for the repository.
GenerateRssFile ()
{
  AcquireLockFile
  ComputeFirstAndLastItemRevisions
  DeleteOldItemFiles
  CreateNewItemFilesFromSVN
  AssembleThePieces
  ReleaseLockFile
  echo "Done."
}

GenerateRssFile
```

Setting Up Variables

Let's take a look at this script, section by section. The first section sets up a number of useful variables that will be used throughout the rest of the script.

```
# Main configuration variables
ReposName=$1
RepositoriesDir=/svnrepos/repositories
MaxItems=100


# Setup misc. variables
Repos=$RepositoriesDir/$ReposName
RssFile=/var/www/html/rss/$ReposName.xml
RssFileTmp=/var/www/html/rss/$ReposName.xml.tmp
```

```
RssHeader=$Repos/rss/header
RssFooter=$Repos/rss/footer
RssItemsDir=$Repos/rss/items
```

The first three variables are the important configuration variables that need to be customized for the specific location of the script. The `ReposName` variable indicates the name of the repository associated with the feed. In this case, that variable is taken from the first argument sent to the script, which is supplied by the `post-commit` hook script that calls the `genRSS` script. The `RepositoriesDir` variable points to the directory where all of the Subversion repositories are stored. So, if you have two repositories, `/var/svnrepos1` and `/var/svnrepos2`, you would set `RepositoriesDir` equal to `/var`. Finally, the `MaxItems` variable stores the maximum number of items that is included in the RSS feed.

Locking the Script

Because commits can occur very close together, it would be possible for this script to end up running concurrently with another instance of itself. To avoid that, and serialize the running of the script, we need to create a lock that will be acquired when the script is run, and released when it is finished. If another script attempts to acquire the lock at the same time, the script will exit.

```
#==================================================
# Attempts to create a lock file so that this script isn't
# affected by other instances that might be started at the same time.
# If a lock-file already exists, this script is exited immediately.
AcquireLockFile ()
{
  LockFile=/svnrepos/locks/$ReposName.rssGen.lock
  if [ -a $LockFile ]; then
    # Another process is currently updating the RSS feed, so exit.
    echo "Lock-file $LockFile exists.  Exiting."
    echo ""
    exit 1
  fi
  # Create the lock file
  touch $LockFile
  echo "Lock-file $LockFile acquired."
}


#==================================================
ReleaseLockFile ()
{
  rm -f $LockFile
  echo "Lock-file $LockFile released."
}
```

This section of the script consists of two fairly simple functions. The first function, `AcquireLockFile()` simply checks to see if the lock file exists. If it does, the script exits. If there is no lock file, the script creates one by running `touch`. When the script exits, the `ReleaseLockFile()` function is called. This function simply removes the lock file that `AcquireLockFile()` created, thus freeing up the next instance of the script to run.

Computing Revision Range

Next, we need to compute the range of revisions that will be included in the RSS feed, which will be made up of a number of revisions equal to the value of `MaxItems` (as set at the beginning of the script), from the HEAD revision back. So, if `MaxItems` is equal to 100, and the repository is currently at revision 1400, the range is from revision 1301 through revision 1400.

```
#=======================================================
ComputeFirstAndLastItemRevisions ()
{
  echo "Computing first and last item revisions:"
  SvnHeadRevision=`svnlook youngest $Repos`
  LastItemToInclude=$SvnHeadRevision
  FirstItemToInclude=$((LastItemToInclude-MaxItems+1))
  if [[ $FirstItemToInclude -lt 0 ]]; then
    FirstItemToInclude=1
  fi

  echo " First revision to include: $FirstItemToInclude"
  echo " Last revision to include : $LastItemToInclude"
  echo " Max items                : $MaxItems"
}
```

The HEAD revision of the repository is found by running `svnlook youngest`, which returns the revision number of the youngest revision in the repository. Then, the beginning of the range is calculated by subtracting the `MaxItems` value from the HEAD revision. If the first revision happens to fall below zero (i.e., there aren't `MaxItems` revisions in the repository), the start of the range is set to the beginning of the repository.

Deleting Old Files

The `genRSS` script creates an item file for each revision contained in the current RSS feed. As new revisions are committed, old revisions fall off the back of the list, and their item files need to be deleted. The `DeleteOldItemFiles()` function shown next handles the cleanup of those files as they become obsolete.

```
#=======================================================
DeleteOldItemFiles ()
```

```
{
  echo "Deleting old item files"
  FirstMissingItem=$((LastItemToInclude+1))
  # Move all items we want to keep to tmp, and then delete all others.
  if [[ ! -a $RssItemsDir/tmp ]]; then
    mkdir $RssItemsDir/tmp
  fi
  for ((Rev=LastItemToInclude; Rev >= FirstItemToInclude; Rev--))
  do
    if [[ -a $RssItemsDir/Item.$Rev ]]; then
      #echo "  Moving $RssItemsDir/Item.$Rev to $RssItemsDir/tmp"
      mv $RssItemsDir/Item.$Rev $RssItemsDir/tmp
    else
      # We need items from FirstItemToInclude -> LastItemToInclude, but ¬
  the current
      # item is missing, so record the revision number so we can later  ¬
  access SVN
      # to create the missing items.
      FirstMissingItem=$Rev
      #echo "  DEBUG: FirstMissingItem=$FirstMissingItem"
    fi
  done
  #echo "  Removing all other Item files in $RssItemsDir"
  rm -f $RssItemsDir/Item.*

  # Now move the items we want to keep back to $RssItemsDir
  #echo "  Moving the files we're keeping from $RssItemsDir/tmp back to ¬
  $RssItemsDir"
  mv -f $RssItemsDir/tmp/Item.* $RssItemsDir
  rmdir $RssItemsDir/tmp
}
```

Because genRSS doesn't have any idea how many revisions have been added since the last time the script was run, figuring out which item files to remove would be a difficult task. So, instead, genRSS figures out which item files it wants to keep (the ones that correspond to revisions in the current range) and moves those into a temporary directory. Then, it removes all of the item files that remain in the RssItemsDir directory. After the obsolete files have been removed, it can then move the still-valid files back and remove the temporary directory.

Inside this function, genRSS also generates the variable FirstMissingItem. This indicates the first revision to be included in the RSS feed for which there is no existing item file. That way, genRSS only has to generate item files for new revisions, instead of wasting time generating files it already has.

Creating the Feed

Now, we come to the heart of genRSS, the functions that actually generate the RSS feed data. There are two functions here. The first, `CreateNewItemFilesFromSVN()`, creates the item files that will contain information about each revision in the feed. Then, the `AssembleThePieces()` function takes those items and creates an RSS feed XML file that it then puts up on the Web server for all (or some, depending on your access controls) to see.

```
#======================================================
# Creates new Items to represent each of the SVN revisions for
# which there are currently no item-files in $RssItemsDir (for revision
# numbers >= FirstItemToInclude, and <= LastItemToInclude).
CreateNewItemFilesFromSVN ()
{
  # Now access SVN to create RSS items for all revisions from $MaxRev ¬
  +1 -> $LatestRevision
  echo "Accessing SVN to create missing items"
  echo "  First missing item: Rev $FirstMissingItem"
  echo "  Last missing item: Rev $LastItemToInclude"
  for ((Rev=FirstMissingItem; Rev <= LastItemToInclude; Rev++))
  do
    echo "  Creating <Item> for SVN revision $Rev"
    RssItemFile=$RssItemsDir/Item.$Rev
    echo "    ItemFile=$RssItemFile"
    echo "    Computing vars..."

    AuthorId=`svnlook -r $Rev author $Repos 2>&1`
    Author=`getent passwd | grep $AuthorId | cut -d: -f 5`
    CommitMsg=`svnlook log -r $Rev $Repos 2>&1`
    CommitDate=`svnlook -r $Rev date $Repos 2>&1`
    CommitDateRss=`echo $CommitDate | sed -e "s/\([^ ]*\) \([^ ]*\) ¬
    \([^ ]*\).*/\\1T\\2+02:00/"`
    # Sample valid date=<dc:date>2004-06-07T17:03:30+02:00</dc:date>
    URL="http://svnserver/viewcvs?rev=$Rev&root=$ReposName&view=rev"
    FirstModifiedPath=`svnlook -r $Rev changed $Repos | cut -b5 ¬
    -1000 | sed -e "s{\([^/]*/[^/]*\).*{\1{" | uniq`
    Category=`echo $FirstModifiedPath | sed -e "s&\(.*\)/\(.*\) ¬
    &\\2 (\\1)&"`
    echo "    Done computing vars"

    echo "  <item>" > $RssItemFile
    echo "    <title><![CDATA[$CommitMsg]]></title>" >> $RssItemFile
    echo "    <link><![CDATA[$URL]]></link>" >> $RssItemFile
```

```
    echo "      <description><![CDATA[$CommitMsg]]></description>" >> ¬
$RssItemFile
    echo "      <category>$Category</category>" >> $RssItemFile
    echo "      <dc:creator>$Author</dc:creator>" >> $RssItemFile
    echo "      <dc:date>$CommitDateRss</dc:date>" >> $RssItemFile
    echo "      <pubDate>$CommitDateRss</pubDate>" >> $RssItemFile
    echo "   </item>" >> $RssItemFile
    echo "CommitDateRss=$CommitDateRss"
  done
}
```

The `CreateNewItemFilesFromSVN()` function loops through all of the new revisions that are to be included in the RSS feed, and uses `svnlook` to get useful information about each revision, which is then parsed (into an RSS-friendly format) and fed into an RSS item file for later inclusion in the RSS feed.

The first bit of information parsed is the author of the revision.

```
AuthorId=` svnlook -r $Rev author $Repos 2>&1 `
Author=` getent passwd | grep $AuthorId | cut -d: -f 5 `
```

The `svnlook author` command is used to get the revision, which is then stored in `AuthorId`. The username that's returned isn't really what we want, though. It would be much better to have the actual full name of the user who committed the revision. So, we instead call `getent passwd`, which returns the contents of the `/etc/passwd` file, and then search it for the username of the author. After that is found, `cut` is used to extract the user's real name, which should be stored in the fifth colon-separated field of the password entry.

Next, `genRSS` uses `svnlook log` to retrieve the log message for the revision, and `svnlook date` to retrieve the time and date of the commit. RSS feeds, however, need a fairly specific format for date information, which happens to be a little bit different from the date format that `svnlook date` returns. Therefore, it is necessary to process the returned date, and massage it into a format suitable for RSS, which is achieved in the code snippet that follows by using `sed` to retrieve the date and time from `svnlook date`'s output and replace the whole string with a modified version that matches the required RSS format. Note the `+02:00` on the replace side of the `sed` expression. That is the time-zone indicator, and shows that the time is two hours ahead of Coordinated Universal Time (formerly known as Greenwich Mean Time, abbreviated UTC). This needs to be modified for your local site, in order to give the correct local time zone.

```
CommitDate=` svnlook -r $Rev date $Repos 2>&1 `
CommitDateRss=` echo $CommitDate | sed -e "s/\([^ ]*\) \([^ ]*\) ¬
    \([^ ]*\).*/\\1T\\2+02:00/" `
```

If `svnlook date` were to output `2004-10-02 17:40:08 +0200 (Sat, 02 Oct 2004)`, the RSS format would look like `2004-10-02T17:40:08+02:00`.

After getting the log and date, the script generates a URL where users will be taken if they click on the link provided for the RSS feed entry in their RSS reader. In this case, the URL generated takes the user to a page in a ViewCVS site that shows the changes for the particular revision. This, of course, assumes that there is in fact a ViewCVS site set up and running. For more information about ViewCVS, take a look at Chapter 8, "Integrating with Other Tools."

```
URL="http://svnserver/viewcvs?rev=$Rev&root=$ReposName&view=rev"
```

Next, genRSS generates a category entry for the RSS item, based on the modified paths. As with the date modification, genRSS uses sed to massage the output garnered from svnlook changed to get a category name that identifies the section of the repository that was modified. This parsing is necessarily very repository specific, and you probably need to generate your own sed commands to parse the output in order to get a meaningful category. If parsing the changed files doesn't make sense as a means to get a category, you may instead want to have the user put a category line in her log message that can be extracted.

```
FirstModifiedPath=` svnlook -r $Rev changed $Repos | cut -b5-1000 | sed ¬
   -e "s{\([^/]*/[^/]*\).*{\1{" | uniq `
Category=` echo $FirstModifiedPath | sed -e "s&\(.*\)/\(.*\)&\\2 (\\1) ¬
   &" `
```

Finally, all of the data that has been gathered is output into an item file, in the appropriate XML format for the RSS feed.

```
echo "  <item>" > $RssItemFile
echo "    <title><![CDATA[$CommitMsg]]></title>" >> $RssItemFile
echo "    <link><![CDATA[$URL]]></link>" >> $RssItemFile
echo "    <description><![CDATA[$CommitMsg]]></description>" >> ¬
  $RssItemFile
echo "    <category>$Category</category>" >> $RssItemFile
echo "    <dc:creator>$Author</dc:creator>" >> $RssItemFile
echo "    <dc:date>$CommitDateRss</dc:date>" >> $RssItemFile
echo "    <pubDate>$CommitDateRss</pubDate>" >> $RssItemFile
echo "  </item>" >> $RssItemFile
```

After the item files have all been generated, it's time to assemble them all into a full RSS feed XML file. This is accomplished by the AssembleThePieces() function, which is shown here.

```
#====================================================
# Echos the contents of RssHeader, followed by each of the Rss Item
# files in revision-number-order, followed by RssFooter to the Rss file
# being generated.
```

```
AssembleThePieces ()
{
  echo "Assembling the pieces"
  cat $RssHeader > $RssFileTmp

  local PubDate=` date +"%a, %d %b %Y %T %Z" `
  echo "    <dc:date>$PubDate</dc:date>" >> $RssFileTmp
  echo "    <pubDate>$PubDate</pubDate>" >> $RssFileTmp
  echo "    <lastBuildDate>$PubDate</lastBuildDate>" >> $RssFileTmp

  # Add all RSS items to the RSS file
  for ((Rev=LastItemToInclude; Rev >= FirstItemToInclude; Rev--))
  do
    cat $RssItemsDir/Item.$Rev >> $RssFileTmp
  done

  # Add the RSS footer
  cat $RssFooter >> $RssFileTmp
  mv -f $RssFileTmp $RssFile
}
```

As you can see in the preceding code, the RSS feed file is generated by successively inserting the RSS header, publication date, each item file, and RSS footer into a temporary RSS file. After the full file is created, that is then moved over to replace the old live RSS file.

The RSS header and footer are stock pieces of XML, which are stored in their own files. The header file contains various pieces of information about the Subversion repository, and needs to be customized for your particular repository.

As an example, here is what the header might look like. Notice that you need to customize most of the tags under the <channel> tag to match your repository.

```
<?xml version="1.0" encoding="iso-8859-1"?>
<rss version="2.0"
    xmlns:dc="http://purl.org/dc/elements/1.1/"
    xmlns:sy="http://purl.org/rss/1.0/modules/syndication/"
    xmlns:admin="http://webns.net/mvcb/"
    xmlns:slash="http://purl.org/rss/1.0/modules/slash/"
    xmlns:rdf="http://www.w3.org/1999/02/22-rdf-syntax-ns#"
    xmlns:content="http://purl.org/rss/1.0/modules/content/">

  <channel>
    <title>InteractV1 Code Updates</title>
    <link>http://svnserver/viewcvs/?root=InteractV1</link>
    <description>News about recent code updates to InteractV1</¬
  description>
```

```
<webMaster>nstrydom@absolutesys.com</webMaster>
<managingEditor>tcl@absolutesys.com</managingEditor>
<dc:language>en-us</dc:language>
<sy:updatePeriod>hourly</sy:updatePeriod>
<sy:updateFrequency>1</sy:updateFrequency>
<sy:updateBase>2000-01-01T12:00+00:00</sy:updateBase>
```

The footer, then, is quite simple, and just closes off a couple of tags that are still open at the end of the RSS feed.

```
  </channel>
</rss>
```

Tying It All Together

Finally, at the end of the genRSS script is the function that ties everything together. The GenerageRssFile() function calls each of the other functions in the proper order, and outputs "Done." when it is finished. After the function is declared, the script immediately calls it.

```
#=====================================================
# Generates a new RSS file for the repository.
GenerateRssFile ()
{
  AcquireLockFile
  ComputeFirstAndLastItemRevisions
  DeleteOldItemFiles
  CreateNewItemFilesFromSVN
  AssembleThePieces
  ReleaseLockFile
  echo "Done."
}

GenerateRssFile
```

Taking Action on the Post-commit

Now that you have the genRSS script, you need to set up your post-commit script to run it, which will give you a script something like the following example.

```
#!/bin/sh

REPOS=$1
REV=$2

REPOSNAME=`/bin/basename $REPOS`
/svnrepos/scripts/genRSS $REPOSNAME
```

For the most part, this is a very straightforward script. The one "gotcha" that you might notice, though, is the REPOSNAME variable, which is constructed using the `basename` command to strip off everything but the trailing repository name. This is because the `genRSS` script takes the name of the repository, not the full path to the repository.

11.2.3   Implement Fine-grain Access Controls

The Authz module for Apache and WebDAV allows you to restrict access to specific directories to individual users or groups of users. What if you use `svnserve` though? It doesn't have the fine-grained access controls of Authz built in. Or, what if you need to restrict write access to a specific file? Authz only allows restrictions to be placed on a per-directory basis. These cases are where `pre-commit` hook scripts can come in handy. With a hook script, you can check the permissions of the user against the directory (or file) where the commit is taking place, before allowing it to be applied (unfortunately, there is no way to run a hook script before a read takes place; as the French say, such is life).

Like e-mailing of commits, access controls are another very common use of hook scripts. As such, Subversion provides two example scripts, similar to the e-mail commit scripts. Each of these scripts allows you fine-grained access control over commits, on a per-file or per-directory basis. If you need to make modifications, there is a Perl script and a Python script, which you can use depending on your language of choice.

commit-access-control.pl

You run the `commit-access-control.pl` script by passing it the repository in question, the transaction name, and a configuration file with the user permissions for the repository. If the script determines that the user performing the commit has the proper permission, it exits with a return status of 0; otherwise it exits with a 1.

The following example shows how you might write a `pre-commit` script that runs `commit-access-control.pl` and decide whether to allow the commit.

```
#!/bin/sh

# Get the pre-commit script arguments
# $1 = The repository path
# $2 = The transaction name

RPS = "$1"
TXN = "$2"

# Check the repository permissions
ACCESS_CONTROL = /usr/local/share/tools/hook-scripts/commit-access- ¬
  control.pl
CONFIG_FILE = /var/repos/svnrepos/access_control.conf
${ACCESS_CONTROL} "${RPS}" "${TXN}" "${CONFIG_FILE}" || exit 1
```

```
# It passed everything appropriately
exit 0
```

The configuration file that `commit-access-control.pl` uses is very similar to the Authz configuration. Each section name is enclosed in brackets (`[sec name]`) and contains entries for a pattern to `match` directories against (for determining which directories the group applies to), a list of `users` to grant the permission to, and an `access` option that determines whether the allowed access is `read-only` or `read-write`.

The following example shows a config file that sets up three permissions sections, giving read permission to everyone, write permission for the trunk to only two users, and write permission to branches to a select few users.

```
[global]
match = .*
access = read-only

[trunk permissions]
match = /trunk
users = fred ethel
access = read-write

[branches]
match = /branches
users = fred ethel joe linda betty
```

The `match` section uses the Perl regular expression syntax to match directories to apply the permissions to. The syntax itself is beyond the scope of this book, but you should have little trouble finding good Perl documentation if you look online or at your local bookstore.

If you know a little bit of Perl, you should feel free to examine the source code for `commit-access-control.pl` to see how it works. You should also feel free to experiment a little and modify the script to better fit your needs. It's not only in the spirit of open source, but it's also a great way to learn.

svnperms.py

If you are thinking that you would like to make a few of your own custom modifications to the `commit-access-control.pl` file, but Perl isn't your cup of tea, you might want to take a look at `svnperms.py`. This script performs almost exactly the same function as `commit-access-control.pl`, but is written in Python instead of Perl. Like `commit-access-control.pl`, `svnperms.py` takes a repository and transaction, and determines whether the user has write permissions based on a supplied configuration file. The syntax of `svnperms.py` is a little different than `commit-access-control.pl`, as is the syntax of its permissions configuration file. If you look at the `svnperms.py` source, you should quickly see how it differs though. You can also run `svnperms.py` by itself with no options to see the usage message.

```
$ ./svnperms.py
missing required option(s): repository, either transaction or a  ¬
  revision
Usage: svnperms.py OPTIONS
```

```
Options:
    -r PATH    Use repository at PATH to check transactions
    -t TXN     Query transaction TXN for commit information
    -f PATH    Use PATH as configuration file (default is repository
               path + /conf/svnperms.conf)
    -s NAME    Use section NAME as permission section (default is
               repository name, extracted from repository path)
    -R REV     Query revision REV for commit information (for tests)
    -A AUTHOR  Check commit as if AUTHOR had committed it (for tests)
    -h         Show this message
```

11.2.4   Enforce Policy

Any software development project is going to have a number of policies that are unique to
that project (even though they may be similar to policies on other projects). One of the jobs
of a project manager is to help ensure that those policies are correctly followed. Due to for-
getfulness, laziness, stubbornness, and occasionally incompetence, ensuring that policies
are followed can be a tough job, and allowing them to slip (even slightly, sometimes) can
cause a lot of headaches down the road.

In many cases, though, the policies that need to be followed are well-defined enough
that a script can be written to parse the source that is being committed to a repository and
check it for compliance with project policies. If that is the case, the script can be run as part
of a pre-commit hook script, which allows Subversion to reject any commits that don't
comply with policy.

Some of the policies that you might want to consider testing in your pre-commit script
are

- Check compliance with source code style rules. Many projects have style rules (in-
  dentation, bracket placement, variable naming, and so on) that all code committed
  to the project should follow. Many of these rules are easily tested by an automated
  checker (GNU Indent is a popular choice for C code), and either fixed or rejected with
  reasons for failure. If your project requires submitters to check their code against a
  standard before committing, you can have a script run the checker when it receives
  the commit and reject any code that doesn't fit the requirements.

- Ensure that submitted source compiles. If a user commits code to the repository that
  doesn't compile, it can cause delays and headaches as other developers have to sort
  out why things no longer work and are potentially blocked in their own development
  until a fix is committed. By running a build of the source before allowing the commit,
  you can help prevent broken source trees. This tends to be a more useful hook if it
  only checks against the trunk (or other shared branches) and allows branches used

only by individual developers to be committed broken.

- Validate submitted changes with the project's test suite. Many projects have a suite of test programs to help ensure that features work (and continue to work after changes are made). If such tests exist, it is usually important for developers to run those tests before submitting changes to the Subversion repository. Unfortunately, that doesn't always happen, and submitted changes may introduce subtle problems in areas other than their main area of operation. By automatically running the project's test suite (or a subset, if it's too large to run on every commit), you can help reduce these instances. This tends to be a more useful hook if it only checks against the trunk (or other shared branches) and allows branches used only by individual developers to be committed broken.

- Use properties to check status of outside processes. For example, you might require that all source code be validated in a peer review before it is placed into the main source trunk. To help ensure that those peer reviews have taken place, you could require that all changes submitted to the repository include a property change that adds the date or the peer review for those changes to a property showing the peer review history of the file.

- Enforce repository modification policies. For instance, users should be able to create new tags in tags/, but you probably don't want them to modify anything in those tags (tags/*/*). Nor do you likely want to have users create files directly in branches/ or tags/. Instead, they should only create directories. Furthermore, you could limit those directories to directories that have history, thus preventing a tag or branch created from a fresh directory addition.

11.2.5 Log Revision Property Changes

When revision properties are changed, the change is applied immediately and the old value is lost forever. This makes revision properties extremely volatile if you allow them to be changed. On the other hand, there are times when changing revision properties can be useful, especially if you add your own revision properties to support your development process. Therefore, the best solution for overcoming the shortcomings of the revision property, while allowing them to be changed for reasonable purposes, is to create a log of each revision property's history. Whenever that revision property changes, you log the previous value of the property into an unversioned file stored somewhere on disk. Then, later, if someone needs to retrieve the old value for a revision property, he can check that file and find the information he wants.

The following pre-revprop-change hook script shows how you might go about logging all of your revision property changes.

```
#!/bin/sh

REPOS="$1"
```

```
REV="$2"
USER="$3"
PROPNAME="$4"

echo "Changing revision property ${PROPNAME} on revision ${REV} at `/¬
  bin/date`" >> ${REPOS}/revprop.log
echo "========== Old Value =========="
echo `/usr/bin/svn propget ${PROPNAME} --revprop --revision ${REV} ¬
  file://${REPOS}` >> ${REPOS}/revprop.log
echo "========== End Old Value =========="
echo

exit 0
```

As you can see, this is a pretty simple script. First, it echoes some information about the property being changed (the property name, the revision number, and the date/time of the change). Then, it retrieves the old value by running `svn propget`, and echoes that value into the log file, too. Finally, it exits with status zero, so that Subversion will allow the property change to take place.

You may be asking why I use `svn propget` instead of `svnlook propget`. The answer is that `svnlook propget` doesn't allow you to retrieve revision properties. Because `svn` doesn't take raw revision paths, though, I have to add the `file://` schema onto the beginning of $REPOS when I put it on the command line.

11.2.6   Make Tags Immutable

One of Subversion's more controversial features is its lack of CVS-style tags (or VSS-style labels), where a particular revision can be "tagged" with an identifier that gives it special meaning. In Subversion, tagging is done with cheap copies, and are technically identical to branches. The only thing that sets tags apart from branches is the convention that copies placed into "branches" directories are branches, and copies placed into "tags" directories are tags. The upside to this is flexibility (hierarchical or alternate branches and tags directories), but the downside is a lack of enforcement for the immutability that is generally desired for tags.

Generally, tags are meant to be static identifiers of the state of the repository at a given point in time. If you want people making changes and committing them to the tag, you would make it a branch, right? The problem with using Subversion copies for tags is that those tags are *not* immutable. In fact, you can check out a tag and freely commit changes to it, just as with any other directory, because Subversion doesn't have any concept of tags being anything special. Of course, your history isn't lost, because the tag will be fully versioned. But if someone accidentally commits a change to a tag, it may not be noticed by others who check out the tag, thinking they are getting a static snapshot of the repository at a specific point in time.

The easiest solution for keeping tags static is to simply make it project policy. Make sure everyone on the development team knows not to modify any files in the `tags` directory, and let the team police itself by occasionally checking histories and ensuring that no one has made any changes they weren't supposed to. Because everything is versioned, it will be relatively easy to undo any changes that are made, and everything should run smoothly.

Are you laughing yet? If you have much experience with development projects (and, more specifically, developers), you will know that relying on everyone to always do the correct thing is setting yourself up for problems. People make mistakes, and occasionally do malicious things (even on a small project). Therefore, if a policy can be enforced through technical means, without unduly causing detriment to the developer's productivity, that is almost always better than just stating the policy and hoping everyone follows it correctly.

One way that you can enforce the immutability of tags in Subversion is to use hook scripts that check data that is being committed, and ensure that nothing in the tags directory is being modified. You can do this, for instance, in a pre-commit script that checks which files are being modified, using svnlook changed, and rejects any commits with changes inside the tags directory. Of course, you still want to be able to add new tags, and probably want to be able to delete tags, too, so you'll want to check specifically for files that have been updated, while allowing adds and deletes. The following example script shows one way that you might implement this functionality using the svnperms.py script.

```
#!/bin/sh

# Grab the repository name and the transaction number from
# the script's arguments.
REPOS="$1"
TXN="$2"

# Run svnperms.py to check the permissions
/usr/bin/svnperms.py -r ${REPOS} -t ${TXN} -s SimpleAuth
exit 0
```

The matching svnperms.conf file should be created in $REPOS/conf/, and will look something like the following example. In this example, the trunk and branches directories are fully modifiable, but users can only create or delete directories at the top level of the tags directory. Any attempts to add, modify, or remove files or directories inside a tag will fail.

```
[SimpleAuth]
trunk/.* = *(add,remove,update)
branches/.* = *(add,remove,update)
tags/*/* = *()
tags/[^/]+/ = *(add,remove)
```

It might be helpful to also be able to set properties on the tags themselves (i.e., the directory contained at the top level of the tags directory). If you'd like to allow properties to be set, you can add `update` to the list of actions that can be performed in the last entry of the `svnperms.conf` file, so that it looks like this:

```
tags/[^/]+/ = *(add,remove,update)
```

Because the only modification you can do to a directory (other than move or delete it) is modify properties, this has the effect of just allowing properties to be set for the tag directories, without allowing the contents of the tag to be modified.

Another common concern with tags: What happens when you do have to change a tag, but modifications have been disallowed? If someone accidentally commits a tag prematurely, or tags the wrong directory, you don't want to be stuck with an incorrect tag. Also, you might find it useful to regularly change some tags to point to a different part of the repository, such as with a "current development tree" or "last successful build" tag. In these cases, you don't want a hook script that disallows modifications to get in the way.

To allow certain users to modify tags, without opening up modification permissions to everybody, you can make use of `svnperms.py`'s groups. By adding an `admin` group, you can assign specific users to have permission to modify tags. The updated `svnperms.conf` file with this added in will look something like the following.

```
[groups]
admins = bill fred

[SimpleAuth]
trunk/.* = *(add,remove,update)
branches/.* = *(add,remove,update)
tags/*/* = *() @admins(add,remove,update)
tags/[^/]+/ = *(add,remove)
```

11.3 Taking Advantage of Metadata

Subversion provides a wealth of metadata about version files, which can be leveraged when writing scripts to automate things in Subversion, both on the client and server side. By knowing what information is available, and how to effectively get at it, you will greatly increase your ability to write scripts that will help to automate Subversion's integration into your software development process.

11.3.1 The Subversion Commands

There are two Subversion programs that you will commonly use when accessing a Subversion repository from your scripts, `svn` and `svnlook`. The choice generally depends on whether you are running server side or client side. In a client-side script, you *must* use `svn`, because `svnlook` requires direct access to the actual repository, rather than access through `svnserve` or Apache. On the server side, though, you are often better off using `svnlook` because it makes a lot of metadata easier to retrieve, and protects you from accidentally modifying a repository in a hook scripts (where such modifications should not occur but are allowed by the system).

svn

The details of using svn are described in detail in Chapter 5, "Working with a Working Copy," so I won't repeat them here. I will, however, briefly review the commands that are useful for examining repository metadata, as well as the specific metadata that you'll be able to retrieve using each of the commands.

svn blame Allows you to retrieve the author responsible for each line in a file, as well as the revision where that line was last modified. In most cases, this is a useful command when run by itself, to provide information to a developer. The author/revision metadata can be useful though, and you may find instances where this is a useful command to use in an automated script.

svn info Provides a variety of pieces of metadata information about an individual versioned file or directory in a working copy (svn info won't work with a URL). Much of this information is useful for automation, and can be easily retrieved from svn info's output. The individual entries that can be retrieved are

- Path (directory, file). This is the path, relative to the base of the repository, where the file or directory is found.

- Name (file). This is the name of the file by itself, without preceding path information.

- URL (directory, file). This is the URL to the file or directory in the repository.

- Repository UUID (directory, file). This is a unique identifier, which identifies which repository the file came from, regardless of URL. It allows the Subversion client to identify a unique repository, regardless of whether the URL is of the form svn://, http://, or something else entirely.

- Revision (directory, file). This is the current revision of the given file in the working copy.

- Node Kind (directory, file). This identifies whether the item being examined is a file or a directory.

- Schedule (directory, file). This is used to identify files that are scheduled for addition or deletion from the repository.

- Last Changed Author (directory, file). This is the last user to make a change to the file or directory.

- Last Changed Rev (directory, file). This is the last revision in which the directory or file was modified.

- Last Changed Date (directory, file). This is the date and time of the last modification to the file or directory.

- Text Last Updated (file). This is the date of the last time the svn update command changed the file's text in the working copy.

- Properties Last Updated (file). This is the date of the last time the svn update command changed a property of the file in the working copy.

- `Checksum` (file). This is a checksum of the file checked out into the working copy. It can be used to make sure that the correct file was downloaded, or to see if the local file has been modified.

svn log You can use this command to retrieve the log history of a file or directory. This is most useful in automated scripts if the log files are structured, so that a script can parse them for useful information. For instance, you might have developers enter the issue tracker ticket number for a commit in a predictable manner, such that an automated script would be able to read through the logs and find all of the revisions that applied to a particular issue.

svn status This command is useful for finding the current state of a repository or working copy. It outputs status in a very strict, easily parsed format, making retrieval of specific items of information fast and trivial.

In addition to these metadata retrieval commands, you can also get information about custom metadata (i.e., properties) using the svn property commands.

svn propget With this command, you can get the individual values of individual properties from a file or directory. The usefulness of any individual property in automation can vary wildly, but well-chosen properties can be extremely useful. On the client side, scripts that validate the state of all project-required properties can be a useful tool for developers, allowing them to see if a commit will be allowed before actually attempting it (which should also give the developer more useful error output if the file doesn't pass).

svn proplist This command allows you to see all of the properties set on a particular file or directory, which can be useful in a client-side automated script to verify the existence of certain properties, and act accordingly. For example, a script could retrieve all of the properties available and process the file based on which properties are there. If there are a lot of optional properties, this is almost certainly faster than testing each property for existence individually.

svnlook

The svnlook command is easily one of the more useful tools available to you when writing scripts that will run on the server, with local access to the repository. It provides you with the ability to inspect a variety of aspects of the repository, including transactions that have not yet been fully committed to the repository. Some of its commands mirror those available in svn (albeit with slightly different inputs and outputs), but many provide information that is difficult to get using the client (or in a form better suited to using with a script).

The svn mirrored commands cover the query commands that don't affect the repository itself in any way. For the most part, they work similar to their equivalent commands in

svn, with the addition of a --transaction (or -t) argument that allows you to inspect a
transaction instead of a revision, given the transaction number. The transaction number is
supplied as an argument to the pre-commit and pre-revprop-change hook scripts, or
can be found by running svnadmin lstxns. Additionally, the svnlook commands take
the local path to the repository, instead of a URL, and won't work with a working copy.

svnlook cat This command works exactly the same as the svn version. It takes a repository and the path to a file in the repository and outputs that file's contents.

```
$ svnlook cat --revision 1492 /var/svnrepos /repos/trunk/groceries.txt
One Gallon Milk
A Dozen Eggs
Steak
Apples
Hamburgers
Bread
```

svnlook diff This diff command is similar to the svn diff command, but with fewer
options. Unlike the svn diff command, svnlook diff is only meant to show the differences that were applied to a repository in a given revision, rather than giving the differences
between two arbitrary versions. Therefore, the following example would output all of the
changes that were applied in revision 1972, using the GNU diff format. Changes are shown
across all files that were changed in that revision. There is no way to specify individual files.

```
$ svnlook diff --revision 1972 /var/svnrepos
Modified: trunk/ParseTree.h
==================================================================
--- trunk/ParseTree.h      2004-09-28 05:15:43 UTC (rev 1971)
+++ trunk/ParseTree.h      2004-09-28 05:52:14 UTC (rev 1972)
@@ -2,33 +2,51 @@
 #define PARSE_TREE_H

 #include "ParsedElem.h"
+#include "UnparsedElem.h"
 #include <string>
 #include <list>
```

svnlook info Instead of giving information about a particular file, this command gives
information about a particular revision in the repository. Specifically, it gives the user who
committed the revision, the date of the revision, the revision number, and the log entry for
that revision.

```
$ svnlook info --revision 1000 /var/svnrepos
bill
```

```
2004-05-11 14:30:43 -0500 (Tue, 11 May 2004)
27
Added ready status output.
```

svnlook log The svnlook log command is identical to the svn log command, except it only gives a single log entry for a specific revision or transaction.

```
$ svnlook log --transaction 34 /var/svnrepos
Implemented a logging algorithm.
```

svnlook propget This command gives exactly the same output as the svn propget command. You just need to feed it a repository, a property name, and a path to a file in the repository.

```
$ svnlook propget --revision 356 /var/svnrepos svn:ignore /trunk/src
*.o
*.so
*.a
```

svnlook proplist Similarly, the proplist command works identically to the svn proplist command, and lists all of the properties associated with a file, at the supplied revision.

```
$ svnlook proplist --revision 558 /var/svnrepos /trunk/src
svn:ignore
svn:keywords
```

If you would like, you can also see the values of each property by passing the --verbose (or -v) parameter.

In addition to the commands that more or less mirror commands from svn, svnlook provides a number of commands that are not available in the Subversion client, but which can be very useful when writing hook scripts, and other server-side automation tools.

svnlook author This command prints the username of the person who committed the designated revision or transaction.

```
$ svnlook author --revision 17834 /var/svnrepos
dwnorth
```

svnlook changed With this command, you are able to see exactly which files have been changed for a particular revision, in a manner similar to the output of svn status. Each file that was modified in that revision is shown, with its full path relative to the root of the repository, preceded by two columns of output that tell what has changed in the file.

```
$ svnlook changed --revision 238 /var/svnrepos
U    trunk/etc/csh.login
A    trunk/etc/httpd.conf
D    trunk/etc/profile.env
_U   trunk/etc/passwd
```

The first column shows changes that have been made to the contents of the file.

   U: The file's contents were modified.

   A: The file was added to the repository.

   D: The file was removed.

Additionally, the second column indicates files that have had a property modified, with a U.

svnlook date   The date command outputs the date that a revision was created.

```
$ svnlook date /var/svnrepos
2004-09-29 18:33:13 -0500 (Wed, 29 Sep 2004)
```

svnlook dirs-changed   This command outputs all of the directories that were changed in a given revision or transaction. Changed directories include directories that had a property modified or directories that contain files which were modified. Directories that had a subdirectory added or removed are also shown.

```
$ svnlook dirs-changed --transaction 19 /var/svnrepos
trunk/
branches/release_1_0_1
```

svnlook history   This command allows you to examine the path that a file has taken, through copies and moves. When you run svnlook history with the path to a file or directory in your repository, it outputs the revision history of that file, showing every revision where that file or directory was modified, along with the path to the file at that revision.

```
$ svnlook history /var/svnrepos /tags/release_1_0
REVISION    PATH
--------    ----
    5630    /tags/release_1_0
    5407    /branches/release_candidate
    5304    /branches/release_candidate
    5207    /branches/release_candidate
    5206    /trunk
    5205    /trunk
     ...
```

```
            3    /trunk
            2    /trunk
            1    /trunk
```

If you give `svnlook history` an explicit revision (using `--revision`, or `-r`), it only outputs the history of the given file up to that point.

```
$ svnlook history --revision 4 /var/svnrepos /tags/release_1_0
REVISION    PATH
--------    ----
        4   /trunk
        3   /trunk
        2   /trunk
        1   /trunk
```

svnlook tree You can examine the hierarchy of files in your repository by using the `svnlook tree` command. If you run the command with no path argument, it shows the entire tree of files in your repository at the supplied revision. If, instead, you provide the command with a path into the repository, it shows that directory and all files/subdirectories contained within.

```
$ svnlook tree /var/svnrepos /branches/release_1_0
release_1_0/
 hello_world/
  hello_world.c
  Makefile
 docs/
  README.txt
```

svnlook uuid Each repository has a unique ID that allows it to be identified independent of the URL used to access it. You can output this ID by running `svnlook uuid`.

```
$ svnlook uuid /var/svnrepos
8ebba8bb-42e5-0310-8fa5-bfaad3eac2b1
```

svnlook youngest You can find the most recently committed revision of a repository by running this command. It has no options, and just takes the path to a repository. Because its output is simply the revision number, it is especially useful in scripts.

```
$ svnlook youngest /var/svnrepos
2592
```

11.4   The Subversion API

Subversion clients interact with a Subversion repository by linking against the Subversion client libraries, which provide a comprehensive API for manipulating the repository. By using the Subversion APIs, you can write complex applications to provide new tools capable of providing new functionality, wrapping old functionality in a manner more conducive to your process, or automating complex tasks. There are even bindings for the API available in a number of different languages (currently, C, C++, Java, Perl, and Python).

The Subversion libraries are a large and full-featured set of interfaces that could probably fill an entire book of their own. So, instead of going into a long-winded (read: *boring*) discussion on how to call this function or initialize that data structure, I'll instead whet your appetite by diving in and showing you a small example program.

11.4.1   svntag

The example program is called svntag. Subversion's tagging via copies can be confusing for some users who are coming from a CVS background. To make the transition from CVS to Subversion easier for them, this program automatically creates a "tag" by copying the trunk into the /tags directory, while requiring only a tag name from the user.

Of course, this particular example could be accomplished much more easily by just writing a script that wraps the svn copy command, but it serves its purpose here of illustrating the Subversion API. To better serve as an example, it is also somewhat incomplete in its error checking and hardcodes a few pieces of information that should never be hardcoded in a production application (such as the base URL for the repository).

```
#include <unistd.h>

#include <svn_client.h>
#include <svn_config.h>
#include <svn_pools.h>
#include <svn_cmdline.h>

/* Define some global structs */
svn_client_ctx_t*       context;
svn_opt_revision_t      revision;

/* Define some path strings */
const char*             baseURL = "http://svn.mydomain.com/testrepos/";
const char*             tagsDir = "tags/";
const char*             trunkDir = "trunk";
const char*             tagname;
char*                   destURL;

/* The base string for tags */
const char*             logBase = "Created new tag: ";
```

```
/* Creates the commit log for the tagging */
svn_error_t* getCommitLog(const char** log_msg, const char** tmp_file,
                          apr_array_header_t* commit_items,
                          void* baton, apr_pool_t* pool)
{
   /* Fill the commit log */
   *log_msg = apr_psprintf(pool, "%s%s", logBase, tagname);

   return SVN_NO_ERROR;
}

/* Initialize the Subversion API context */
svn_error_t* initializeContext(apr_pool_t* pool)
{
   /* Create a new context */
   SVN_ERR(svn_client_create_context(&context, pool));

   /* Get the configuration data structure for the context */
   SVN_ERR(svn_config_get_config(&(context->config), NULL, pool));

   /* Set the callback function for setting the commit log */
   context->log_msg_func = getCommitLog;
   context->log_msg_baton = NULL;

   return SVN_NO_ERROR;
}

/* Parse the command line */
int parseCmdLine(int argc, char** argv, apr_pool_t* pool)
{
   if(argc != 2) {
      printf("Usage: svntag TAGNAME\n");
      return -1;
   }

   /* Set the tag name */
   tagname = argv[1];

   /* Construct the destination URL */
   destURL = apr_psprintf(pool, "%s%s%s", baseURL, tagsDir, tagname);

   return 0;
```

```
}


int main(int argc, char** argv)
{
    apr_pool_t* pool;

    /* Perform command-line application initializations */
    svn_cmdline_init("svntag", stderr);

    /* Initialize the memory pool */
    pool = svn_pool_create(NULL);

    /* Parse the command line */
    if(parseCmdLine(argc, argv, pool) < 0) return -1;

    /* Initialize the Subversion API */
    SVN_INT_ERR(initializeContext(pool));

    /* Set the revision */
    revision.kind = svn_opt_revision_head;

    /* Perform the copy */
    {
        svn_client_commit_info_t* commitInfo;
        char* trunkURL;

        trunkURL = apr_psprintf(pool, "%s%s", baseURL, trunkDir);
        SVN_INT_ERR(svn_client_copy(&commitInfo,
                                    trunkURL,
                                    &revision,
                                    destURL,
                                    context,
                                    pool));
    }

    return 0;
}
```

That's it. That's the whole program. I'll explain how to compile it in a little while, but first, let's look at what each part of the program does, and why.

Initial Includes and Defines

At the beginning of the program, you see a number of includes, as well as the definitions for several global variables. Let's start by looking at the includes.

```
#include <unistd.h>

#include <svn_client.h>
#include <svn_config.h>
#include <svn_pools.h>
#include <svn_cmdline.h>
```

The Subversion API consists of a large number of header files that segregate the API into different subsets of functionality. For example, if you need to deal with contextual diffing, you would include `svn_diff.h`. If you you need to deal with authentication to a repository, include `svn_auth.h`. In this program, as you can see, we've included four Subversion API header files (plus the common `unistd.h` header). Three of these, `svn_cmdline.h`, `svn_config.h`, and `svn_pools.h`, provide common functionality that is needed in almost every application. The third, `svn_cmdline.h`, provides the interface to the `libsvn_client` library, which includes functions for implementing the familiar Subversion client commands.

After the header includes, you see a number of global variable defines.

```
/* Define some global structs */
svn_client_ctx_t*        context;
svn_opt_revision_t       revision;

/* Define some path strings */
const char*              baseURL = "http://svn.mydomain.com/testrepos/";
const char*              tagsDir = "tags/";
const char*              trunkDir = "trunk";
const char*              tagname;
char*                    destURL;

/* The base string for tags */
const char*              logBase = "Created new tag: ";
```

The first two of these are structures from the Subversion API that probably make no sense to you. That's okay; ignore them for now. I'll discuss their purpose later, when I show where they are actually used. After the structures are a bunch of strings. These are used for storing the URLs given to the Subversion API, as well as the log message for inclusion with each tagging.

Memory Pools

Before we continue with our program, let's take a minute to talk about *memory pools*. The Subversion libraries are built atop the Apache Portable Runtime (APR) project. APR is a library designed to give a portable interface to programs, which then communicates with the platform-specific interfaces of different operating systems. This library is the reason why Subversion is runnable on such a wide array of different platforms. One of APR's more complex interfaces is its memory pool system. To allow memory to be allocated and disposed of cleanly and efficiently, APR allows programs to create a memory pool that provides a dynamically allocated block of memory. Programs can then use that memory as they see fit, and then deallocate the entire block at an appropriate time. Additionally, APR allows blocks of memory to be chained together (and intelligently shared behind the scenes). Chained memory pools can then be cleared individually or all at once (a very powerful feature).

The Subversion libraries make extensive use of APR memory pools, and expose them frequently in the Subversion API. To make their creation a little bit easier in the context of Subversion, though, the Subversion API wraps the APR memory pool manipulation functions with its own versions. In the case of our program, we'll use the svn_pool_create() function, which acts as a wrapper to the apr_pool_create_ex. I'll explain its use in a little more detail when I discuss the main() function in a little while.

Initializing the Client Context

Moving to the list, we'll skip over the getCommitLog() function (for now) and look at the next function, initializeContext().

```
svn_error_t* initializeContext(apr_pool_t* pool)
{
    /* Create a new context */
    SVN_ERR(svn_client_create_context(&context, pool));

    /* Get the configuration data structure for the context */
    SVN_ERR(svn_config_get_config(&(context->config), NULL, pool));

    /* Set the callback function for setting the commit log */
    context->log_msg_func = getCommitLog;
    context->log_msg_baton = NULL;

    return NULL;
}
```

The Subversion svn_client_ctx_t structure is used to store context for a client program's repository access session. This includes callback functions that are used by various client command functions, as well as configuration information. Contexts also include the concept of a *baton*, which is used to pass state information to the various callback functions (each callback function has an associated baton). The client context structure is defined as follows.

```
typedef struct svn_client_ctx_t
{
    svn_auth_baton_t *              auth_baton;
```

```
svn_wc_notify_func_t          notify_func;
void *                        notify_baton;
svn_client_get_commit_log_t   log_msg_func;
void *                        log_msg_baton;
apr_hash_t *                  config;
svn_cancel_func_t             cancel_func;
void *                        cancel_baton;
} svn_client_ctx_t;
```

Looking back to the `initializeContext()` function, you'll see that it starts off by calling `svn_client_create_context()`. This takes our empty context pointer and allocates a new context structure for us to use. Notice how it also takes a pointer to our memory pool, which it uses for allocating the actual context.

You'll also notice that the whole `svn_client_create_context()` function call is wrapped with the SVN_ERR macro. This is a convenience macro that is used for checking the return value of the enclosed function for an error. If `svn_client_create_context()` returns a non-null `svn_error_t` pointer, the SVN_ERR macro will return the error value from the current function.

Next, we make a call to `svn_config_get_config()` and pass a pointer to the `config` field in our context, along with our memory pool. This function is used to load standard Subversion configuration information from the standard Subversion configuration files. If we had passed a string with the path to a directory (instead of NULL) as the second argument, `svn_config_get_config()` would have loaded the configuration from that directory instead of the standard system-wide and user-specific sources.

Finally, the last remaining item we need to initialize in our context is the log message callback function. This function is called whenever Subversion needs to obtain a log message for a commit. In this case, we set it up to point to `getCommitLog()`, which I will discuss in the next section. Because our commit log function doesn't need any state propagated from one call to the next, we can set the log message baton to NULL.

Setting the Commit Log

Let's go back up a little ways and look at the `getCommitLog()` function that we skipped over earlier.

```
svn_error_t* getCommitLog(const char** log_msg, const char** tmp_file,
                          apr_array_header_t* commit_items,
                          void* baton, apr_pool_t* pool)
{
    /* Fill the commit log */
    *log_msg = apr_psprintf(pool, "%s%s", logBase, tagname);

    return SVN_NO_ERROR;
}
```

The `getCommitLog()` function is responsible for supplying a log message to the Subversion client library backend, on demand. The function is never directly called by our program, but instead, a pointer to it is set in the client context structure and called internally by various other client library functions. When this function is called, it receives pointers to two unallocated strings (which it is responsible for filling). It also receives an array consisting of some or all of the items being committed, a pointer to the commit log baton that was set for the client context, and a pointer to the pool that should be used for all allocations.

The two unallocated strings that the commit log function is responsible for allocating are the log message (`log_msg`) and a path indicating a temporary file that contains the log message (`tmp_file`). If there is no temporary file, the `tmp_file` parameter can be set to NULL. Similarly, if you want to cancel the commit, you can set the `log_msg` variable to NULL.

In the case of our `getCommitLog()` function, though, we just want to set a simple log message that gives the name of the tag that was created. So, we use the `apr_psprintf()` function to generate our log message, and set `log_msg` to point to it. The `apr_psprintf()` function works the same as an `sprintf()`, but takes a pointer to the memory pool to allocate the string.

The Main Program

Finally, we come to the main function of our program. This is where the previous functions are all tied together. It is also where the actual copying of the `trunk` directory occurs.

```
int main(int argc, char** argv)
{
    apr_pool_t* pool;

    /* Perform command-line application initializations */
    svn_cmdline_init("svntag", stderr);

    /* Initialize the memory pool */
    pool = svn_pool_create(NULL);

    /* Parse the command line */
    if(parseCmdLine(argc, argv) < 0) return -1;

    /* Initialize the Subversion API */
    SVN_INT_ERR(initializeContext(pool));

    /* Set the revision */
    revision.kind = svn_opt_revision_head;

    /* Perform the copy */
    {
        svn_client_commit_info_t* commitInfo;
        char* trunkURL;
```

```
    trunkURL = apr_psprintf(pool, "%s%s", baseURL, trunkDir);
    SVN_INT_ERR(svn_client_copy(&commitInfo,
                                trunkURL,
                                &revision,
                                destURL,
                                context,
                                pool));
}

  return 0;
}
```

At the top of the main() function, you'll see a pointer of type apr_pool_t declared. This is the main memory pool for our program, and it is passed around to every other function that needs it.

After the memory pool is declared, the first thing our main() function does is call the svn_cmdline_init() function, which performs initializations for the underlying Subversion library, specific to a command-line program. After that, we'll initialize our memory pool with a call to svn_pool_create(). Normally, svn_pool_create() takes a pointer to the pool's parent pool, but because this is our base memory pool, we have no parent, and pass NULL instead.

The next part of the main() function parses the program's command-line parameters. The parseCmdLine() function is one local to our program that extracts the tag name from the command parameters. The function itself is self-explanatory enough that I won't go into it specifically.

Following the command-line parsing, we call the initializeContext() function that was discussed earlier. You'll notice that the initializeContext() function call is wrapped by the SVN_INT_ERR() macro. This is a convenience macro supplied by the Subversion API that checks the return result of the function for an error. If an error occurs, it outputs the error to stderr and returns EXIT_FAILURE.

The revision structure is set to point to the HEAD revision (because our program always copies from HEAD).

Finally, the actual copy of the directory is performed. This is done using the function svn_client_copy(), which takes the path to be copied from, a pointer to the revision, the destination URL, the context that we set up earlier, and our memory pool. It also takes a pointer to an svn_client_commit_info_t structure, which will be filled with some information about the commit that occurred.

Compiling the Program

Our program needs to be compiled with a few references to the Subversion libraries, as well as the APR libraries and the Neon library. The best way to get these libraries is through the svn-config program. In some versions of Subversion, though, the output of svn-config is broken and won't produce valid values for passing directly to gcc. Instead, you may have to run `svn-config` separately and copy the valid parameters by hand (or if you're using a Makefile, write a filter to strip out the invalid values). In this case, I compiled the preceding application using the following command lines. You'll note, though, that I had to also add `-lsvn_client-1` to the command line for linking, even though it is not included by `svn-config -libs` output.

```
$ svn-config --cflags
 -g -O2 -march=athlon -fomit-frame-pointer   -pthread  -DNEON_ZLIB - ¬
 DNEON_SSL
$ svn-config --includes
 -I/usr/include/subversion-1 -I/usr/include/neon   @SVN_DB_INCLUDES@  - ¬
 I/usr/include/apache2    -I/usr/include/apache2
$ gcc -g -O2 -march=athlon -fomit-frame-pointer   -pthread  -DNEON_ZLIB ¬
  -DNEON_SSL -Wall -I/usr/include/subversion-1 -I/usr/include/neon  -I ¬
 /usr/include/apache2    -I/usr/include/apache2 -c svntag.c
$ svn-config --libs
-lneon -lz -lssl -lcrypto -ldl -lxml2 -lz -lpthread -lm  -L/usr/lib - ¬
 laprutil-0 -lgdbm -ldb-4.1 -lexpat  -L/usr/lib -lapr-0 -lrt -lm - ¬
 lcrypt -lnsl  -lpthread -ldl
$ gcc -g -O2 -march=athlon -fomit-frame-pointer   -pthread -DNEON_ZLIB ¬
  -DNEON_SSL -Wall -lneon -lz -lssl -lcrypto -ldl -lxml2 -lz -lpthread ¬
  -lm  -L/usr/lib -laprutil-0 -lgdbm -ldb-4.1 -lexpat  -L/usr/lib - ¬
 lapr-0 -lrt -lm -lcrypt -lnsl  -lpthread -ldl -lsvn_client-1 svntag.o ¬
  -o svntag
```

11.5   Summary

In this chapter, you have learned a lot of things about automating your use of Subversion. You saw how you could make use of hook scripts to verify commits to a repository, as well as to use those hook scripts to perform other actions in response to commits. Additionally, you saw a number of different example scripts that can be used in your hook scripts or modified to fit your particular needs. You also learned about how to take advantage of Subversion's metadata when automating things and, finally, you saw an example of how to use the Subversion API to write programs that directly interact with Subversion.

Part IV

The Software Development Process

Chapter 12

Development Process Policies

A version control system is just one of the many tools that are used in your development process. Certainly, it is an important tool, and a good version control system is vital to an effective development methodology, but even the best VCS is still only as effective as the process it is used in. In Part IV, I will examine the many aspects of the software development process, and the ways in which Subversion can best fit into those policies. By the end, you should have a solid grasp on the concepts necessary to design your own development process to fit Subversion into *your* development environment.

Any good process is made up of policies that proscribe what should be done in certain situations. Therefore, if you are going to design your development process to make use of Subversion, it only makes sense to start by looking at the policies that should be considered when integrating with version control. In this chapter, we'll examine different version control policies and how they should be integrated into an overall software development process.

12.1 Effective Branching and Tagging

Branching and tagging inside Subversion is one of its more flexible features, due to the use of simple cheap copies for both actions. Within an organized software development process, though, flexibility is only good to a point, before it becomes a hinderance to people trying to work together. To avoid this chaos, you need to develop guidelines for branching and tagging. If you have simple rules for what branches and tags should be created, when they should be created, and what they should be named, you will find that you have greatly increased the ability for your developers to make use of the project's branches and tags to aid in collaboration on the project.

12.1.1 Branch and Tag Creation and Organization

Before you can effectively make use of branches and tags, you need to decide what circumstances warrant the creation of branches and tags, and how those branches and tags will be organized in the repository. Because creating branches and tags is fast, and essentially uses no space, there is little reason to be stingy with their use. On the other hand, you don't want to waste time creating branches and tags that hold no value for anyone. If the copies just sit around collecting dust and littering your repository hierarchies, the useful branches may become harder to find and use.

If you're coming from a CVS background (or another similar VCS), you will find that tags are much less necessary in Subversion than they were in CVS. For example, CVS users often use tags to preserve the state of their work before a large commit in case the commit was interrupted (which would cause an incomplete commit that could be hard to recover from). With Subversion, though, all commits are atomic, so this is no longer a concern. Similarly, it is a common practice with CVS to create tags before and after feature commits, so that the differences can be easily examined later. This is also no longer necessary, because Subversion's global revision numbers make it easy to compare the state of the entire repository before and after any commit. Subversion also makes the timing of tag creation less important, because you can use the `--revision` option when you use `svn copy` to create a new tag, in order to create a tag from a revision other than the current HEAD revision.

There are a number of different things that you might use branches and tags for, and for each there is a different set of issues to consider when deciding your policies for creating and organizing them. Let's take a look at a few of the different branch and tag categories that you might have, and the policies you might use.

Software Version Branches

Often, you will have multiple versions of a project being developed simultaneously. For example, say you have a project that is creating an application called FooMatic. When version 1.0 of FooMatic is released, you want to mark the point in development where that occurred, and then continue developing the main trunk in preparation for FooMatic 2.0. Now, say it's six months after the release of FooMatic 1.0, and you're well on the way to FooMatic 2.0. Despite all of your careful beta testing, though, version 1.0 wasn't perfect, and someone finds a bug. The version 2.0 development group, however, has completely changed that section of the code, and the bug doesn't even apply anymore. You don't want to tell all of your customers that they'll have to wait for the next version to get the bug fixed though. They need it fixed now. Fortunately, when you released 1.0, you created a tag for that version. Now, when bugs are found, you can create a new branch from the 1.0 tag, fix the bug, and release a new (tagged) bug-fix version without interrupting development on version 2.0. When a fix applies to both versions, you can use a merge to copy the changes from one branch to another.

Alternately, you can make a branch every time you release a version of the software to the public that you want to support with fixes in the future and maintain it as a separate line of development. If you release version 1.0, it is likely that you'll want to release minor versions that fix bugs and security issues before the release of version 2.0. So, make version 1.0 a separate branch from development of 2.0 when you make the 1.0 release. Then, create tags of minor releases from that branch as they are developed. If you release minor feature releases (1.0, 1.1, 1.2, and so on), you'll probably want each of those to be a separate branch, too, so that you can release 1.0.1 while you're developing 1.1.0.

Your best choice is to pick a version number level and make a unique branch for each release at that granularity. So, if you pick the major revision numbers, you'd have a branch for 1.0, 2.0, 3.0, and so on. If you pick the first level of minor revisions, you'd have branches named 1.0, 1.1, 1.2, 2.0, and 2.1. The choice of the exact level to branch on is dependent on the way any individual project releases software, but consistency is much more important than one particular choice of branch point. In general, I suggest standardizing on one or two levels of minor revision numbers.

When it comes to organizing these revision branches, there are a couple of ways to approach the process. The first is to see the release branches the same as any other branch. Your current main line of development occurs in /trunk, and whenever a release is made, you create a new branch in /branches/releases/. If you think about it, all of your development is really occurring on a release branch, regardless of whether you call the development on the trunk a release branch. So, instead of having a /trunk, you might want to consider having two top-level directories named /releasedev and /releases, as shown in Figure 12.1. In /releasedev, put a branch for each release of the project that is currently being developed. Then, when a version is actually released, move it into the /releases directory (where the release will be treated as an immutable tag) and create a copy of the new release in /releasedev that will become the next development version.

Quality Assurance Branches and Betas

Many projects have a development team and a quality assurance team. In such a case, it can be helpful to have two branches of development—one that the developers use for their day-to-day work and another that the quality assurance (QA) team uses for its testing. When

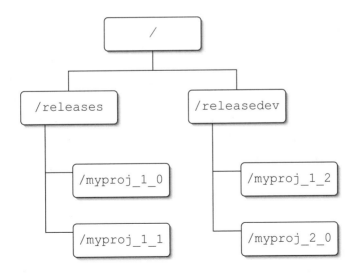

Figure 12.1. A repository with release branches instead of a trunk.

the development team finishes a feature or fix (or on a fixed schedule), the changes on the development branch are merged to the QA branch for the testers to inspect.

One approach to this setup is to have two fixed branches. All development occurs on one branch, and is then merged over to the QA branch for testing. Another approach is to have a single QA branch, with multiple development branches. For instance, each developer could be working on her own branch, which would be periodically merged into the QA branch. Then, when a QA tester finds an issue, she can create a new branch with the state of the project where the issue occurred. A developer would then be able to fix the issue on that branch and merge the fix back into the QA branch when it's finished.

To organize QA branches, we can build on the release branches structure suggested in the previous section. Instead of having a single directory for each project release, create two branches, so that you have a structure where you will have something like `/releasedev/version_1_0/dev/` and `/releasedev/version_1_0/qa/`. This gives you a development branch and a quality assurance branch for each version of the software that is being actively developed.

As development on a project advances, you will invariably release beta versions of the software to testers outside of your quality assurance team. These versions are generally created from your quality assurance branches, and will be immutable releases, just like a final version release. One option for organizing beta releases is to store them in `/releases/`, just as you would a final version release. Or, you can make a distinction by creating another top-level directory named `/betas/` where beta releases can be tagged.

Task Branches

Another area where branches can be useful are in task branches. For each individual feature or issue that a developer is going to work on, she creates a task branch. On the task branch, the developer can make small, incremental changes and commits until that particular task is finished. When the task is complete, it can be merged back into the main trunk, or into a QA branch. For example, in Figure 12.2, you can see how task branches are created from the last release of the project, and then merged into a QA branch, which is then moved to create the next bug-fix release of the project.

There are a few policies that you need to decide on when using task branches. Who will create the branches? When will task branches be created? What granularity of task requires a task branch? How will the branches be organized? There is, of course, no universal "right answer" to these questions. Instead, the answers are based on the myriad of intricacies that define your project.

Who will create the branch? The obvious answer is to have the developer who will be working on that particular task create the branch. Whenever a developer starts a new task, he creates a new branch. It's simple, and it works well for projects with a lot of developer freedom. If you have a large project with lots of managerial oversight, though, it might be easier to keep track of the tasks currently in progress if task branches are created by a project manager responsible for assigning tasks. When a task is assigned, the branch is created and handed to a developer to implement. This might also be a good choice for sensitive projects where the main trunk would not be available to every developer for security reasons. When a developer is assigned a task, the project manager would only have

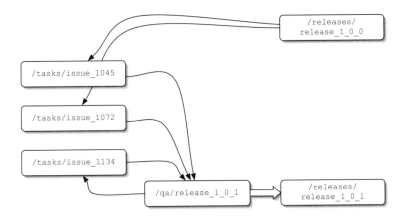

Figure 12.2. Task branches used for fixing issues in a release.

to create a branch of the small subsection of the project necessary for implementing the task and give permission for that branch to the appropriate developer(s). On a mature project, you may even have most (or all) of the tasks generated by QA testers who are handling bug reports from users.

When will task branches be created? There are really only two major options here (with small variations). Task branches can either be created when the task is scheduled or when work on it begins. For tasks that are responding to a particular base state of the project (such as bug fixes), it is usually a good idea to create the tasks when the task is scheduled, because there is usually a well-known baseline to work from at that point. Later on, when work on the task actually begins, it's possible that the changes made to the project in the interim may have modified the base project to a point where there is no good baseline to start implementation of the task. On the other hand, for other tasks that are adding new features to an evolving project, it may be better to create the branch when the developer starts working on the task. This way, the branch is up-to-date when it is begun, which will make merging it back into the main trunk a little easier.

What granularity of task requires a branch? This is largely a matter of taste. If you want very fine-grained project organization, you may want individual task branches for each atomic feature enhancement or bug fix. Or, if you prefer a more coarsely managed project, it might make sense to only create branches for major tasks that will require large code changes or additions.

How will the branches be organized? The way you organize task branches has a lot to do with who is creating and using them. If, for instance, each developer maintains her own task branches while working on the project, you might want to give each developer her own directory for storing them. However, if the task branches are generated by a project manager or QA tester, it might be better to have a common directory for task branches. Then, if you want to keep the branches that are being worked on separate, each developer could move the branch from the common directory into her own task branch directory when she begins work on the task.

Sliding Tags

Sometimes, you have a tag that you want to point to a changing target while retaining the same name. As an example, say you create a daily build of your project. In addition to a tag that will always point to that particular build, it might be useful to have a tag called `daily_build` that always points to today's build. That way, anyone who needs access to the most up-to-date daily build can check out the `daily_build` tag and can just update to get the latest release.

There are a couple of ways you can approach creating these sorts of tags. One way is to delete the old tag and recreate a new one by the same name whenever you want to move the tag. This has the advantage of being fairly easy to execute, but it requires two steps to perform the change (if anyone updates between the two steps, his directory will be deleted on disk and he'll have to redownload the whole thing). Using delete/re-add also has the disadvantage that it makes an `svn log` on that directory useless, because it won't show the history of the tag.

An alternative to using copy and delete is to make use of the `svn:externals` property to create your sliding tag. With the externals property, you can create a directory that holds the tag, and then set `svn:externals` to point to the correct directory and revision number. Then, when the path or revision number is changed to move the tag, you will have a log record of where the tag has pointed to. The downside to using `svn:externals` is that the syntax for creating and moving the tag is a little more complex than using copy and delete; but in most cases, I would suggest it as the better alternative.

Merge Tracking with Tags

Subversion doesn't do a particularly good job of tracking merges—yet. In fact, Subversion's poor merge tracking is arguably its weakest point as a version control system. The commonly suggested practice for tracking merges is to use the log files to keep track of which range of revisions were merged, and where they were merged from, in the log message for each committed merge.

Keeping track of merges is important, because subsequent merges need to account for the past history, in order to avoid applying incorrect changes. If you create a branch of `/trunk` at revision 50 and then merge changes on the trunk made between 50 and 100, it's important to make sure the next merge applies the changes from 100 to 150, not 50 to 150. Using the log messages to note that you merged 50 to 100 already is a serviceable solution, but it's not the only one. Subversion merges apply the difference between two arbitrary sections of the repository. Using different revisions for a single path is only one way to get those two sections for the merge. Another way is to give two entirely different repository paths. So, if you made a tag of `/trunk` at the last point where you performed the merge, you could instead use that in the merge, instead of needing to know the revision number.

Merge tags can either be stored in a common location, such as `/tags/merges`, or they can be stored alongside the specific branch where the merge occurred. You could, for

example, create a directory named /branches/proj_branch_1_merges/ where all of
the versions involved in a merge into /branches/proj_branch_1/ would be tagged.

Tagging Project Builds

If you have an automated build system that performs nightly (or hourly, or even more
frequent), it may be useful for it to automatically generate tags that reference those builds.
So, for instance, if it creates a build on June 4th at 3:00 in the morning, it could create a tag
named something like /builds/build-060405-0300. Then, when the build system runs
your test harness to do regression testing, it can include a reference to the specific build
in the Subversion repository as a part of its results output. That way, you have a durable
reference to the exact state of the repository at the time of the test run, and can recreate it
at a later date if you need to in order to fix any issues that arose during the tests.

Milestone and Release Point Tags

One of the most common uses for tags is to mark important milestones in the code. One
example would be tags that mark releases of the project. By creating a tag at every such
milestone, you can create an easily accessible record of your project's history that is significantly more useful than simply knowing what the project looked like on a certain date,
or at a particular revision number.

   The first policy to adopt when deciding on milestone tags is to determine which milestones you will tag. Some people may spend a lot of time thinking about this in order to
decide on a detailed policy. Don't. Tags are cheap. They take up almost no space in the
repository. You could sit and make tags from full copies of your repository all day long and
not make a significant dent in the size of your repository. Therefore, there is no reason to
be stingy with them. Release a beta? Create a tag. If you release a daily build, create a tag
for each release. Even if you create hourly project builds for in-house development, there
is little reason not to keep track of those builds by creating tags.

   Milestone tags are best organized by collecting different types of milestones into their
own directories. For example, you might have directories named /tags/releases/,
/tags/betas/, and /tags/builds/. Or, if you don't want to hide them away in the
/tags directory, you can move those directories up to the top level. If you have multiple
projects, you might want to put all of those directories in a project directory, or you might
want to put just some of them in a project directory. For instance, you could have a top-
level /releases/ directory that stored the releases for every project, and project-specific
directories for holding builds and beta releases.

Saved Working Copies Snapshots

At times, it can be very useful to save the current state of a working copy, without committing all of the changes to the current trunk or branch. This can be especially useful if you
have a working copy that is made up of several switched directories and you want to save a
snapshot of that layout. Because Subversion allows you to copy from a working copy, this
is easy to do. All you need to do is take a directory in your current working copy and copy

it to a repository URL.

The best place to store a working copy snapshot depends on the purpose of the snapshot. If you make a snapshot for purposes of releasing a project beta, obviously, you would want to store your snapshot along with other tags of beta releases—similarly for full releases, builds, or any other sort of tag. Rarely will you find the need to make a mixed revision snapshot that doesn't have some sort of other purpose; but if you do, it may be useful to have a special tags directory (such as `/tags/snapshots/`) for storing them.

12.1.2   Merging Policies

Merging is currently Subversion's biggest weak point. It can be difficult to perform merges correctly, and it is fairly easy to perform an incorrect merge that causes unintended consequences. The best way to avoid problems is to set out clear policies for when to perform merges, who should perform the merges, and how they should be documented.

When to Merge

The best time to merge depends a lot on what is being merged. Merges can be done on a timetable. They can be done whenever changes occur (or whenever relevant changes occur). Generally, you'll find that you want to use a mix of the two. If, for example, you have a build engineer who manages performing a daily build of your project, she might want to standardize on a daily routine of merging from the available development branches in order to create the day's build—especially if you have multiple independent development branches for different developers that need to be merged and tested every day.

Conversely, if your developers use a more rapid XP-style test-edit-build-test cycle, developers may need to do frequent merges to and from the project's trunk in order to continuously make sure that the rest of the project continues to work with the changes they are making on their branch.

Who Should Merge

In general, it's good policy to allow the same people who should be performing modifications to a trunk or branch directory the ability to perform merges from other branches. Merges should be performed by people who are familiar with the target branch, as well as the source that is being merged in. Because Subversion doesn't have any context for the merges it performs (they're just dumb textual merges), it's important that any merges be thoroughly tested before they are committed. Even if there are no conflicts, merges can easily break working code, and it's important for the person performing the merge to be able to detect and fix any errors that are introduced.

If you have a build engineer or quality assurance tester, it can be useful for him to maintain a QA or build branch, and may be prudent for him to perform merges from other branches into the branch that he maintains. That way, he maintains complete control over what goes into the branch. That also means, though, that he will almost certainly be merging in source code that he didn't write himself. Therefore, if conflicts occur, he may not have the proper background necessary to make a decision on how the conflicted sections should be merged. One solution would be to have the person performing the merge make an educated guess as to the proper resolution, and then test it. This is probably the fastest way to resolve the conflict, but it's also the least reliable (and most likely to introduce subtle errors that don't get caught). Another, possibly better, solution is to have the merger resolve the conflict, but then send a detailed description of what was done to any developers who might have more information about the conflict. Then, they can examine what was done and hopefully catch potential issues. Or, as a third potential solution, the merge could be blocked when a conflict occurs, until the developers who wrote the merged code in the first place can resolve it. This is probably the safest solution, but it is also the most time-consuming. In the end, there really isn't a universal *best* solution here. Ideally, you should try to avoid merge conflicts as much as possible by maintaining an organized development process. If you never have two people working on the same section of code, you never have to worry about merge conflicts. If you do have two people working on the same section of code, they should be talking to each other.

Documenting Merges

Some day, Subversion will have built-in merge tracking that allows you to easily sync two directories without worrying about which revisions have already been merged, or which direction the merges have happened in. In the meantime, the best way to maintain good clean merges between branches and the trunk is to keep detailed documentation about exactly what you've done. Whenever a developer performs a merge, she should record in the log message what repository paths were involved in the merge, as well as the revisions of each path that were involved. Additionally, the log messages that record a merge should always follow an agreed upon standard format that includes a keyword, such as `Merged`, to allow developers to easily use `grep` to filter the output of `svn log` for merges that have previously occurred. If you are using tags to mark the merge history of a trunk or branch directory, developers should also make those tags whenever they perform a merge (you might want to use a script to automate this process and ensure that the tags always get created).

12.2 Checking In Code

As soon as code is committed to a repository, it becomes available for other developers to check out and use (barring permission restrictions). If the code is committed on the trunk, or a public branch, it not only becomes available, but it enters the HEAD revision and any developers performing an update will find those changes merged into their own working copies. This means that if a developer commits changes that break the source on a trunk or branch in a way that blocks other developers from continuing with their work, there will be a lot of wasted labor as developers scramble to figure out why their working copies no longer work and either fix the problems or roll back all or part of their working copy to previous revisions in order to be able to continue their own work.

To avoid time-wasting problems from prematurely committed code, it is important to have a set of policies that define when developers should be performing commits. There's nothing radical here, and most of the policy suggestions I make are commonsense etiquette. They're also mostly universal. They may not always be appropriate for every project, but I would think hard before throwing any of them out.

- Never commit code that hasn't been compiled. If it doesn't compile for you, it probably won't compile for anyone else either. By committing a revision that doesn't even compile, you are costing at least a few wasted minutes for most of the other developers on the project, and possibly more if the reason for the failed compile isn't immediately obvious (for example, if other developers think the problem may be caused by the interaction of their changes and yours). You will also introduce a broken revision that can cause confusion (and headaches) in the future.

- Avoid committing untested code. For essentially the same reasons that you should never commit source code that can't be compiled, you should also avoid committing code that hasn't been thoroughly tested. Unfortunately, it is hard to make this as hard and fast as the compile rule. Sometimes, it just isn't possible to test code before you commit it. For instance, you may not have the environment necessary to test the application on your development machine, or you might require modifications from another developer before thorough testing can take place, or in some cases it just might not be your job to do thorough testing before you commit. If the committed code is destined for a QA testing team, they may be the ones doing the thorough testing. You also may sometimes make changes to the source that are so trivial that there is little reason to actually test. In most cases, you should test anyway, but if testing is hard and the change is truly trivial, it may be acceptable.

- Always update and test before committing. If you have been working on a modification for a while, and are finally ready for a commit, it is possible (probable, even) that other developers have committed their own modifications in the meantime. So, even if you have thoroughly tested your modifications in your own working copy, it is important to do an update of all the project components that may be affected by your change and test against the updated version.

- Use a diff to check exactly what will be committed. It's easy to forget to remove one-off debugging code, or to make a minor change that should be committed as a separate revision and then forget you made it. By actually looking at the changes you will be committing before you run the actual commit, you can make a sanity check to make sure you're committing what you think you're committing. To perform the diff, run `svn diff` with no options on the working copy directory (or file) that will be committed.

- Try to commit only one distinct modification per commit. When you commit a modification to the repository, it should be a single atomic modification. That way, it is easy to roll back just that modification if you need to at a later point. For instance, if you modify a function that adds up a series of numbers, and at the same time add in a dialog box for confirming database modifications, you shouldn't commit both to the same revision. If at all possible, commit one modification and then the other (which is easy if they're in completely different files—just commit one set of files and then the other). The best way to avoid accidentally committing two modifications, though, is to commit frequently.

- Don't commit incomplete changes on a common branch. There is wisdom in committing atomic modifications, but be careful with committing modifications that are too small. If you commit incomplete features, you may find that rolling back those changes is more difficult (because there are more revisions involved). You will also likely find that commits that are too small will tend to break the branch, because they are not complete features in and of themselves. If you are going to be making a lot of changes that would be well-served by multiple commits, but aren't logically multiple feature modifications, you may be well-served by creating a branch for making those changes. That way, you can do a lot of little commits, and then combine them all into a single merge that puts those changes into the main trunk (or another branch) in a single step.

12.3   Log Data

It's easy to write bad log messages. I've seen it done countless times (and, I must admit, have done it a few times myself). After long hours of coding, it's easy to top it off with "Added a bunch of stuff," "Fixed all the compile errors," or even "Fixed an off-by-one error." It is so easy, in fact, that despite all levels of experience or good intentions, you're almost certain to get a few similar log messages in your repository at some point. You'll rue their entry, though, the day you need to search out the exact point where a feature was added or a bug was fixed. With poor log messages, you find yourself frantically searching through diffs and guessing dates in order to pinpoint an exact revision amidst a sea of commits, instead of being able to do a quick search through the log messages.

In general, the more detailed your log messages, the more useful they'll be in the future. As a rule of thumb, every log message should be detailed enough that you would want to decipher exactly what changed for the project in that revision 10 years from now. By that point, you will have completely forgotten all context for the commit, and will not likely remember any information that is left out of the log. One way to help jog your memory and ensure that you don't forget to include a description of every modification in the log is to use `svn diff` to review the changes made before performing the commit.

The best way to ensure good log messages from everyone involved in a project is to develop a clear set of policies for what should (and should not) go into a log message. If the expectations for log messages are clear, it is much harder for individual developers to slack off and say, "This revision doesn't matter. I'll just dash off a quick message and move on to something else." Additionally, if you have a clear format for log messages, searching through them to find a particular piece of information will be much easier. In some cases, you may even find that rigid log formats help with scripts that parse the logs to add automated functionality.

12.3.1   Policies for Informative Logs

The most important consideration for log messages is to make them informative. Log messages that don't tell you anything are like comments in code that just restate the obvious — useless. Good log messages inform the reader as to what the revision adds to the project and why the revision was needed. To help you generate an overall policy that draws useful log messages from your project's developers, here are some of the specific policies that you should consider. If developers have what is essentially a checklist of points to include in their logs, useful log messages will quickly become second nature.

- State the specific issue solved by this revision. Explain, in as much detail as you need, exactly what functionality has been added to the project or what bug has been fixed. If the revision is in response to an issue in an issue-tracking system, you should reference the issue with an issue number or URL (or other reference, as appropriate). If there are any other external documents that describe the issue, you should also make reference to them, with enough information for a later developer to find the appropriate documentation.

- Briefly explain why the issue needed solving. With the exception of Easter eggs, features are rarely added to a project for no reason. You should include a brief description of why a change was made in your log messages. This is especially important for future reference. Two or three years down the road, some other developer may be searching through the log messages, trying to fix a bug or add a new feature, and if he doesn't know why your revision was put in, he may accidentally remove it without fully understanding the consequences.

- List any known side effects. If you know of any side effects caused by your revision, you should make sure they are explicitly enumerated, because they will likely not be obvious to the next person to work around the revision. As with the description of why, this helps avoid many long hours of debugging obscure changes far (or not so far) in the future. Listing known side effects is also important for other developers currently working on the project, so that they know what they can expect from updating their working copy to include your revision.

- List any interface changes. Knowing what changed in the interface is important for other developers working concurrently on the project, by helping to inform them of potential changes that need to be made to the sections of the project that they are responsible for. They can also act as an important tool for future developers tracking the project's history. By being able to clearly see points where interfaces changed, it is also easier for developers to identify modifications that need to be made to code that is reused from older revisions.

- Explain what, if anything, was removed. If the revision removes any functionality from the project, it is important to explicitly list it. Even if the functionality removed seems minor and inconsequential to the rest of the project, other parts of the project may depend on it. If that dependent functionality breaks as a result of the revision, it will be much easier for the developers responsible for fixing it to find the problem if they are able to clearly see that something was removed when they look at the logs.

- Reference other relevant revisions or tags. For instance, if the revision you are committing builds on a previous revision, you should mention that revision and how they are related. This makes it easier for future developers to trace the history of the project when they are making a modification. It is easy for the many interdependencies in a project to get lost after a relatively short period of time (especially if the original developers leave), so this little bit of extra information can greatly reduce the risks of future modifications to the project.

- Include any Subversion commands that are part of the revision. When you perform an `svn merge`, Subversion doesn't explicitly record everything that went into the merge. Similarly, `svn copy` and `svn move` can be difficult to trace effectively. You can make these commands much easier to track by explicitly referencing their use in your log messages. This is especially important for merges, because future merges can end up working incorrectly if you don't know the merge history of the directories involved.

- Don't be afraid of humor in log messages. As long as humorous log messages are not offensive, and don't detract from the information being conveyed, developers should be encouraged to occasionally have fun with log entries. Not only does this give developers a good outlet for their creativity, but it helps to encourage developers to write good log messages (and gives them an incentive to pay attention to the log messages that others write).

12.3.2   Parseable Log Messages

Creating automated tools that can make use of log messages is very powerful. The problem is making the tool understand what the log messages are saying. If log messages are completely free-form, this can be impossible to do with any accuracy. It can also be difficult to use hook scripts to validate log messages that don't contain any predefined structure. Therefore, if you want to use scripts that look at your log messages, you will be well-served to develop a log message structure that every log message should conform to.

- Use section tags to explicitly partition the log message. If you have specific points that you want made in your log messages (such as purpose, description, and an issue tracker reference), it may be useful to begin each point with a well-known tag. For example, you might format your log messages like the following example.

```
ISSUE:       1758
PURPOSE:     Fixes the bug that was causing a crash when the
             program was closed.
DESCRIPTION: Removes an incorrect reference in the Window class
             destructor that was accessing m_mybutton after it was
             destroyed.
```

This way, you can easily search for the revision where issue #1758 was fixed, or check the log message on commit to ensure that the purpose and description have been filled in.

- Define strict formats for external references. Whenever a log message references an external source, such as an issue-tracking system or design document, you should have a well-defined format for making that reference. For instance, you could reference an issue-tracking system with a format such as [ISSUE:##]. In the following log message, the explicit reference would allow a script to find the issue referenced.

```
Fully implemented the requirements in [ISSUE:453].
```

- If a log message references changes to an interface in the project, you should be able to parse that information in a script to identify exactly which interfaces were changed. That way, you could write a script that would automatically identify interface changes and send warnings to the appropriate developers, or even perform an analysis on the project and identify places where modifications need to be made. The following interface change section from a log file shows how you might structure those changes.

```
INTERFACE_CHANGES:
ADDED int Button::on_clicked(int btn) TO button.h
CHANGED void Button::on_mouseover(void) IN button.h TO int Button ¬
  ::on_mouseover(void)
REMOVED void Button::destroy(void) FROM button.h
```

- Define a standard set of terms and keywords for your project. Developers should use explicitly defined common terminology when talking about common project details. That way, searching becomes a more useful tool for examining the project's history. Additionally, scripts can be written that discern meaning from log messages by looking for certain terms and phrases.

12.3.3   What Not to Include

Log messages should be detailed, but there is such a thing as too much information in the logs. If each log message is a novel unto itself, no one will be able to glean anything useful from a quick read-through. Therefore, to help keep things short without sacrificing utility, there are some things you *shouldn't* include in your log messages.

- Don't use source code from the revision in your log messages. If developers need to see the actual source code changes, they can use svn diff to obtain that information. If you need to reference the actual code that was modified, use references to the source code itself (don't use line numbers, as those will quickly end up out of date).

- Don't list the files that were changed. Subversion already gives you the ability to see what files have changed by using the svn log -verbose command, so this information is redundant.

- Avoid going into too much detail for things described elsewhere. In general, it is better to give a brief description of what you are referencing, and let the user go to the referenced material if she needs more detail.

12.4 Project Builds

Integration of work is an important aspect of any software development process. With multiple developers working on the same project, it is important to frequently integrate everyone's work, build the entire project, and test that all of the changes work together. Linking the version control system into this process is vital, because the VCS is generally one of the primary tools for performing the integration of work.

With Subversion, there are a couple of different approaches that you can take toward accommodating project build integration, which I will discuss in a little while. When setting up project builds, though, you also need to take into consideration how you will run your build process (automated or manual), and how individual bits of the build will be configured.

12.4.1 Configuration

Project builds generally require some sort of build configuration file, such as a makefile for a version of the classic UNIX Make program, a `build.xml` configuration for that Java-based Ant build system, or a Visual Studio `.dsp` file. Often, with these build configurations, you have a base configuration file that needs to be used by everyone who is working on the project; however, each developer also often needs to make local modifications that shouldn't be fed back to the version stored on the repository.

The naïve approach to local build configurations is often to commit the base configuration file to the repository, and then have individual developers modify the file in their working copy to meet their needs. This works fine until someone accidentally commits their local changes to the repository (better not run `svn commit` with no options). Furthermore, if a developer needs to commit some of his local changes to the base version in the repository, but not others, it can be a major pain to do.

A better approach to local build configuration files is to commit the base configuration file as a template, under a different name. Then, add an `svn:ignore` property entry to force Subversion to ignore the real configuration file. When developers check out a working copy of the project, they can then copy the template to create a new configuration file that can be edited locally. So, for example, if you have a project that is built using GNU Make, with a makefile named `Makefile`, you would create a makefile template named `Makefile.tmpl`, which would be added to the repository. When you check out a working copy of the repository, you would then copy `Makefile.tmpl` to `Makefile` and make any necessary local changes.

Even better still is to have two configuration files (if your build system supports this). In one, you place the bulk of your base build configuration and commit it as-is. It then includes a second build configuration that holds values likely to change from one local installation to another. For that file, you commit a template instead of the actual file, and use svn:ignore as I mentioned previously. The advantage of doing things this way is that it allows changes to be made to the base build configuration, without requiring you to hand-merge those changes in each working copy to the local build configuration every time a change is made to the base.

12.4.2   Daily Builds

Traditionally, a big part of most software development processes has been the daily build of the entire project, which integrates everything and allows the full project to be tested, either with automated tools or by a QA testing team. Recently, as the popularity of rapid development techniques grows (as well as the available computing power), daily builds are more frequently becoming multiple builds per day. If you are going to be performing frequent full-project builds like this (especially if your project is large), it is important for you to know how to best accommodate the daily build (I will refer to them as daily builds, even if you perform them more frequently than once per day) in your Subversion repository.

There are two major overall policies for handling your build process. You can either have a manual build, with a build engineer (which may be a regular developer doing double-duty or a full-time job for large projects), or you can have an automated build system that runs the build, and possibly a test suite, without any regular human interaction.

From a Subversion perspective, manual daily builds are the easiest to accommodate. The build engineer simply needs to have his own working copy of the project's main development branch, which he can update before every build. For more information on the process of getting each developer's work integrated into the development branch in preparation for the daily build, see Section 12.4.3, "Integration."

Manual daily builds may be the easiest to prepare your Subversion repository for, but in the real world, there are a lot of compelling reasons to use automated daily builds instead, such as reliability, cost, and speed. If the build is going to be run automatically, though, you need to put a little more thought into how the automated build will interact with Subversion.

A simple approach to automated builds is to have a script that runs at a set interval (daily, hourly, and so on) to execute the build. When the script runs, it should create a tag for the build, switch the automated tests working copy to the new tag, and then run the build system against the newly created tag. Additionally, you might want to have a test suite run (although that may be built into the build system), and add notification about the build's results, which could be e-mailed, added to a Web site, or included in an RSS feed.

Here is a simple example of a script that you might have run your automated build. It uses the svn commands to interact with the repository, and uses make to run a build and a test suite. To set it up for a daily build, you could configure cron to run it every night and report the results to a build engineer, or post them to a Web site.

```
#!/bin/sh
# run_daily_build.sh

# Get the repository working copy path from the script's arguments
WORKING_COPY=${1}
```

```
# Get the URL of the main branch, and the URL of the tags directory
TRUNK_BRANCH=${2}
TAGS_DIR=${3}

# Check to make sure the working copy exists.
# If it doesn't exist, exit with an error message.
if [ ! -f "${WORKING_COPY}" ]; then echo "No working copy\n"; fi

# Change directories to the working copy
cd "${WORKING_COPY}"

# Update the working copy
# Redirect the results into a status file
svn update . > build_results.txt

# Get the current revision
REV=` svn info . | grep "^Revision: " | cut -c 11-`

# Execute the build and test suite
make && make testsuite

# Make a daily build tag of the build
svn copy -m "Tagged daily build" -r ${REV} ${TRUNK_BRANCH} ${TAGS_DIR}/ ¬
  build-` date "+%m%d%Y"`
```

CruiseControl

Rather than rolling your own scripts for doing automatic scheduled builds, you can make use of a system designed for doing automatic scheduled builds. The CruiseControl system (cruisecontrol.sourceforge.net) is a framework that checks your Subversion repository on a configurable schedule to see if any changes have been committed. If they have been committed, it downloads the changes, builds your system, and runs all of your unit tests. If you do any sort of rapid development, this can be a huge timesaver. It is a Java-based system, and uses Ant for its project builds, which makes it specifically suited for development of Java-based projects, but you should be able to make it build other projects (possibly with a bit less integration) if you are so inclined.

To set up CruiseControl to build your project, you first need to install CruiseControl on your build system, by following the instructions for CruiseControl installation that can be found on the project's Web site or in the CruiseControl distribution. Then, to set up CruiseControl to talk to your Subversion repository, there are a few things you need to configure in the config.xml file for CruiseControl.

The first elements to add are two `<plugin>` elements to load the two Subversion plug-ins.

```
<plugin name="svnbooststrapper" classname="net.sourceforge. ¬
  cruisecontrol.bootstrappers.SVNBootstrapper"/>
<plugin name="svn" classname="net.sourceforge.cruisecontrol. ¬
  sourcecontrol.SVN"/>
```

Then, you need to add the `<svn>` element to the `<modificationset>` element.

```
<modificationset>
    <svn localWorkingCopy="svnrepos/trunk"
        repositoryLocation="https://myserver.com/svnrepos"
        username="bill"
        password="mypass"/>
</modificationset>
```

Also, in your Ant build, you need to add an `<exec>` element to make Ant update the Subversion repository.

```
<exec executable="svn">
    <arg line="up">
</exec>
```

12.4.3   Integration

If you are doing a daily build of your full project, it is important for you to have the project's developers integrate their work into a single development branch. The biggest question, though, is when this should happen. A developer making a single minor change to the project is unlikely to cause major integration problems, but a developer working on a more in-depth feature will likely be making numerous intermediate commits, which may temporarily break the project in relation to other developers. Avoiding broken builds is important for obvious reasons, which means that you need to put some thought into how you are arranging your Subversion repository to accommodate both the work flow of individual developers and the overall integration problem for full-project daily builds.

Continuous Integration

One approach to integration is to have a policy whereby every developer works on the main development branch, committing their changes as they go. This has the advantage that there are no worries about merges, and everyone stays very up-to-date with the current state of the project. It is also the easiest for people to understand, and lends itself to small to medium-sized projects that are undergoing small incremental development. The downside, however, is that because all commits go onto the same branch everyone else is working on, every commit needs to integrate perfectly with the rest of the project or it breaks the build. Although this encourages careful committing and conservative changes, it also discourages frequent commits and may lead to larger commits that don't encapsulate a single change to the project.

Task Integration

An alternate approach to integration is to use task branches. With this integration policy approach, each developer does all of her nontrivial project development (more than a couple of lines of code) on a branch created for that specific task, where she can freely commit small changes without fear of breaking the project build. Then, as soon as an individual task is complete, the task branch can be merged into the main development branch for inclusion in the full project's daily build.

The biggest downside to this approach is its complexity. Each developer needs to have a working understanding of Subversion branches and merges, along with the discipline to use the task branches properly. It also splits the project's history off into a large number of branches, which can make finding a specific change more difficult.

On the positive side, task branches encourage frequent small commits, while maintaining the integrity of the main project build. They also keep the history of the project's main branch clean, because small commits get aggregated into a single merge log message for each task. These advantages make task integration a good choice for large, complex projects with a large number of developers, as well as for projects that use fewer daily builds with automatic unit testing. If the integrated build is only built and tested a few times a day or less, task integration tends to make it easier to find and repair broken builds. On the other hand, if you are doing very frequent builds with continuous testing, task branches may get in the way for all but the most complex of tasks.

12.5 Testing and Quality Assurance

Testing is another major component of any software development process, and any successful project has some sort of policy in place for assuring that a sufficient amount of testing is done. Although most of the actual testing is beyond the purview of Subversion, a good set of policies for project organization within the repository can lend strong support to your quality assurance process.

Some of the policies that I discuss in this section were already touched upon in the previous sections of the chapter, but here they are brought together into a coherent structure. I note this not to assure you that I didn't forget that I already mentioned them, but rather to stress the total interdependency of the various policies that make up a total software development process. The policies that you ultimately make a part of your strategy for using Subversion in your software development process are not a set of unrelated policies tacked together. Instead, your interaction with Subversion should be considered for how it fits into the whole of your software development process.

12.5.1 The Parts of Testing

There are a number of different types of testing that make up the full gamut of testing that a project undergoes during its development. Not every project uses all of the testing methods that I talk about in this section, but I find it unlikely that any successful project has ever avoided all of these methods (as much as some have tried). For each of these different areas of testing, I will talk about what they are, and what sort of policies you might adopt to integrate Subversion into the process.

Individual Developer Testing

In most cases, developers do their own personal testing of the code that they write, before integrating it with the main public development branch of a project. Even in projects where it is difficult or impossible for an individual developer to personally test her code against the full project before committing, most developers will do some sort of private testing to ensure to the best of their ability that the code does what it is supposed to do. Often, this involves local test harnesses or throwaway unit tests.

For the most part, Subversion doesn't play a particularly big role in individual developer testing. Most such testing is done on the developer's personal workstation, in her working copy, without anything getting committed to the repository until the testing is finished. However, there are a few policies that you can use to support individual developer testing.

- Give developers a place to version their personal test code. When developers write local test code, it often consists of throwaway tests that either get erased or tossed in a random directory on the developer's hard drive after they've been used, or they continue to sit in the working copy as unversioned files. If developers have a place in the Subversion repository dedicated to storing those test programs, they will be more likely to keep them around and reuse them in the future.

- Use task branches for developer work. By using task branches, the individual developer's work is segregated from the rest of the project until it's tested and ready to be merged back into the main branch. That makes it much easier for the developer to perform incremental local testing on the code as it's written, without interfering with the rest of the project. This is especially useful if the developer can't do local testing against the full project.

- Allow developers to create private branches, for testing multiple potential solutions to a problem. In the case of most nontrivial development tasks, there are many different ways that a problem can be solved, and it's not always clear to the developer what the best method is. If you allow the developer to make private branches for testing different potential solutions, it is easy to write two versions of the solution and then run tests that compare the two to see which is better.

Automated Unit and Regression Testing

Automated tests are a big part of many software development processes. They generally make up a comprehensive test suite that exercises a project in order to make sure it's doing what the specification says it should, and as changes are made to the project, the test suite also helps to ensure that previously working components of the project continue to work. How often these tests are run depends on an individual project (and is often dependent on how long the tests take to run). When integrating your automated testing process into Subversion, the biggest questions to answer are "Which branches will the automated tests be run on?" and "What role, if any, will Subversion play in triggering those tests?"

One way to trigger automated tests is to have them run whenever someone commits something to the repository, or even to a specific branch. The commit can trigger a hook script that runs the test suite and reports any errors to the author of the commit and any-one else appropriate. This could work well as a policy if you have a main development branch and use task branches for feature development. Whenever a feature is deemed com-plete enough for the main branch, the task branch can be merged in and committed. The automated test suite could then run regression tests on the full main branch to make sure everything still works. Or, if you want an extra layer of redundancy, you could have an in-termediary branch. When a task branch is finished, it can be merged into the testing branch. If all of the regression tests pass, the testing branch could then be merged (or copied) over to the main development branch.

The QA Team

Some projects (especially large ones) make use of a dedicated quality assurance team whose sole job is to rigorously test the work of the project's developers. As I have touched on previously at several points, there is a lot that you can do organizationally with your repository to support the interaction between a development team and a testing team. The policies that you set in regard to support for testing in your Subversion repository not only can support your QA process, they can help to shape it.

One of the areas where you will find a wide range of policy choices for supporting QA is in the use of a branching/merging structure that supports the transfer of data from developers to testers in an organized manner. I talked previously about what there is to know on this subject. If you would like to review my thoughts on the subject, you can reread Section 12.1, "Effective Branching and Tagging."

Another place where you can use Subversion to support your QA testing process is through the use of properties. For example, you could set a property, `qa:tested`, to label the current testing state of a file or directory. Or, you could use a property to allow the tester to "sign off" on a section of code. You could even set a property to a digitally signed md5 sum of the repository revision on which the tester is signing off, if there are safety critical issues for which someone is required to take legal responsibility.[1]

Beta Testing

Beta testing is the point in a project's life cycle when it is sent out to real users to allow them to stress test the product under real (or at least semi-real) working conditions. In many ways, beta versions are handled just like a final release. Generally, unless it is an open source project, the release is binary only, and the beta testers have no knowledge of the inner workings of the application, or even any knowledge of programming. However, since it is still not a final release of the project, you are usually expecting a large number of bug reports to come back as a part of the beta test process. How these bug reports are supplied to you is, of course, outside the purview of Subversion, but it can be helpful for you to have some policies for what you do to the repository in response to the bug reports.

When you release a beta, you will almost certainly want to create a tag of the revision of the project that made up the beta release. That tag can then be used as a basis for

---

1.   I am not a lawyer, and make no claim as to how well this would stand up legally. If you are doing something critical to require that level of liability, I strongly suggest speaking with a real attorney.

creating branches dedicated to fixing issues raised in bug reports. You can either create task branches for each reported bug or you can create a single beta branch for fixing the bugs and then have each individual developer create branches as he sees fit.

Shipping the Final Product

It may seem a little counterintuitive to have a section on shipping the final product in a section on testing the project during development, but the fact is that shipping the product is really nothing more than another step in the product's development path. Except in very rare cases, no product ships without flaws, and flaws mean that bug reports will continue to come in even after the product is in full release. To that extent, a full product release is really no different from a beta release in the eyes of Subversion, and the policies you set in place for handling beta tests are likely the same policies that you will want to have in place for maintaining the full release of the project.

12.6   Communication

It is easy to think that Subversion is an alternative to good communication. Because it is flexible, and supportive of distributed concurrent development, it can seem at first that there is little need to discuss a project with your co-developers at the same level of detail required with no version control in place (or even a less flexible version control system). After all, you can always move things around, roll back to a previous revision, or create a new branch.

Now is the part where I'm supposed to tell you that's all wrong. That communication is just as vital with Subversion as without, and you should communicate with Subversion at exactly the same level, and in exactly the same manner, as if it weren't there. The problem is that I wouldn't be telling you the truth if I did that. Subversion doesn't require you to communicate at exactly the same level as without. It does provide you with a flexible versioning tool that allows you to drop much of the communication that was necessary in a pre-Subversion environment. In fact, a small project could probably be worked on by a group of reasonably competent developers with no communication outside of the Subversion repository, except for a brief end-project goal agreed upon prior to starting the project.

Wait, though. Before the project managers of the world band against me, or my old software engineering professor hunts me down and takes back my degree, I am not saying that you don't need to communicate if you are using Subversion. In fact, I believe that good, effective communication is vital to any software development project. What is not needed with Subversion, however, is to ignore the tool and communicate as if it didn't exist. Instead, you need to integrate Subversion into your communications policies.

12.6.1   Communicating through Subversion

Subversion is, in essence, a communications tool. At its core, it communicates the history of a software development project, of course, but it can also be used to communicate other more immediate bits of information from one developer to another. By setting policies to shape Subversion's use as a communications tool, you allow the developers working on the project to obtain the greatest possible gain in efficiency from using Subversion.

Log Messages

Good log messages are vital for good intraproject communications. As I talked about in Section 12.3.1, "Policies for Informative Logs," it is important to set policies that ensure informative log messages. Additionally, if you do regular reviews of code that has been committed to the repository, you should also have a policy of review for the logs that describe the committed changes. After a week, you will probably still be able to remember what was placed in a revision, and log messages can be edited if need be. In six months, though, a mildly uninformative log message can become incomprehensible.

Properties

Make use of properties as a communications tool. So far, I have mostly discussed properties in terms of how you can use them in automation of tasks, but they can also be an effective tool for communicating information to other developers. Log messages are good for describing meta-information about a particular revision. Properties should be used to describe meta-information about the current state of a file or directory, in order to communicate that information to other developers (and yourself, six months from now).

Some of the items of information that you might want to store as properties so they can be efficiently communicated to others include

- Testing status of the file, along with a list of known issues (or references to them in an issue-tracking system)

- Design document for the file (either the actual document or a reference to allow others to find the document)

- A TODO list for the file

- The names of the reviewers who have looked at the file, along with the date and time of the reviews

- Licensing or ownership information (especially if that information varies from file to file)

Branches and Tags

Branches and tags may not seem like an obvious means for communicating information to other developers, but if used correctly, they can be useful. Whenever you create a branch or tag, that branch or tag's existence can convey information to other developers—if there is a clear policy in place for defining the circumstances for creating branches/tags, along with policy that describes their naming and organization. For example, if you use task branches, you can use the branch's location to indicate status. The project manager (or QA tester) can create task branches when scheduling the task, and place it in a `/tasks/unassigned/`

directory. Then, when the task is assigned and a developer begins work, the task can be moved to `/tasks/in_progress/`. The task branches could even be cross-referenced to an issue-tracking system by using a naming scheme that includes the issue number, or by storing an issue reference in a property.

12.6.2   Communicating about Subversion

Equally important to using Subversion to communicate is making sure that you communicate sufficiently *about* Subversion. When working on a software development project, it is extremely important to make sure other developers know what is going on. When you start work on a long task or create a branch, let everyone working on the project know. That way, you can avoid wasted and redundant work. You can also gain the benefit of others spotting problems before they occur. If no one knows until after the fact what you are doing, you are relying entirely on yourself to recognize potential problems, and multiple sets of eyes are always better than one.

Communication always works more smoothly if you set out clear policies for what should be communicated, and how it should be communicated (e.g., e-mail, instant message, or weekly meetings). For instance, you should have policies on communication of the following Subversion-related activities.

- A developer begins work on a particular task, regardless of whether it has been explicitly scheduled.

- A branch or tag needs to be created for a purpose other than those normally used.

- There is a need to perform a nontrivial merge in a branch used by other developers.

- A revision is (accidentally) committed that breaks previously working areas of the project.

- A bug is found in a public branch of the project.

- There is any restructuring of the repository, such as the renaming of branches or creation/deletion of publicly used directories.

12.7   Enforcing Policies

In a perfect world, there is no need to enforce policies, because every developer would follow every policy as close to the letter as prudent, but no closer. Of course, we don't live in a perfect world, and even the best developers fail to follow policy occasionally. There are, of course, many established methods for enforcing policies, such as banning or firing (depending on the nature of the project), as well as a number of lesser punishments. I won't go into any of those methods in any detail here. Their use is well beyond the scope of this book. However, there are some ways in which you can use Subversion (along with some external scripts) to self-enforce some of these policies to varying degrees.

- Use `pre-commit` hook scripts to parse log files and ensure that all of the necessary information has been entered.

- Similarly, use `pre-commit` hook scripts to check for the existence of properties, and ensure that they contain valid values.

- Set up read/write permissions to ensure that branches and tags are created by the right people, and that tags are not modified.

- Use properties to indicate the validity of actions. For instance, if QA testers sign off on a file or directory by setting a value in a property, you can use a `pre-commit` hook script to check for the sign-off before allowing tester branches to be merged into the main development branch.

12.8 Summary

In this chapter, you learned about setting a variety of policies for a software development project preparing to use Subversion, including policies for branching/tagging, committing of changes, log messages, project builds, and quality assurance. In addition to learning about the potential policy areas, you saw a number of examples for different ways to implement policies, depending on the type of project. At the end, you read short discussions on ensuring that the project is supported by good communication, as well as some ways that you might enforce policies within Subversion.

Chapter 13

Integrating SVN with the Development Process

Subversion is only one tool in the software development process, and as such it works best when integrated with the rest of the software development process. In this chapter, I will talk about a number of other aspects of software development, and how Subversion can best help support them.

13.1 SVN in Different Developers' Workflows

To start, let's take a look at the developer's daily workflow, and how Subversion fits into that process. Of course, every developer's workflow is different, and depends largely on a combination of each developer's work habits and the work environment; however, there are plenty of commonalities that we can examine, and those commonalities tend to fall into different developer types. Of course, no individual developer fits a stereotype, but for the sake of illustration, I've broken the discussion down into six archetypal developers. For each one, I've taken a look at how Subversion might fit into that developer's workflow (of course, project policies could radically alter each archetype's workflow).

13.1.1 The Methodical Programmer

The methodical programmer is the diligent developer who sits at his desk quietly and steadily churns out line after line of clean, well-documented code. In a typical day, he may come in to the office, get a cup of coffee, then sit down at his desk and do an `svn update`. After checking his e-mail, he will see what was updated in his working copy and test any changes to make sure they didn't affect anything he was working on.

After the methodical programmer is up to speed with the changes, and certain that everything is working properly, he will get a list of tasks for the day and begin working his way through them. For each task, he will do the following.

1. Make a branch in his own private branches directory, for implementing the task.

2. Use `svn switch` to switch the appropriate sections of his working copy of `/trunk` over to that branch.

3. Implement the task, testing and committing after each distinct, testable change.

4. When the task is tested and complete, he will use `svn switch` to go back to the trunk, followed by an `svn merge`.

5. With the task merged into the trunk, he will do an `svn update` and thoroughly test the feature with any new changes.

6. The task now complete, he will commit with a detailed log message and move on to the next task on his list.

The methodical programmer is also very exacting with all of his work, and everything is done in small chunks with detailed documentation (comments, logs, and so on) at every step of the way. By using small, distinct changes for each commit, he allows himself to take maximum advantage of Subversion's merge system. If a change ever needs to be removed, he will also find merge useful, because his detailed documentation allows him to pinpoint exactly which revisions contain the change (and because each revision is a single change, `svn merge` can be used).

At the end of the day, the methodical programmer makes sure that all of his work has been committed to the repository, and uses `svn info` to make sure that every part of the working copy has been switched back to the trunk (wouldn't want to forget and accidentally commit work to the wrong place, or miss an important update). Then, he makes a list of the tasks that need to be completed the next day, before logging everything off and packing up for the day.

13.1.2 The Collaborator

The collaborator works in a team environment and shares her work frequently with others as she goes along. When she gets into work in the mornings, she first spends a few minutes chatting with her coworkers while she sips her morning latte, to catch up on what everyone else is working on. Then, she gets together with her pair-programming partner, and they discuss the day's tasks.

With a rough plan for the day put together, the collaborator and her programming partner begin implementing the days tasks. Individual tasks tend to flow together in a much more fluid manner than the rigid separation of tasks that the methodical programmer used, and branches are less commonly used. In general, the collaborator's workflow for tasks runs something like this:

1. She updates frequently to get the latest changes from the other developers on the project, discusses those changes with them over e-mail or instant messaging (or occasionally by shouting across the room) if any clarification is necessary, and tests her changes thoroughly with any new updates when they occur.

2. She and her programming partner implement tasks in their working copy, and commit frequently, as new bits of features are tested. For experimental changes, she may create a branch to avoid breaking the project build for other developers.

3. When one task is complete, she moves on to the next, but this process tends to be somewhat fluid, with one task flowing into the next. There often are no clear breaks between broad tasks.

The collaborator also makes heavy use of tools that integrate her work with that of her coworkers. For instance, she is very "at home" in an environment where a site such as Trac (Section 13.3.2, "Automating Interaction with Issue Tracking") has been implemented. When she has access to Trac, she makes heavy use of it to document all of her work for others. She also keeps running RSS feeds of commits to each project or project component that she is interested in displayed on her secondary display at all times. Any new designs or potential changes to the structure of the application under development are drawn up and described using the Trac wiki, or some other collaborative tool that allows her ideas to be viewed and commented on by her coworkers.

The best way to accommodate the collaborator is to ensure that she has access to the best collaborative development tools that you can provide. Getting her to use them isn't a problem. Instead, she spends her time proselytizing the tool's uses to her coworkers. The collaborator wants to work with others. She wants to communicate what she's doing to everyone else, but more importantly, she wants to understand the work that is being done on the rest of the project. She isn't productive if she cannot see what is going on with other aspects of the project. If she doesn't have that information, she seeks it out, possibly disturbing the productivity of others if she doesn't have ready access to the information she wants. By introducing policies that help ensure that information about the project is available at all times, you allow the collaborator to get information whenever it is useful, without interrupting her coworkers unnecessarily and without needing to wait unproductively for information to be delivered.

13.1.3 The Lone Hacker

The lone hacker is a cowboy who codes rapidly, and without regard for a regimented development process. He keeps odd hours, and tends not to communicate with other developers more than necessary. The results of his work are technically exemplary, but can be lacking in documentation and adherence to prescribed style. To him, Subversion is a minor part of the software development process, and exists mostly as a tool for adding changes to the project in large blocks. He is unlikely to make a lot of use of Subversion's advanced features, and mostly uses `svn update` and `svn commit`, with the occasional `svn status`.

The lone hacker can (and does) often make excellent contributions to the project itself, but can wreak havoc on carefully designed development processes. He comes in late, and goes home late—really late. When he sits down at his computer to work, he picks a task from his to-do list (which is often at least partially in his head) and dives right in. As far as he is concerned, tasks are easiest to complete in large chunks, so that's how he does them. Often, he forgets to commit after individual tasks. Frequently, he only makes a single commit at the end of the day—with log messages that are cryptic and only marginally useful to all but himself.

The best way to handle a lone hacker depends a lot on the environment he is working in. If his contribution is valuable, and the development process allows it, you may be best served by giving him the freedom to be creative and productive. By using task branches and/or `pre-commit` hook scripts that validate commits against policies, you may be able to gently conform his process to a more collaborative effort, without making him feel as if his creative freedom has been stifled. If the overall development process is more strict, the strictness of automated checks can be increased accordingly. Automation of mundane policy tasks can also serve to help constrain a lone hacker. For example, if he has to create his own task branches, he may be inclined to forget and commit directly to the trunk or combine multiple tasks into one branch. On the other hand, if the task branches are automatically created when a task is assigned to a developer, he may be more inclined to use them properly.

13.1.4   The Guru

The guru has been around the block several times, and has all the tricks up her sleeve. She draws on her experience to both develop and help others less experienced. Her workflow often floats between personal implementation of tasks and offering aid to others. As such, she frequently makes use of `svn switch`, `svn cat`, and `svn diff` to view and test other's work, which is usually discussed over e-mail or instant messaging. Additionally, she often has multiple working copies that have different revisions or sections of the repository checked out.

The most valuable resource a guru provides is her knowledge. That knowledge, applied to the project at hand, can be invaluable. However, by imparting that knowledge on others in the project, the value of her knowledge is increased ten-fold. Therefore, it is important that the Subversion repository be set up in such a way as to maximize her ability to transfer knowledge.

- Provide Web-based repository browsing, to make it easy for the guru to check out other developers' source in order to comment or answer questions. The repository browsing features of Apache/WebDAV may be sufficient, but a Web frontend such as WebSVN, which allows for additional features such as examination of previous revisions and graphical diffs between files, is a much better choice.

- Define properties that can be used for providing comment on files in the repository. If a developer seeks the guru's advice on a problem, the guru may not be in a position to provide her help at that particular moment in time (she may also not be in the same geographical location as the developer seeking help). It would, of course, be possible for her to provide her response via an external route, such as e-mail or instant messaging; however, if she can attach the comments to a property associated with the relevant file, it will never be lost, and can be easily retrieved in the proper context.

- Sometimes, it is useful for the guru to make actual modifications to code in the repository in order to properly illustrate an answer to a question from another developer. It isn't usually appropriate for the guru's changes to be immediately committed to the main trunk of the repository though, as she isn't the person responsible for that section of code and may not always have the opportunity to know all of the consequences of her change. In these cases, it can be useful to provide every developer with areas where she can create private branches. Then, the guru can create a branch and make the changes there, leaving it up to the original developer to merge those changes back into the main development trunk as appropriate.

13.1.5 The Rookie

The rookie is just starting out as a developer, and hasn't developed a personal workflow process yet. He is prone to experimentation and tends to make a lot of mistakes from lack of experience. In addition to routinely seeking out advice from the guru, he needs to make frequent use of `svn help`, as well as any policy documentation specific to the project (a good reason to develop such documentation).

Automation can be a great aid to the rookie programmer. Like the lone hacker, he is prone to forgetting small details and has a tendency to incorrectly follow policy procedures (not because of a cavalier attitude, but due to a lack of experience). In addition to safeguards put in place to automatically check for adherence to policies, custom tools that automate common tasks can be very useful, as can a good GUI-based Subversion client. It may also be a good idea to perform frequent peer review sessions that look at his use of Subversion and other tools in addition to the actual code he is writing. It is much easier to change a log message a week after the commit than it is six months after the commit, when no one remembers why the changes were made.

13.1.6 The Hobbyist Programmer

The hobbyist programmer is not developing as a nine-to-five career, but rather as an evening hobby. That means that she is much more interested in fun than she is in following a complex procedure designed to improve the manageability or efficiency of a project. This doesn't mean that she is an amateur, just that her priorities are likely to be different than those of a professional developer. She is unlikely to be a Subversion guru, nor is she likely to have much desire to become one. In most cases, many (if not most) of the developers involved with any given open source project fit this archetype, which means that most open source projects will needs to accommodate her development efforts. There are several approaches that can work.

- Keep the process simple. Make sure most development is done on a single branch, and don't use complex processes that involve specially formatted log messages or custom properties. Provide clear documentation for what should be in a commit log, as well as any other (simple) policies for committing new revisions. Where possible, use hook scripts to enforce minimum compliance. For example, you might have a hook script that checks to make sure that there is never an empty log message, or that the submitted code passes a style check.

- Make use of trusted "core developers" who receive code changes from contributing developers and then perform the actual Subversion repository commit themselves. In addition to allowing you to take advantage of more complex policies for using Subversion (due to a developer base that is presumably more dedicated to the project and thus willing to learn), this also allows your project to readily accept contributions from a wide range of contributors and test them before applying the contributions to the repository.

- If you want to readily allow a wide variety of developers to commit code directly to the repository, but don't want the hassle of vetting each developer's ability to properly apply changes to the project, a third option is to make use of individual developer branches. Each developer can be given his own branch of the main development trunk, with permission to commit. It then becomes his responsibility to maintain that branch and make changes, which can then be merged into the main trunk after being tested by a smaller core developer group. This has the advantage of allowing more developers the ability to preserve their work in the repository, while maintaining the integrity of the primary project.

13.2   Using SVN in Peer Reviews

Peer reviews can be a useful tool for helping to ensure code quality, but no one likes them. They tend to feel like wastes of time, even when they're not, and are extremely prone to devolving into chaos. Many developers feel like their time could be better spent doing "real work," and few cherish losing a day, or even an afternoon, to reviewing others' work. Subversion doesn't have some magical key to making peer reviews perfect, of course, but you can use Subversion to help organize them so that they can at least feel more productive. In distributed development environments (such as open source projects), you can even use Subversion to help support distributed peer review.

13.2.1   Tracking Peer Review Status

The most obvious use of Subversion in peer reviews is as a tool to track what has been peer reviewed already and what has not. By using Subversion properties and other metadata, you can easily track peer reviews on a per-file basis, per-directory basis, or even per-project basis. That way, when you're ready to do a peer review, it's already obvious what needs to be reviewed in that session. Developers can prepare ahead of time, and a checker script can ensure that no code accidently slips through unreviewed.

The exact methods used for tracking peer reviews depends mainly on what code you want to have reviewed, how often you want reviews, and in what granularity of code. To give you some ideas for how you might go about tracking reviews, here are a number of different ways to keep track of them.

- You can track reviews per-revision, recording which revisions have been reviewed and which have not. When you perform a review, you would then be able to call up all of the changes made to the repository in a given block of unreviewed revisions.

  To track the revisions that have been reviewed, you can use a property set on the root directory, called something such as `review:last_rev`. Whenever you perform a review, modify that property to hold the revision number of the last reviewed revision. If you would rather separate your reviews by project (or even "part of project"), you can use the base directories of each project to store the property, instead of the root directory of the repository.

- Another method of tracking reviews is to do them based on revision dates. For instance, you could hold regular peer reviews twice a month, and always review the changes that have been committed to the repository since the last peer review.

  In this scenario, you may not even need to explicitly store something in the repository to track the reviews. Instead, you could just use Subversion's capability to retrieve revisions by date to always get the correct revisions. Of course, it could still be useful to store the dates in the repository (just in case), which can easily be done with properties, the same as when tracking by revision number.

- If reviews aren't always done sequentially, storing the last reviewed revision or date doesn't do you much good. In this case, it might be more useful to use revision properties to store review status. When an individual revision is reviewed, set a revision property on that revision that indicates it has been reviewed.

  Alternately, you could use a single versioned property to store a list of nonsequential reviewed revisions. Using the single versioned property has the advantage of allowing you to easily view (or parse in a script) all of the reviewed revisions for a particular project. On the other hand, it decouples the indicator of review status from the revision itself, making it difficult to figure out when a revision was reviewed.

- As an alternative to using properties to signify peer review status, you can also use tags. For instance, you could keep a sliding tag of the last reviewed revision for each of your projects. When you have a new review, you can use the tag to see what has changed since your last review, and then recreate the tag against the HEAD of your repository.

Finding Unreviewed Revisions

If you are using revision properties to mark which revisions have been reviewed and which haven't, finding unreviewed revisions can be a difficult process. The following script, however, could be used to automate the process. It takes a URL into a repository that points to the base of the project being checked, as well as a range of revisions to check. It then searches through the revision properties for that project, and finds any revisions where the designated project was changed but the revision has never been reviewed (it also outputs revisions that have not had the property set). Because it has to search linearly through the revision properties, this can be a slow script to run (especially on large repositories), but presumably you don't need to run it frequently. In this version of the script, the revision range must be given in the form of revision numbers. The script could be expanded to parse dates or symbolic revision labels though.

```
#!/bin/bash
# review_status.sh
# Finds all revisions with the review:status property set to 'false'
```

```
# The URL of the repository
URL=$1

# The range of revisions to check
LOW_REV=$2
HIGH_REV=$3

# Cycle through the range of revisions
for i in ` seq ${LOW_REV} ${HIGH_REV} `
do

    # Check the review status of this revision
    REVSTAT=` svn propget reviewstat --revprop -r ${i} ${URL} `

    # If the revision hasn't been reviewed, output the revision number
    if [ ${REVSTAT} = "false" ]
    then
        echo ${i}
    # If the reviewstat property hasn't been set,
    # output the revision number with an asterisk
    elif [ ${REVSTAT} = "" ]
    then
        echo "${i}*"
    fi
done
```

This script can be run from the command line, as in the following example.

```
$ review_status.sh https://svn.mydomain.com/repos 425 780
```

13.2.2   Distributing Material for Peer Reviews

When it comes time to do a peer review, it helps greatly to distribute the code to be reviewed to the reviewers a few days ahead of time. That way, when everyone comes together for the review, they are prepared for the discussion. The process of getting that code to the reviewers is where Subversion comes in. There are several ways that you can go about distributing the code to be reviewed, each with different advantages and disadvantages.

- You can inform each reviewer of the revisions that will be reviewed, and allow her to examine the revisions as she wants. This has the advantage of putting the least amount of burden on the organizer of the review, while maximizing the flexibility of the reviewers to examine the changes as they wish. However, flexibility is not always the best virtue, as reviewers tend to be less likely to examine the changes to be reviewed if they have to work at getting at them. Additionally, in some cases, the reviewers may not readily have a working copy of the revision to play around with. Also, I should note here that none of my other suggestions for distribution in any way limit the developer from using Subversion to get more information about the changes, nor is there anything I talk about in the following examples that wouldn't normally be available for the reviewer to personally generate.

- You can distribute diffs of all the changes in the revisions under review. These can be easily obtained using Subversion, and they give you a tangible set of changes that can be sent to reviewers or posted on a mailing list. The downside is that many developers find diffs hard to read, and next to useless as part of a code review. On the other hand, they do put something heftier than a couple of revision numbers into the reviewer's hands, which may improve the chances that the code under review will at least be looked at before the review takes place.

- Distribute `svn blame` output for the project to be reviewed. This has the advantage of putting the entire source of the project being reviewed in front of the reviewer. However, it can make it difficult to pinpoint exactly what changes need to be reviewed, because every line is annotated, not just the lines added in the desired revisions. A potential solution to that problem, though, is to process the output of `svn blame` to generate a reviewer's version that has all of the annotations for irrelevant revisions stripped out.

- Instead of distributing the source directly to reviewers, you could generate a Web page to display the changes to be reviewed. The Web page could then be generated from the output of `svn diff` or `svn blame`, wrapped in markup text that could color-code sections or provide links to other parts of the project that are referenced. Every developer participating in the review would then be able to view this Web site to get up to speed on the changes. Or, if a Web site isn't practical, you could also use the output to generate an annotated and colored version of the source to be reviewed.

An `svn blame` Postprocessor

If you would like to use the output of `svn blame` to create a peer review copy of your source files, it can be useful to filter `svn blame`'s output to only annotate the specific range of revisions that you are reviewing. The following example shows how you can create a Perl script that will do just that.

```perl
#!/usr/bin/perl
# blame_filter.pl
# Filters the output of svn blame for specific revisions

# Get the range of revisions to include in the output
$LOW_REV = $ARGV[0];
$HIGH_REV = $ARGV[1];
```

```
# Iterate through each line of svn blame output and filter the ¬
  annotation
while ($LINE = <STDIN>) {

    # Get the revision number for this line
    $CUR_REV = substr $LINE, 0, 6;

    # Compare the revision number to the revision range
    if(($LOW_REV <= $CUR_REV) && ($HIGH_REV >= $CUR_REV)) {

        # This revision is in our range, include the annotation
        print $LINE;
    }
    else {

        # This revision is outside the range, strip the annotation
        print "                    " . substr($LINE, 18);
    }
}
```

This script can then be run as a filter for the output of svn blame from the command line or in a script, as in the following example (which includes the annotation for revisions 435 through 502).

```
$ svn blame test.cpp | blame_filter.pl 435 502 | test-annotated.cpp
```

13.2.3   Performing Peer Reviews

When it comes time to actually perform peer review, there are a few areas where Subversion can be a useful tool. How it can best be used as a tool depends on what type of peer review you are looking to use. There is the traditional (and often dreaded) code review that consists of several developers sitting around a table and critiquing sections of code, or a more one-on-one style review, where each developer's work is sent to directly to one or more other developers who review and comment directly back to the developer at their own convenience. Alternately, peer review can be accomplished through a forum style review (usually hosted on a message board or e-mail mailing list), where sections of a project to be reviewed are made available for comment by a wide array of interested parties. This sort of review is especially popular for open source projects, where the project's developers are widely scattered and diverse.

Group Reviews

For a group review, developers get together either as a group to critique each other's work or as a panel to critique the work of one or more reviewees. The code to be reviewed is usually either disseminated in paper or electronic form (i.e., to developer's laptops), or displayed on some sort of overhead projection for all to see and comment on.

The logistics of getting the code to be reviewed to the reviewers has already been discussed in some detail, so I won't bore you further. As for getting the code so that it can be displayed on an overhead projector, that should be trivial to do, and doesn't require any special tricks from Subversion. Just check out the code and display it, possibly in an `svn blame` format. There is, however, one other component to the review that Subversion can be useful for, which does require more than trivial implementation. During any review, there is useful commentary provided by the reviewers involved—if there weren't, you wouldn't be having the review in the first place. Obviously, you want to keep a record of those comments as they are made, and what better place to keep that record than in the form of Subversion properties that are tied to the individual files and easily accessible after the review.

Individual Review

With individual reviews, the reviewee's code is sent to one or more reviewers, who examine the code and make comments directly back to the developers in their own time. For the most part, the discussion on group reviews holds true for individual reviews. Distribution of source for review can usually be handled the same, and the suggestions for using properties for storage of reviews holds equally useful. There is one catch with using properties in the context of individual reviews, though. One of the weaknesses of the Subversion property system is its lack of support for searching through properties. If another developer attaches reviews to your source files, it can be difficult to figure out exactly which files have had the reviews attached. One solution is to use log messages to indicate where reviews have been added, but that is error prone and inelegant. A better solution is to set up a post-commit script, which watches for changes on the peer review properties. When a change is made, the modified peer review can be sent via e-mail to the target developer. That way, you always have a complete record of all peer review, readily accessible along with the file itself, but each developer is also given a much more immediate indication of peer reviews.

Forum Review

The final sort of review is a forum review, which is the sort of review most likely to be used in an open source project. In this type of review, changes to a project are made available through some sort of public forum (although "public" could well be limited to within a company or project group) where developers are free to view the changes and comment as they feel necessary. An example of this sort of review would be the Linux Kernel Mailing List, where potential additions to the kernel are sent to the mailing list in the form of patches, to be put up for comment and discussion prior to possible inclusion in the repository.

With Subversion, you can support this sort of review by setting up the repository to automatically send diffs and log messages to a mailing list whenever commits to certain project branches are made. For instance, if you have branches for each developer authorized to commit to an open source project, you could set up a `post-commit` script that would use `svnlook diff` and `svnlook log` to retrieve the changes made for each commit to one of those branches and send it to a developer mailing list. Then, when the discussion on the commit is concluded, the appropriate developers can merge the changes into the main project trunk. It is even possible to have a script that receives the mails sent to the developer list and automatically archives peer review discussions into properties on the appropriate files (the downside being that thread tracking isn't always perfect, and you might end up missing some e-mails, or getting other unrelated ones thrown in).

13.3   Tying Revisions to Issue Tracking

Issue tracking and development go hand-in-hand, so it makes sense to have your issue-tracking system and Subversion work together. With a little bit of forethought and setup, you can do just that. For most issue-tracking systems, there are ways that they can control external systems, and vice versa. So, by hooking Subversion and your issue-tracking system up to each other, you can automate a lot of the drudgery that is involved in keeping both systems in sync.

13.3.1   Issue-tracking Properties

The TortoiseSVN GUI interface for Subversion has an interesting extra feature that adds integration with bug tracking to Subversion. By setting certain properties on project directories, you can control how the TortoiseSVN interface is able to automatically query the user about issue-tracking information, and store it in a manner that allows the GUI to present bug-tracking data to the user. Also, in addition to being used by TortoiseSVN, these properties are also gaining traction as a standard for Subversion issue-tracker integration, and are also used by WebSVN now. The full standard for these properties can be found in the document `issuetracker.txt`, which is located in the TortoiseSVN project's Subversion repository (`svn.collab.net/repos/tortoisesvn/trunk/doc`).

bugtraq:label

This property allows you to specify a label for the text box that the Subversion client displays to ask you to enter an issue number to associate a revision with. If this property is left unset, the client displays some sort of default value (something like `Issue ID:`). This allows you to personalize the bug-tracking interface, to appropriately match the terminology used by your issue-tracking system.

bugtraq:message

This property is used to turn issue-tracking integration on or off in a compliant Subversion client. If the property is unset, no issue-tracking integration is used. If it is set, integration is turned on, and the client uses the value of this property to set a special line in the log files of your commits. The line is added to the end of each log message, and `%BUGID%` is replaced with the appropriate issue numbers (usually; see `bugtraq:append` later in this section).

For instance, if your `bugtraq:message` property is equal to this:

```
Associated issues: %BUGID%
```

Then a commit that is given the issue IDs 247, 342, and 771 will have the following line added to the end of its log message:

```
Associated issues: 247, 342, 771
```

bugtraq:number

This property is used to indicate whether your issue-tracking system identifies issues with numbers exclusively, or if it allows other characters. If only numbers are allowed, this property should be set to `true` (or left unset). If other characters are allowed, you should set this property to `false`.

bugtraq:url

This property is used to allow a Subversion client to present you with a link to the issues referenced by the log message. The value of this property is a URL, which contains `%BUGID%`. Just like in the `bugtraq:message` property, this URL replaces `%BUGID%` with the appropriate issue ID when the link is displayed.

bugtraq:warnifnoissue

Subversion revisions aren't always associated with a specific issue in your issue tracker, but for some projects, unassociated revisions are the exception, not the norm. If this is the case for your project, you may want to have the Subversion client warn the user if he doesn't enter an issue number when he commits. To turn that warning on, you have to set this property to `true`. If you don't want the warnings, just leave this property unset.

bugtraq:append

The default for adding the issue message to your log messages is to append the message to the end of the log. If you would rather have the message appear at the top of each log message, you can set this property to `false`. In either case, the message appears on its own line.

13.3.2 Automating Interaction with Issue Tracking

If you're up for a little bit of scripting, much of the Subversion issue-tracking interaction can be automated, which allows you to keep your issue tracking system more consistently in sync with your Subversion repository, as well as alleviate some of the drudgery of entering information into both systems.

- You can use a `post-commit` hook script to automatically send messages to an issue-tracking system. Many systems, such as Bugzilla (`www.bugzilla.org`), have Web-based interfaces that can be interfaced with through a script that emulates a user manipulating the system by hand (Python is a good language choice for these scripts). Other systems, such as the up-and-coming Scarab (`scarab.tigris.org`) or the e-mail-based RT (`bestpractical.com`) have interfaces specifically designed for remote control by external programs.

Messages can be controlled through formatted log messages. Commands placed in log messages can be used to determine which issue(s) a revision applies to, and what should be done with that revision. Useful commands for manipulating the issue tracker include

- Setting the resolution status of an open issue

- Appending a log message to the comments for an issue

- Associating a revision in Subversion to an issue in the tracker

- It may also be possible to make things work in the other direction. Most issue-tracking systems can send out e-mails notifying people of activity on the issue-tracking system. If you have messages carbon copied to a Subversion-specific e-mail address, and write a program to listen for those messages, you can set up automated tasks to manipulate the Subversion repository in response to changes in the issue tracker. For instance:

  - New bug reports in the issue tracker could automatically trigger the creation of a task branch in the repository for fixing the bug. If security is a major concern, this could also set the proper permissions for the developer assigned to fix the bug.

  - When an issue is closed, the task branch for that issue could be moved into a closed issues directory, or deleted altogether.

Trac

Another option for integrating Subversion with issue tracking is the Trac project management system (`www.edgewall.com`). Trac provides a Web-based environment for managing projects, including an issue tracker and a wiki that integrate with a Web-based interface to Subversion. Log messages can directly reference issues (called tickets) and wiki pages (with links generated by Trac when viewing the log message from the Trac interface), and ticket/wiki pages can reference specific repository revisions (also with links). Trac even includes a `post-commit` hook script that allows you to automatically update the status of Trac tickets based on information provided in the log message. Figure 13.1 shows the Trac interface displaying its repository browsing screen.

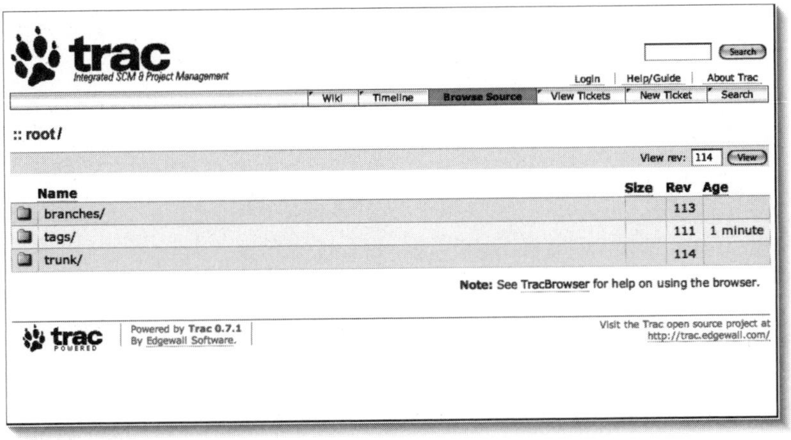

Figure 13.1. The Trac repository browser.

13.4 Summary

In this chapter, you've seen a variety of information on integrating Subversion into your overall development process. The developer studies showed some of the quirks you may have to deal with when it comes to developer personalities and work habits, along with suggestions for integrating their workflow into Subversion (or vice versa). Additionally, you saw ways in which you can integrate Subversion with a rigorous peer review process and issue tracking. In the next chapter, we will look at several case studies of different project environments (both archetypal and real world) and how Subversion fits into their process.

Chapter 14

Case Studies in Development Processes

Understanding is always easier with a few examples. So far, we've looked at a lot of small examples, but haven't really tied everything together. In this chapter, we'll do just that, and look at some case studies of full Subversion repositories.

14.1   Archetypal Studies

In this section, we'll look at several development project archetypes. For each one, I will describe the sort of development philosophy that such a project is likely to have, as well as key points of process and policy that define the archetype. Then, I'll examine the choices that such a project will have to make when integrating with Subversion, such as laying out the repository and using properties, hook scripts, and other Subversion features. I'll also look at the limitations of Subversion that you may run into with each archetype, and how you can work around them.

14.1.1   Managed Chaos

The managed chaos project is one with little managerial oversight over the day-to-day details of development. Instead, managerial duties are limited to integration and high-level design. In fact, in many such projects, the project manager is really more of a project maintainer, and may even be officially titled that way. You are most likely to find this sort of a project in an academic or open source project setting.

In this case study, we will look at a hypothetical managed chaos project and open source program called BogeyTalk, which allows text on your computer to be read to you in the style of Humphrey Bogart. BogeyTalk is a mature project, with dozens of contributors, as well as a small team of five maintainers, handpicked from the project's major developers by the creator of the project, who we'll call Bob. Significant project releases are frequent (a couple of times a year), and the project follows the Linux Kernel version numbering scheme (even minor numbers for releases, and odd minor numbers for development versions).

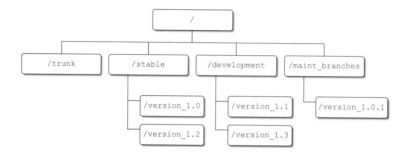

Figure 14.1. The BogeyTalk repository layout.

Repository Layout

Because BogeyTalk is the only project hosted in its Subversion repository, the entire project resides at the top level of the repository. The main development branch of the project resides in the /trunk directory. Additionally, there are /stable, /development, and /maint_branches directories, as you can see in Figure 14.1. The /maint_branches directory is used to store maintenance branches (as I will explain shortly), whereas the /stable and /development directories are tag directories that store snapshots of various releases of the project.

Branches and Tags

Because most BogeyTalk developers do not have access to make direct commits to the repository, task branches make little sense. Therefore, BogeyTalk uses branches and tags primarily to signify different versions and releases. For each release of the project, a tag of the project is created in either /stable or /development, depending on whether the release was a stable release or a development release (the different directories help ensure a logical separation between the two release categories). Both of these directories are used as immutable tag directories (i.e., copies are created here from elsewhere and nothing is changed once created), but the repository is not set up to enforce that policy. Instead, Bob made the decision to trust the maintainers and make it easy for them to make a correction if there is an error when creating a release tag. Because there are only a few maintainers, this works out well.

Most actual development on BogeyTalk occurs in the /trunk directory, but occasionally there needs to be further development on an older version of the program in order to patch security holes or maintain compatibility with other projects. To support these security patches, the BogeyTalk project maintains maintenance branches for each stable version of the project (1.0, 1.2, 1.4, and so on) in the /maint_branches directory. These branches are created at the time of the stable version's release, and are identical to that version's tag in the /stable directory at the time of the release. When security or compatibility patches need to be made, they are committed to these branches, which are then tagged to create subminor version releases (1.0.1, 1.0.2, and so on).

Properties

The BogeyTalk makes use of the `svn:keywords` property to embed repository information in the comment header of each file, using the `$Id$` tag. Because most BogeyTalk users get their copy of the project's source code from a release package, and not directly from the repository, this makes sure that the information necessary for finding a particular file in the repository will always be available.

BogeyTalk also uses several custom properties for storing additional meta-information relevant to the project.

- Each release tag stores packaged tarballs and RPM files in `pkg:tgz` and `pkg:rpm` properties, respectively. This allows a script to automatically maintain the downloads directories on the project's Web site, by scanning the releases directories for new packages. If it discovers a release that does not have associated packages (or has out-of-date packages), it sends an e-mail warning to Bob to make sure the problem is corrected. Bob could have opted to use a directory in the repository to store package files, but he decided to use the properties to maintain a logical connection between packages and the source they're associated with. Because the package files are created from the tag itself, and then attached to the tag after it is created, the possibility that a tag will have an out-of-date package associated with it is minimal.

- Most of the BogeyTalk project is licensed under the GNU General Public License (GPL), but a few key sections are licensed under the GNU Lesser General Public License (LGPL) to allow external programs to link to BogeyTalk without requiring them to follow the GPL's restrictions. To keep clear which files fall under which license, each file maintains a `license` property that states the license for that file. For GPL licensed files, it has a value of GPL, and for LGPL licensed files it has a value of LGPL. The project's documentation is also licensed under the GNU Free Documentation License (FDL), and those files have a `license` property of FDL.

- Because most of the developers who contribute to the BogeyTalk project do not have direct write access to the repository, the repository commit logs do not reflect that actual author of a change. One way around this is to always note the author's name in the log files, but for this project Bob wanted to go one step further. He wanted his Web-based Subversion blame tool to show the actual author of specific bits of code, rather than just the developer responsible for the commit. So, in addition to noting who the author of a committed revision is, the BogeyTalk project also makes use of a `developer` revision property, where the real name of the contributing developer is stored.

Scripts

BogeyTalk uses a custom script that automatically maintains the project's download directories, which contain packaged versions of the project in source and binary form. Each night, the script is run as a `cron` job on the project server.

1. The script first iterates through each of the immediate subdirectories in /stable, of which there is one for each release.

2. For each stable release, the script checks the pkg:tgz and pkg:rpm properties to see if they contain an up-to-date package.

   (a) If either property is empty, or contains a package that is older than the latest revision of that release, the script sends an e-mail to the project maintainer.

   (b) Otherwise, the script checks to see if the package already exists on the project's Web server. If it does not, the package is copied to the server.

3. The script then repeats steps 1 and 2 for all of the development releases in the directory /development.

4. Finally, the script creates a tarball (.tgz) of the /trunk directory, names it with the current date, and places it on the Web server as a nightly snapshot of the development.

BogeyTalk also has a custom script for creating its contributer annotated blame output for the BogeyTalk developer's Web site. The BogeyTalk blame script takes the raw output from svn blame and compares each entry with the developer property for the appropriate revision (to improve performance, it caches values it has already discovered). It then replaces the author label in the blame output to match the value of developer. To ensure that this script is able to run at a reasonable speed, due to the large amount of svn propget commands that it must call, the script is run from the same machine as the repository itself.

14.1.2   Rapid Development

The rapid development project is aimed at getting rapid functional output, without a long upfront development cycle. The project is often subject to frequent requirements changes, and developers need to be able to react quickly to shifts. Because development cycles are short, development needs to perform frequent integration, and Subversion plays a big role as a supporting framework that helps support changes.

For this case study, we'll look at a hypothetical Web database application, being developed by the software development consulting firm, Programmers, LLC. The client on the project, Internet Sales, Inc., wants to put the application into use on its internationally known online sales Web site, but the exact requirements are fluctuating rapidly due to changing market needs. Because the application is a custom development job, there is no intention to market it as a prepackaged product, but Programmers, LLC will likely be contracted in the future to support the software for Internet Sales, Inc.

Repository Layout

The repository for Programmers, LLC holds all of its ongoing projects, not just the database application for Internet Sales, Inc. Therefore, the top level of the repository consists of subdirectories for each project, which in this case is referred to as ISDB (Internet Sales DataBase). The developers at Programmers, LLC are no fans of extra work, though,

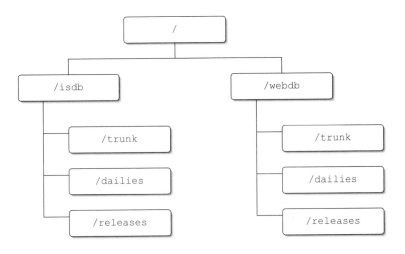

Figure 14.2. The Programmers, LLC repository layout.

and many of their projects tend to have overlapping functionalities. Therefore, they have also developed a number of in-house projects that contain libraries used by their contract projects, which they also store in top-level directories. In the case of ISDB, there is one Web database project, stored in /webdb, that is used.

Inside the /isdb project directory, the project is split into a main /isdb/trunk directory, an /isdb/dailies directory, and an /isdb/releases directory (see Figure 14.2). The trunk directory is where the main project development occurs. They store daily project build tags in the dailies directory, and versions of the project released to the client in releases.

Branches and Tags

Because the ISDB project is on a rapid development schedule, the project's developers are using continuous integration of their work. That puts all of their development work on the main trunk, and alleviates the need to use branches for separating work. There is also no need to use branches for supporting multiple versions of the software, because there will only be a single client that they need to support. If the project were to be "branched" for development for a different client, the developers would instead make a copy of the /isdb top-level project to create a new project for their new client.

The Programmers, LLC developers do make frequent tags of the ISDB project trunk, though. Each day, they make a snapshot of the trunk directory in the dailies directory to store the state of the project at the end of that day's development. Additionally, they make tags of the trunk directory whenever they release a version of the software to the client (either for testing purposes, or as a version to be used in production), and place them in the releases directory.

Properties

Programmers, LLC makes use of the `svn:externals` property to link their in-house libraries to the projects that use them. In the case of ISDB, it makes use of their custom Web database library, located in `/webdb`. To link that to the ISDB project, `/isdb/trunk` directory has the `svn:externals` property set to

```
libs/webdb        https://svn.programmers.com/repos/webdb/trunk
```

Programmers, LLC also makes heavy use of properties to store project information at the top level of each project. For each project, the top-level directory for that project stores

- The name of the client for the project, in `proj:client`

- Client contact information, in `proj:contact`

- Scheduling information for the project, in `proj:schedule`

- Project budget information, in `proj:budget`

As a part of the ISDB project's rapid development cycle, the project uses automated regression tests to ensure that no developer's contribution breaks other parts of the project. To facilitate these tests being run automatically, the top-level project directory stores two properties, `tests:daily` and `tests:hourly`. These properties contain a list of the tests that should be run on a daily basis and the tests that should be run on an hourly basis (respectively). Additionally, each source file has a property named `tests:commit`, which lists tests that should be run whenever changes to that file are committed to the repository.

Scripts

The ISDB project uses a number of scripts to perform automatic testing on the project, in order to help facilitate Programmers, LLC's rapid development and integration schedule.

- A script runs each day to generate a snapshot of the daily build in the directory, `/isdb/dailies`. This script also builds the daily snapshot and runs the tests specified in the project's `tests:daily` property. Any errors are reported to the project Web server (which shows build statistics) and e-mailed to the appropriate developers.

- Another script performs hourly builds and runs the tests contained in the project's `tests:hourly` property.

- Finally, a `post-commit` script runs the appropriate `tests:commit` tests whenever a commit is made.

14.1.3   Central Planning

A centrally planned project has a high degree of rigidity in design and process. Project design is likely done up-front (or at least in large iterative cycles), and although individual developers may not be micromanaged by the project manager, they generally are required to follow rigid policies. This sort of development project is often necessary for managing very large projects, or complex projects that require a large amount of high- and low-level project design.

To examine this project archetype, we'll look at the hypothetical government contractor, GovCon. GovCon develops a wide variety of different projects for various government agencies. Many of the projects are quite large, and all must conform to detailed and exacting government specifications. In order to maintain the level of control necessary to meet these specs, GovCon maintains a strict project hierarchy of project management, with clearly defined task descriptions for each member of a project team. Each project team (there may be more than one per project) is further split into two sides: developers and quality assurance testers. Communication between the two sides of the team is important, and Subversion is used as a key tool in facilitating that communication.

Repository Layout

GovCon uses separate Subversion repositories for each project, so individual projects exist at the top level of their respective repository. The project then consists of four subdirectories: /qa_builds, /dev_builds, /tasks, and /releases (as shown in Figure 14.3). The /qa_builds and /dev_builds projects are used for compiling and storing integrated project builds, whereas the /tasks directory is used for individual developer work on specific tasks. Released versions of the projects are stored in the /releases directory.

Branches and Tags

GovCon makes heavy use of branches in its project development to separate tasks in order to allow each individual developer's work to be thoroughly tested by a QA tester before integration into the rest of the project. For each development task that needs to be completed, a project manager creates a branch of the project in the /tasks directory, from that day's development build (located in the dev_builds directory) or from the daily QA build (in

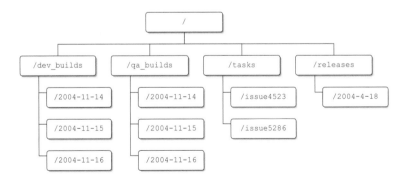

Figure 14.3. The GovCon repository layout.

/qa_builds). Then, after the task has been completed, it is marked for QA testing. Completed and tested tasks are then integrated into a QA build (in the /qa_builds directory) where the integrated build is tested before using it to create a new development build.

Properties

The GovCon projects use properties as a tool for facilitating communication between QA testers and developers. The top-level directory for each project branch contains a status property (qa:status), which indicates whether a branch has been tested yet. When a task is created, its status is set to untested/inprogress, and the qa:tester property is unset. As soon as a developer feels that the current task is ready for testing, that developer changes the value of qa:status to untested/ready. QA testers can then go through and test all of the tasks with a status that is marked as ready. If the tester is happy with the results, the qa:status property is set to tested/passed. If the task is not satisfactory, qa status is set to tested/failed. When a task is tested, the QA tester's username also is entered into the qa:tester property.

Scripts

All of the GovCon projects use pre-commit hook scripts to ensure that a variety of project policies are being followed correctly.

- Log messages are checked to ensure that they match the proper log format.

- Committed source code is run through a style checker, to ensure that it matches the prescribed coding styles for the project.

- QA properties are checked to make sure they have valid values.

Additionally, a post-commit hook script checks the QA property values for changes, and sends e-mails to the appropriate people to inform them of the current status for tasks.

14.1.4   Small Teams

In small-team projects, there are very few developers working on a project—generally 10 or less. Development process tends to be relaxed, because there are few enough people to still keep it manageable, and individual development style has a much greater influence on project policy.

For this case study, we'll look at an imaginary startup company named SmallCo. SmallCo was started by five friends who graduated from college together, and has since added three new developers. Of the five original founders, though, only three are developers themselves (the fourth is a business guy and the other is in marketing). That leaves a current full development team of six people for SmallCo, all of whom are working on developing the company's ground-breaking new Internet product.

Repository Layout

SmallCo currently has only a single product, which is stored in its own repository. With so few developers, SmallCo hasn't seen much of a need to be particularly creative with its repository layout, either. Following standard convention, the top level of the SmallCo repository is laid out with /branches, /tags, and /trunk directories, as you can see in Figure 14.4.

Branches and Tags

SmallCo does all of its project development in the main /trunk directory, with each developer committing changes as they are made and tested. Tags of the project are made at both development milestones (i.e., beta or alpha releases) and at releases. Branches are only used when problems need to be fixed with a previously released version, in which case the tag for that release is copied into the branches directory, where it can be modified as necessary. When the fix is finished, the branch is moved back to the tags directory as the new release. For instance, if a bug is found in version 1.1 of the software, the developers would copy /tags/version_1.1 to /branches/version_1.1.1 and make the necessary changes. When the new bug-fix release is ready, it is moved back to /tags using svn mv.

Properties

Because of SmallCo's size, its developers tend to handle project management and communication more informally than a larger operation might. As a result, it hasn't yet found a large need for custom properties to store or communicate project metadata, and to date has not instituted any such properties. The only properties that are used in the repository are the predefined Subversion properties, which the developers use as the situation warrants.

Scripts

As with properties, SmallCo has not found a pressing need to automate any of its practices or policy enforcement with custom scripts. It is small enough that policy enforcement is more easily done offline (if someone messes up, the developers fix it), and the development process is handled too informally to benefit from automation.

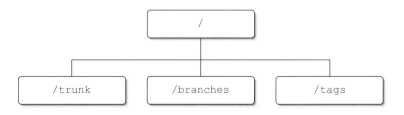

Figure 14.4. The SmallCo repository layout.

14.2   Real-world Studies

Hypothetical case studies based around common project archetypes have their uses, but it can also be helpful to take a look at some real-world projects, and how they manage many of the issues associated with using Subversion. As with the archetypal studies, in this section I will examine the different choices made by these projects, and how those choices fit in with the topics discussed in previous chapters.

14.2.1   KeyGhost Ltd.

KeyGhost, Ltd. is a developer of embedded and PC software and hardware that uses Subversion for storing not only software source code, but also documentation in the form of Open Office files, and hardware designs. It chose to use Subversion based on indications that it is poised to become the next open source version control standard.

Repository

KeyGhost arranges its projects into 29 separate repositories, one for each project, most of which are legacy projects that see little activity. Its more active projects have around 500 revisions, with a total repository size of 1GB. In total, the repositories are used by less than 10 developers who all have rights to commit changes.

Each repository is organized into a top-level directory, named for the project, with `trunk`, `branches`, and `tags` directories in each project. Under the `trunk` directory, developers categorize project files into source code, documentation, and hardware designs (using `source`, `docs`, and `pcb`, respectively). Figure 14.5 shows an example of the standard layout for a KeyGhost repository. KeyGhost makes use of tags for storing project releases, and uses branches whenever it has an appropriate need for branching a project's development.

The repositories themselves are hosted on a Microsoft Windows 2000 server, using the Berkeley DB database backend. To share the repository, KeyGhost uses the Apache server, largely due to its ease of setup and administration. It also uses secure HTTP over SSL to secure the repository for remote access. The KeyGhost developers access Subversion from Windows 2000 client machines, and use TortoiseSVN as a GUI client.

Migrating to Subversion

The KeyGhost migration to Subversion involved a conceptual change, from using a paradigm where files were locked to limit a single developer to making modifications to a particular file at a time, to the Subversion merge paradigm without locking. Additionally, they had to overcome the hurdle of a user base without previous experience in version control. To overcome this issue, developers were given training in version control, and provided with the TortoiseSVN GUI client to make the learning curve significantly less steep.

Storing Binary Files

In addition to storing text-based source code files, KeyGhost also uses its Subversion repository for storing binary files from Open Office and its circuit board design package. Despite

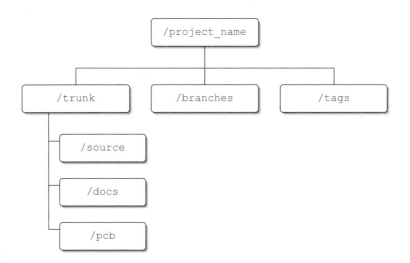

Figure 14.5. The standard KeyGhost repository layout.

Subversion's use of a binary difference algorithm to store only changes to a binary file, developers found the storage requirements from one version of a file to the next to be hefty. In order to limit unbounded exponential repository growth, KeyGhost has made a policy of limiting commits to its binary files.

Repository Migration

Subversion makes a valiant attempt to make restructuring of a repository a simple process. However, KeyGhost discovered that simple does not mean trouble free, and it can be prudent to put some long-term thought into structure. KeyGhost began with a single Subversion repository, using a single top-level `/trunk` directory with individual projects in subdirectories under that. After using Subversion for a while, however, KeyGhost decided to migrate to its current structure of multiple repositories, with one project per repository. Because a number of files had been moved or deleted, KeyGhost found that `svnadmin export` and `svndumpfilter` were unable to properly migrate all of the projects with their full histories. In the end, KeyGhost was forced to resort to checking out working copies and reimporting those into a new repository (which still caused a loss of history).

14.2.2 Error Free Software

Error Free Software (EFS) develops a proprietary trading system, which it stores in a Subversion repository. EFS chose Subversion after examining a number of different version control systems, and settled on Subversion due to its snug fit with the EFS environment. The developers found it to have a full feature set, without any undue complexity.

Repository

The EFS repository is arranged with a number of different top-level directories with a variety of purposes, as you can see in Figure 14.6.

/branches This directory stores project branches. EFS doesn't make very much use of this directory, and as of this writing only had a total of six branches.

/dailyLibraryBuild Daily builds of the repository are stored here. Each daily build is placed in its own directory. The directories are named for the date of the build, using two-digit year, month, and day numbers (YYMMDD).

/releases Project releases are stored here.

/doc This directory is used to store documentation for individual projects.

/projects The EFS trading system consists of a large number of application suites and libraries. This directory is used to store individual application suites, which are linked to the various libraries using svn:externals properties.

/src The actual source code for the repository (which is linked via svn:externals in /projects) is stored in this directory. This acts as EFS's /trunk directory.

/spd EFS stores its design documents for its software in this directory.

The repository itself is very large, totaling more than 35,000 revisions in a 2GB database. Much of the repository, however, was preexisting when EFS migrated to Subversion, and was carried over from SCCS. The repository is hosted on a machine running RedHat Linux, and uses Berkeley DB as its repository database backend.

The repository is also accessed by about 30 people every day, most of whom perform regular commits. The developers access the repository from a mix of machines running

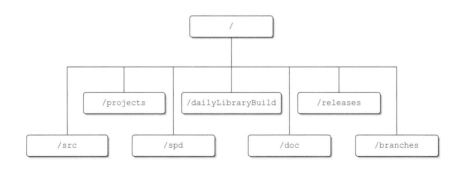

Figure 14.6. The Error Free Software repository layout.

Sun's Solaris and machines running Microsoft's Windows XP. Remote access to the repository is done through Apache, which was chosen due to its ease of integration into the existing authentication infrastructure, previous familiarity with Apache, and general all-round good looks. It also made it easy to make the repository accessible from a Web browser.

14.2.3 Teledata Communications

Teledata Communications, Inc. (TCI) uses Subversion to store all of its source code, documentation, and build projects, as well as information from data providers, and development documentation. TCI began testing Subversion fairly early on in its development, at around version 0.24, and have been using it in a production setting since July of 2003, after giving it a thorough run through all of its paces.

One of the major reasons for switching to Subversion from TCI's previous (commercial) version control system was to save costs on per-seat developer licensing. As the company was growing in size, it came to the conclusion that its previous VCS solution wasn't worth the cost. So instead of shelling out more money to license new developers, TCI decided to make the jump to Subversion instead. Even though their developers had experience with the previous system, as did most of their new hires, the benefits of moving to Subversion outweighed the costs of training.

The other reason for TCI's switch to Subversion is best illustrated by Mark Bohlman, the Software Development Manager at TCI.

> As we were utilizing a commercial version of RCS, all the developers had developed habits of locking/unlocking and utilizing e-mail or instant messaging to indicate that they needed a particular code file in order to make changes. Within two weeks of my arrival at TCI, it became apparent that a fairly large stumbling block existed within the team when changes were needed. We have development staff broken up into three distinct groups, backend Java coders, mid-level JSP coders, and frontend HTML developers. As the boundaries between these groups are fairly loose at any given time, one developer would need to access code from another level. At the time, we also were dispersed in a location where the physical separation between the teams made it difficult to communicate without the use of e-mail and/or IM. A number of times in the first weeks of my employ here, it became clear that deadlines would be missed solely because of the inefficient usage of the tools, and the way that locking was implemented.

> The straw that broke the camel's back for me was trying to get a build release for a client only to find that a developer in the Java group had checked code back in to allow a frontend developer to make a change to a logo, and failed to complete needed changes. This ended up costing us with the customer, which we managed to hold onto, but at the expense of nearly a week's worth of client testing, QA testing, and development time (saying nothing of the ill-will it generated).

Repository

Teledata Communications' data is split into three separate repositories, each of which holds a different type of data.

- The developer repository holds all of TCI's source code, as well as its third-party vendor tools and all associated documentation. It is used by TCI's developers, and is laid out according to the standard /trunk, /branches, and /tags scheme. Clocking in at a little over 2GB in size, this repository has over 11,000 revisions and uses Berkeley DB as its storage backend. All of TCI's developers, QA testers, and systems engineers access this repository daily, and have both read and commit access.

- The next repository holds all of the information that TCI's data providers supply them with, such as credit bureaus, valuation providers, and criminal background data sources. This data is continually undergoing modification by the vendors, and the number of vendors themselves is also increasing regularly. It is important for TCI to keep track of these changes in order to maintain all of the versions of its software that is being used by clients. This repository is laid out with top-level directories for each data provider, and no branching or tagging is used. Read access to this repository is provided to the entire company, but commit access is limited to just a few developers and a maintainer.

- The final repository is a client requirements repository that stores customer requirements, use cases, scenarios, and design thoughts for each project and client. Documents are arranged in the repository by application, with each application in a top-level directory. Below that, documents are arranged by client, with a directory for each of an application's clients under the directory for that application. Access to this repository is also provided to all in the company for checkout purposes, but commits are limited to systems engineers and managers.

Branches and Tags

The TCI developer repository uses tags in its automated build process. The Java applications that developers build run under WebLogic and have an Ant-based build process that involves creating a tag for each build provided to a development test, QA test, or production environment. To ensure consistency between the three builds, they are all done at the same time. Custom properties are used to indicate the configuration files that should be used for determining build environments.

TCI also makes use of branches for a variety of uses. Changes in branches are periodically merged back into the trunk, as appropriate.

- New development lines for a code base.

- Custom changes for an individual client.

- Experimental development.

Branches are also sometimes used for bug fixes. Whether to do bug fixes in a branch or in the trunk is dependent on the development state of an application (i.e., QA, beta, or production).

Hook Scripts

Hook scripts are used for

- Repository access control. This allows them to prevent commit access for unauthorized persons.

- Sending commit notification e-mails for the client documentation repository. This ensures that all involved parties (sales, sales engineering, development, QA, MIS, and support) are informed of any changes to client requirements.

14.2.4   GladeSoft

This case study looks at GladeSoft, Inc. GladeSoft is the smallest company among the various case studies (it has three developers accessing the repository). GladeSoft migrated to Subversion under familiar circumstances, after finding CVS too painful to continue using. Within the company, Subversion repositories are used to store source code, corporate data, and the GladeSoft Web site.

GladeSoft's choice to use Subversion came down to a variety of different requirements it had for a version control system.

- The ease of migrating from an existing CVS repository, while preserving the repository history.

- Subversion's clean and useable design.

- The ability to use HTTP and SSL for authenticated communication with the repository, without needing shell accounts.

- The transactional atomic commits, which GladeSoft found to be especially important in the storm-prone area of Florida where the company is located (frequent power loss).

Repository

GladeSoft uses three separate repositories for storing information.

- A primary repository holds the source code for the product.

- The second holds GladeSoft's corporate data.

- The final repository holds the GladeSoft Web site.

The source code repository is arranged with a standard /trunk, /branches, and /tags. Inside /branches are several subdirectories that allow them to categorize their branches. Tags are created to mark feature freezes and release points in the source code, and branches are used mainly for making customer-specific changes. The repository is small, holding less than 20MB of data, in over 1500 revisions, and is accessed by three developers who commit changes.

The other two repositories don't make use of branching or tagging, and simply have their main file tree at the top level. These repositories are even smaller than the source code repository, clocking in at around 5MB, with even fewer revisions—Gladesoft doesn't like doing paperwork.

All three repositories are served via Apache, from an old 200MHz PowerPC running Gentoo Linux. HTTP was chosen for its capability to work without local shell accounts (for individual users), which provides extra security. It is also used for its source browsing capability, which makes it easy for GladeSoft to quickly check a source file or do an informal code review. Client connections are made from a menagerie of operating systems, including Windows, Linux, various BSDs, and OS X.

Hook Scripts

GladeSoft also uses two hook scripts for its source repository.

- The first sends out commit notification e-mails.

- The second automatically runs the build server against the latest source using a variety of compliers and targets.

14.2.5   ExCo

In this case study, we will look at a company that uses Subversion to store its complete source code base, as well as its build tools. The company declined to have its real name mentioned, so to protect the innocent I will call it "ExCo" instead.

ExCo began using Subversion after migrating from its CVS repository in 2003, which it had previously migrated to from Microsoft Visual SourceSafe in 2000. The migration occurred because CVS was not meeting ExCo's needs (although it was still better than VSS). Subversion allowed ExCo to maintain a similar development paradigm (thus less training) while making almost everything easier to perform.

Some of the other reasons for the migration include

- The branching and tagging paradigms, which were easier to learn, especially for developers who didn't want to invest much time in training

- The atomic commits, which eliminated the need for complicated commit processes

- The possibility of allowing individual developers to perform branching and merging, which allowed for a "task branch" model of development

- Easy migration of existing tools to work with Subversion instead of CVS

- The well-known names such as Karl Fogel and Collab.net that were associated with Subversion

Repository

ExCo's repositories are set up with a fairly standard arrangement. The top-level directories are made up of `/trunk`, `/branches`, and `/tags`, as well as a directory named `/devbranches`, where individual developers can create their own task branches (see Figure 14.7).

ExCo has three repositories, which hold 8,000, 9,600, and 2,400 files, respectively, and are used to store different sets of projects. Access to the repositories are through an Apache server, due to its stability and security (via SSL). Because ExCo has developers overseas, the security was an important feature. Commits to the repository are allowed for all developers who have access, which comprises approximately 20 to 28 developers. The server is hosted on a Solaris machine, with users connecting from Windows 2000 clients.

Branches and Tags

Branches and tags are heavily used inside the ExCo Subversion repositories.

- Tags are created for each successful build performed by their automated build system.

- Branches are created for each individual task, which is then merged into its final destination when the task is complete.

- Production ready builds are branched in order to stabilize them before they are deployed.

Because of ExCo's heavy use of branches, it has found it necessary to deal with merge tracking (which Subversion lacks in any real form). Instead of having an overall merge tracking plan, however, ExCo relies on individual developers to track their own changes and merges. To date, this has worked well and not caused any real problems.

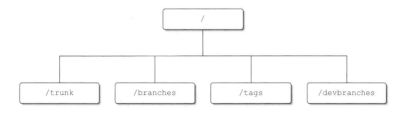

Figure 14.7. The ExCo repository layout.

The People Problem

One of the issues noted by ExCo as a problem to be dealt with was not technical at all. It is the problem of getting developers to integrate their work process with a version control system. Ron Bieber (of "ExCo") explained this issue.

> The biggest problem we've had in whole [has] been people problems. Your average developer doesn't care about source control and doesn't see why they have to learn it. If you look at most companies (at least for people I've either talked to or interviewed for positions), they use very primitive methods to keep track of source control (including just storing things on a network drive), or they know just enough to check out and do not know anything about branching. You usually have to have a completely full-time employee just to manage concurrent development. It was a challenge to get people to learn [Subversion], but once they did, the process became self-sufficient without the extra head count.

14.2.6 Wye Corp

In this case study, we'll look at a company that does embedded development, and uses Subversion to store its firmware and hardware specifications, as well as source for device drivers and testing applications. The company in question declined to be identified by name for this book, so I'll refer to it as "Wye Corp."

Wye Corp switched to Subversion after hitting one too many walls while dealing with CVS's limitations. Many of its projects had started out for internal use only, but as time passed, its customers started using their tools, which inevitably led to requests from the customers to add features and expand the projects. Attempts to expand the projects, however, quickly hit a wall with CVS, as developers attempted to restructure file and directory layouts and found it impossible without breaking CVS's file history.

Repository

Instead of setting up a single repository, Wye Corp uses a different repository for each project, 16 in all. The repositories range in size up to 400MB, but have relatively low revision counts (under 500). Some of the repositories are as old as two years. Overall, the company has 14 developers accessing its various repositories, and limits access to only those people who have a need.

Repository layout for Wye Corp is a fairly standard /trunk, /branches, and /tags setup, with the addition of a dedicated /releases directory. The releases directory allows Wye Corp to separate internal tags used for marking milestones (such as points where support for a special feature was incorporated) from releases that were delivered to a customer, which is something Wye Corp needs to keep careful track of. Inside /releases, there is also a directory called info, which contains a file releases.txt. Wye Corp uses the releases.txt file to keep track of which customer received each released version of its software. Figure 14.8 shows how this layout is arranged.

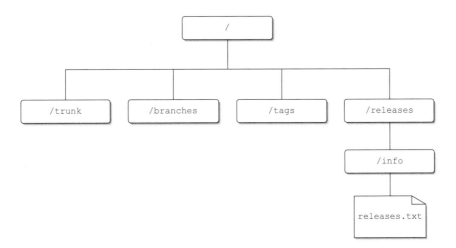

Figure 14.8. The Wye Corp repository layout.

The repository itself is hosted on a Dell server with 400GB of RAID5 storage space and 1GB of memory, running RedHat Enterprise Linux. Remote access to the repository is served via Apache. Originally, HTTP was chosen because it was the only network capable server available (Wye Corp was a very early adopter of Subversion, starting at version 0.17). Later on, however, it began to rely on the convenience of browsing the repository over the Web, as well as the ability to authenticate against its LDAP servers.

Branches and Tags

Wye Corp has a few different uses for branches and tags.

- Tags are used for the occasional internal milestone that bears remembering.

- Releases to customers are also copied and placed in the `/releases` directory.

- Branches are used for significant changes to the code base.

- Branches are also used for trying out a potential solution to a problem, without breaking the main trunk for everyone else.

For the most part, Wye Corp has found little reason to do many merges from one branch to another, because most of their development occurs on the main trunk, which it uses to directly create release tags. Occasionally, however, circumstances have required merges to a release that used only certain revisions. In those cases, Wye Corp has used a separate file in the repository to keep track of all merges.

Hook Scripts

Wye Corp has several hook scripts in place to enforce policy and provide automatic notifications.

- A script is used that updates the internal developer Web site with information when commits are made.

- Another notification script is used for sending e-mails whenever a commit occurs.

- Wye Corp prevents any changes to `/tags` or `/releases` except to create a new tag or release.

- A script checks to make sure that no developer makes a commit with an empty log message.

14.2.7   ZedCom

For our final case study, let's look at one more company that decided not to have its name used. We'll call it "ZedCom." ZedCom uses its Subversion repository to store firmware for multimedia embedded systems. Like many of the previous case studies, ZedCom migrated to Subversion from CVS, due to the limitations that I've already exhaustively discussed.

Repository

The ZedCom repository is arranged with four top-level directories: `/trunk`, `/users`, `/branches`, and `/tags`. The familiar directories have the functions you would normally expect, although I should note that the `/trunk` directory contains subdirectories for individual projects. Additionally, the `/users` directory contains subdirectories for each Subversion user (named after his username), where individual users can create their own private branches.

The repository has relatively few users, with 10 who can access the repository and six who perform commits. It contains about 600MB of data in 1,800 revisions. Access is performed via `svnserve`, due to its ease of setup (ZedCom has no need for secure authentication).

Branching is limited to user branching, and although ZedCom has a `/branches` directory, it has never actually used it. Merge tracking of the branches is done manually via commit logs, which works, but serves as a source of irritation for the developers.

Part V

Reference

Chapter 15

Command Reference

In this final chapter, I'm going to change the format a bit. Instead of walking you through how to do things, the remaining portion of the book is a reference manual for the Subversion command-line utilities. Each command-line utility has its own section, and within that section, the individual commands are arranged alphabetically.

Much of the information covered in this reference section can also be found by running `help` for each individual command. I've tried to expound on that information wherever possible though.

The commands covered are

- svn

- svnadmin

- svnlook

- svnversion

- svndumpfilter

15.1 svn

The svn program is the basic command-line client for interacting with Subversion. It contains a full array of commands that can be used for interacting with a Subversion working copy or repository.

Online help for each of svn's subcommands can be obtained by running the program as: `svn help [COMMAND]`.

Options

- `--version`

    Outputs version information about svn.

Subcommands

The svn commands (with alternate names in parenthesis) are

- add
- blame (praise, annotate, ann)
- cat
- checkout (co)
- cleanup
- commit (ci)
- copy (cp)
- delete (del, remove, rm)
- diff (di)
- export
- help (?, h)
- import
- info
- list (ls)
- log
- merge
- mkdir
- move (mv, rename, ren)
- propdel (pdel, pd)
- propedit (pedit, pe)
- propget (pget, pg)
- proplist (plist, pl)
- propset (pset, ps)
- resolved
- revert

- status (stat, st)

- switch (sw)

- update (up)

15.1.1 svn add

This command schedules new files or directories to be placed under Subversion's control. This command doesn't actually send the file to the repository, but merely marks it for addition in the working copy. The actual addition to the repository occurs on the next svn commit command.

Basic Usage

$ svn add PATH

Options

- --targets arg

  Parse the files pointed to by arg, and add them to the list of arguments for the command.

- -N [--non-recursive]

  Don't recurse into subdirectories and add their contents.

- -q [--quiet]

  Supply the minimum output possible.

- --config-dir arg

  Load the user configuration files from the directory pointed to by arg, instead of the default directory.

- --auto-props

  Automatically set properties based on the type of file added to the repository. This overrides any defaults set in your Subversion configuration files.

- --no-auto-props

  Don't automatically set properties on any files added to the repository. This overrides any defaults set in your Subversion configuration files.

15.1.2   svn blame (praise, annotate, ann)

This command outputs the contents of one or more files, with an author and revision number listed for each line of the file. The author is the username of the last user to modify that particular line, and the revision represents the revision where the modification occurred.

Note that it's the *last* user to modify the line who is listed, even if she made a nonfunctional change such as adjusting whitespace. The output of this command is useful, but you should generally use other commands like svn log and svn diff to double-check what it tells you before relying on the author information it supplies you with.

Basic Usage

```
$ svn blame PATH...
```

   or

```
$ svn blame URL...
```

Takes one or more PATHs or URLs that point to files. Attempting to run svn blame on a directory results in an error. You can mix URLs and PATHs on the same command line.

Options

- -r [--revision] arg

  Use the version of files in revision arg when processing the command. Takes either a single revision number, or a range of revisions, separated by a colon.

  ```
  --revision REV
  --revision LOW:HIGH
  ```

- --username arg

  Use the username arg when contacting the repository. If a username is not given, Subversion uses the username that has been cached in the current working copy, or if a URL is given instead of a PATH, it uses the current login username.

- --password arg

  Use the password arg when contacting the repository. If a password is needed and not supplied, Subversion prompts for one.

- --no-auth-cache

  Don't keep the authentication information for use with future repository connections.

- --non-interactive

  Don't ask the user for any additional information. Useful for running the command in a script.

- `--config-dir arg`

  Load the user configuration files from the directory pointed to by `arg`, instead of the default directory.

15.1.3 svn cat

This command dumps the specified file(s) to standard output.

Basic Usage

```
$ svn cat PATH...
```

  or

```
$ svn cat URL...
```

Takes one or more PATHs or URLs that point to files. Attempting to run `svn cat` on a directory results in an error. You can mix URLs and PATHs on the same command line.

Options

- `-r [--revision] arg`

  Use the version of files in revision `arg` when processing the command. Takes only a single revision number. Ranges are not allowed.

- `--username arg`

  Use the username `arg` when contacting the repository. If a username is not given, Subversion uses the username that has been cached in the current working copy, or if a URL is given instead of a PATH, it uses the current login username.

- `--password arg`

  Use the password `arg` when contacting the repository. If a password is needed and not supplied, Subversion prompts for one.

- `--no-auth-cache`

  Don't keep the authentication information for use with future repository connections.

- `--non-interactive`

  Don't ask the user for any additional information. Useful for running the command in a script.

- `--config-dir arg`

  Load the user configuration files from the directory pointed to by `arg`, instead of the default directory.

15.1.4 svn checkout (co)

This command retrieves the contents of a repository (or part of a repository) and places them in a new working copy on the local machine.

Basic Usage

```
$ svn checkout URL [PATH]
```

Subversion checks out a working copy from the URL given. If the URL points to a directory other than the root of a repository, Subversion recursively checks out that directory and its contents. If the URL points to the root of the repository, the whole repository is checked out. URLs must point to a directory. Single files cannot be checked out (use svn cat).

If a PATH is given, Subversion uses that as the location and name of the working copy (the basename of the PATH is the root of the working copy). If no PATH is given, the working copy is created in the current directory, with the same name as the directory being checked out (or the repository, if the root is being checked out).

Options

- -r --revision] arg

  Use the version of files in revision arg when performing the checkout. Takes only a single revision number, not ranges.

- -q --quiet]

  Supply the minimum output possible.

- -N --non-recursive]

  Don't recurse into subdirectories and process their contents. Only the specified directory and top-level files that it contains are checked out.

- --username arg

  Use the username arg when contacting the repository. If a username is not given, Subversion uses the username that has been cached in the current working copy, or if a URL is given instead of a PATH, it uses the current login username.

- --password arg

  Use the password arg when contacting the repository. If a password is needed and not supplied, Subversion prompts for one.

- --no-auth-cache

  Don't keep the authentication information for use with future repository connections.

- `--non-interactive`

  Don't ask the user for any additional information. Useful for running the command in a script.

- `--config-dir arg`

  Load the user configuration files from the directory pointed to by `arg`, instead of the default directory.

15.1.5   svn cleanup

This command can be used to clean up a working copy if a command fails and leaves the working copy unusable. It removes all locks and completes any unfinished operations in order to get the working copy back into a usable state.

Basic Usage

```
$ svn cleanup
```

   or

```
$ svn cleanup PATH...
```

Options

- `--diff3-cmd arg`

  Use the command pointed to by `arg` for performing two- and three-way diffs, instead of the built-in functions.

- `--config-dir arg`

  Load the user configuration files from the directory pointed to by `arg`, instead of the default directory.

15.1.6   svn commit (ci)

This command sends local modifications to files or directories to the repository, creating a new revision.

Basic Usage

```
$ svn commit
```

   or

```
$ svn commit PATH...
```

Options

- **-m --message] arg**

  Use `arg` as the log message for the commit. If this option isn't used, an editor is opened to request the log message (if a default editor has been configured or the --editor-cmd option is also used).

- **-F --file] arg**

  Read the log message from the file `arg`.

- **-q --quiet]**

  Supply the minimum output possible.

- **-N --non-recursive]**

  Don't recurse into subdirectories and process their contents.

- **--targets arg**

  Parse the files pointed to by `arg`, and add them to the list of arguments for the command.

- **--force-log**

  Force the provided log message source to be accepted as valid. This may be needed if Subversion thinks that a provided log message or file containing a log message is meant as something else (for instance, if you use a versioned file as the source of your log message).

- **--username arg**

  Use the username `arg` when contacting the repository. If a username is not given, Subversion uses the username that has been cached in the current working copy, or if a URL is given instead of a PATH, it uses the current login username.

- **--password arg**

  Use the password `arg` when contacting the repository. If a password is needed and not supplied, Subversion prompts for one.

- **--no-auth-cache**

  Don't keep the authentication information for use with future repository connections.

- **--non-interactive**

  Don't ask the user for any additional information. Useful for running the command in a script.

- **--editor-cmd arg**

  Use the command pointed to by `arg` as the editor to open when asking for a log message, rather than the system-wide default editor.

- --encoding arg

  Use to indicate that the log message is encoded in a different encoding than the system default. The encoding used is given as arg.

- --config-dir arg

  Load the user configuration files from the directory pointed to by arg, instead of the default directory.

15.1.7 svn copy (cp)

This command copies files or directories within a repository or working copy (or from one to the other).

Basic Usage

```
$ svn copy SOURCE_PATH DESTINATION_PATH
```

Either the source path or destination path (or both) can be URLs that point to a point in the repository. If the destination is a URL, the copy is committed immediately, instead of being scheduled for the next svn commit.

Options

- -m --message] arg

  Use arg as the log message for the commit. On repository-side copies, if this option isn't used, an editor is opened to request the log message (if a default editor has been configured or the --editor-cmd option is also used).

- -F --file] arg

  Read the log message from the file arg.

- -r --revision] arg

  Use revision arg as the source for the file being copied. Only takes single revision numbers, not ranges.

- -q --quiet]

  Supply the minimum output possible.

- --username arg

  Use the username arg when contacting the repository. If a username is not given, Subversion uses the username that has been cached in the current working copy, or if a URL is given instead of a PATH, it uses the current login username.

- --password arg

  Use the password arg when contacting the repository. If a password is needed and not supplied, Subversion prompts for one.

- `--no-auth-cache`

  Don't keep the authentication information for use with future repository connections.

- `--non-interactive`

  Don't ask the user for any additional information. Useful for running the command in a script.

- `--force-log`

  Force the provided log message source to be accepted as valid. This may be needed if Subversion thinks that a provided log message or file containing a log message is meant as something else (for instance, if you use a versioned file as the source of your log message).

- `--editor-cmd arg`

  Use the command pointed to by `arg` as the editor to open when asking for a log message, rather than the system-wide default editor.

- `--encoding arg`

  Use to indicate that the log message is encoded in a different encoding than the system default. The encoding used is given as `arg`.

- `--config-dir arg`

  Load the user configuration files from the directory pointed to by `arg`, instead of the default directory.

15.1.8   svn delete (del, remove, rm)

This command marks files or directories in a working copy for deletion. The next time a commit occurs, they are removed in the repository. The command can also operate directly on a repository, in which case the removal occurs immediately (as if an `svn commit` had been executed immediately following the deletion).

Basic Usage

```
$ svn delete PATH...
```

   or

```
$ svn delete URL...
```

Takes one or more PATHs or URLs. Must use all PATHs or all URLs. You cannot mix the two.

Options

- `--force`

  Turns off any precautions meant to ensure that you don't accidentally lose data. This can be useful in some instances, if you know what you're doing, but use it with caution.

- `--force-log`

  Force the provided log message source to be accepted as valid. This may be needed if Subversion thinks that a provided log message or file containing a log message is meant as something else (for instance, if you use a versioned file as the source of your log message).

- `-m --message] arg`

  Use `arg` as the log message for the commit. On repository-side deletions, if this option isn't used, an editor is opened to request the log message (if a default editor has been configured or the `--editor-cmd` option is also used).

- `-F --file] arg`

  Read the log message from the file `arg`.

- `-q --quiet]`

  Supply the minimum output possible.

- `--targets arg`

  Parse the files pointed to by `arg`, and add them to the list of arguments for the command.

- `--username arg`

  Use the username `arg` when contacting the repository. If a username is not given, Subversion uses the username that has been cached in the current working copy, or if a URL is given instead of a PATH, it uses the current login username.

- `--password arg`

  Use the password `arg` when contacting the repository. If a password is needed and not supplied, Subversion prompts for one.

- `--no-auth-cache`

  Don't keep the authentication information for use with future repository connections.

- `--non-interactive`

  Don't ask the user for any additional information. Useful for running the command in a script.

- `--editor-cmd arg`

  Use the command pointed to by `arg` as the editor to open when asking for a log message, rather than the system-wide default editor.

- `--encoding arg`

  Use to indicate that the log message is encoded in a different encoding than the system default. The encoding used is given as `arg`.

- `--config-dir arg`

  Load the user configuration files from the directory pointed to by `arg`, instead of the default directory.

15.1.9   svn diff (di)

This command outputs the differences between two files, or two revisions of the same file. Both files used for the comparison can come from the current working copy, or from a given revision in the repository.

Basic Usage

```
$ svn diff -r N:M URL...
```

Or, if you want to take the difference between two different URLs in a repository

```
$ svn diff URL1@N URL2@M
```

or

```
$ svn diff -r N:M URL1 URL2
```

Finally, the long form of the command is

```
$ svn diff -r N:M --old OLD_URL --new NEW_URL [PATH...]
```

If one or more PATHs are used, Subversion restricts the diff output to those paths, relative to each URL.

In Subversion 1.1 and later, use of the @ sign indicates peg revisions. If a peg revision is used, Subversion takes the file of the given URL at that particular revision. If the normal `--revision` option is used, Subversion instead looks for the file of the given URL in the HEAD revision and follows it back to the requested revision. Normally, the distinction is unimportant, but if a file was moved or deleted and then later replaced by a file of the same name, using the wrong form might not give you the file that you really want.

Options

- -r --revision] arg

  The two revisions to use when performing the diff, in the form N:M, where N is the old revision and M is the new revision.

- --old arg

  The URL (given as arg for the older revision used in the diff). This option must be accompanied by --new.

- --new arg

  The URL (given as arg for the newer revision used in the diff). This option must be accompanied by --old.

- -x --extensions] arg

  Pass the value of arg to the GNU diff program, when performing the diff operation. If you use this option, you must also use the --diff-cmd option.

- -N --non-recursive]

  Don't recurse into subdirectories and process their contents.

- --diff-cmd arg

  Tell Subversion to use arg as the diff command for performing the diff.

- --no-diff-deleted

  If a file has been deleted, don't print the differences. This prevents an entire file from being dumped if it has been deleted in one of the versions compared.

- --notice-ancestry

  Look at a file's ancestry when comparing two files. If two files have similar contents but different ancestry, they are considered different.

- --username arg

  Use the username arg when contacting the repository. If a username is not given, Subversion uses the username that has been cached in the current working copy, or if a URL is given instead of a PATH, it uses the current login username.

- --password arg

  Use the password arg when contacting the repository. If a password is needed and not supplied, Subversion prompts for one.

- --no-auth-cache

  Don't keep the authentication information for use with future repository connections.

- `--non-interactive`

  Don't ask the user for any additional information. Useful for running the command in a script.

- `--config-dir arg`

  Load the user configuration files from the directory pointed to by `arg`, instead of the default directory.

15.1.10   `svn export`

This command is used to get a local copy of a repository (or portion of a repository) without any Subversion-specific information (i.e., without the `.svn` directories).

Basic Usage

```
$ svn export URL [DESTINATION_PATH]
```

  or

```
$ svn export WC_PATH [DESTINATION_PATH]
```

    The URL or WC_PATH must point to a directory. Individual files cannot be exported (use `svn cat`). If no DESTINATION_PATH is given, the exported directory is placed in the current working directory, using its name from the repository. If a DESTINATION_PATH is given, the exported directory is created with the path and name supplied as the destination.

Options

- `-r --revision] arg`

  Use the version of files in revision `arg` when performing the export. Takes only single revision numbers, no ranges.

- `-q --quiet]`

  Supply the minimum output possible.

- `--force`

  Turns off any precautions meant to ensure that you don't accidentally lose data. This can be useful in some instances, if you know what you're doing, but use it with caution.

- `--username arg`

  Use the username `arg` when contacting the repository. If a username is not given, Subversion uses the username that has been cached in the current working copy, or if a URL is given instead of a PATH, it uses the current login username.

- --password arg

  Use the password arg when contacting the repository. If a password is needed and not supplied, Subversion prompts for one.

- --no-auth-cache

  Don't keep the authentication information for use with future repository connections.

- --non-interactive

  Don't ask the user for any additional information. Useful for running the command in a script.

- --config-dir arg

  Load the user configuration files from the directory pointed to by arg, instead of the default directory.

- --native-eol arg (1.1 only)

  Allows you to specify an end-of-line indicator to use for files that use the default system EOL indicator (i.e., have svn:eol-style unset or set to native). The argument for this option can be LF, CR, or CRLF.

15.1.11   svn help (?, h)

This command outputs documentation for the svn command. To get help on a specific subcommand, run help with the name of the command.

Basic Usage

```
$ svn help [COMMAND]
```

Options

None

15.1.12   svn import

This command is used to bring an unversioned file or directory into a repository. Unlike svn add, this command performs an immediate commit. It also doesn't need a working copy to function.

Basic Usage

```
$ svn import URL
```

  or

```
$ svn import PATH URL
```

If just a URL is given, the current working directory is recursively imported into the repository pointed to by URL. If a PATH is given, the directory pointed to by PATH is imported.

Options

- `-m --message] arg`

  Use `arg` as the log message for the commit. If this option isn't used, an editor is opened to request the log message (if a default editor has been configured or the `--editor-cmd` option is also used).

- `-F --file] arg`

  Read the log message from the file `arg`.

- `-q --quiet]`

  Supply the minimum output possible.

- `-N --non-recursive]`

  Don't recurse into subdirectories and process their contents.

- `--username arg`

  Use the username `arg` when contacting the repository. If a username is not given, Subversion uses the username that has been cached in the current working copy, or if a URL is given instead of a PATH, it uses the current login username.

- `--password arg`

  Use the password `arg` when contacting the repository. If a password is needed and not supplied, Subversion prompts for one.

- `--no-auth-cache`

  Don't keep the authentication information for use with future repository connections.

- `--non-interactive`

  Don't ask the user for any additional information. Useful for running the command in a script.

- `--force-log`

  Force the provided log message source to be accepted as valid. This may be needed if Subversion thinks that a provided log message or file containing a log message is meant as something else (for instance, if you use a versioned file as the source of your log message).

- `--editor-cmd arg`

  Use the command pointed to by `arg` as the editor to open when asking for a log message, rather than the system-wide default editor.

- `--encoding arg`

  Use to indicate that the log message is encoded in a different encoding than the system default. The encoding used is given as `arg`.

- `--config-dir arg`

  Load the user configuration files from the directory pointed to by `arg`, instead of the default directory.

- `--auto-props`

  Automatically set properties based on the type of file imported into the repository.

- `--no-auto-props`

  Don't automatically set properties on any files added to the repository.

15.1.13 svn info

This command is used to output a variety of information about files and directories in a working copy.

Basic Usage

```
$ svn info [PATH...]
```

If no PATH is given, the info for the current working directory is displayed.

Options

- `--targets arg`

  Parse the files pointed to by `arg`, and add them to the list of arguments for the command.

- `-R --recursive]`

  Recursively descend into any directories supplied in the path, and process all of the files contained therein.

- `--config-dir arg`

  Load the user configuration files from the directory pointed to by `arg`, instead of the default directory.

15.1.14 svn list (ls)

This command lists the contents of directories in a repository.

Basic Usage

```
$ svn list [PATH...]
```

  or

```
$ svn list [URL...]
```

  Takes one or more PATHs or URLs. You may mix PATHs and URLs in the same command.

Options

- -r --revision] arg

  List the files as of revision `arg`. Only accepts single revision numbers, not ranges.

- -v --verbose]

  Print extra information about each file and directory. For each item listed, `svn list` tells you the last revision where that item was modified, the last user who modified the item, the size of the item (if it is a file and not a directory), and the date that the item was modified.

- -R --recursive]

  Recursively descend into any directories supplied in the path, and process all of the files contained therein.

- --username arg

  Use the username `arg` when contacting the repository. If a username is not given, Subversion uses the username that has been cached in the current working copy, or if a URL is given instead of a PATH, it uses the current login username.

- --password arg

  Use the password `arg` when contacting the repository. If a password is needed and not supplied, Subversion prompts for one.

- --no-auth-cache

  Don't keep the authentication information for use with future repository connections.

- --non-interactive

  Don't ask the user for any additional information. Useful for running the command in a script.

- --config-dir arg

  Load the user configuration files from the directory pointed to by `arg`, instead of the default directory.

15.1.15   svn log

This command can be used to output the log message history of a file or directory.

Basic Usage

```
$ svn log [PATH...]
```

or

```
$ svn log URL [PATH...]
```

If no URL or PATH is given, the log history for the current working directory is displayed. If just PATHs are given, the log history for the files or directories pointed to is displayed. If a URL is given, the log history for the repository file or directory pointed to by the URL is displayed. If the URL points to a directory, and one or more PATHs are given after the URL, those PATHs are considered relative to the URL, and the logs for all file or directories pointed to are displayed.

Options

- -r --revision] arg

  Limit the logs messages displayed to a specific revision or range of revisions. To enter a range, use the form -r N:M, where N and M are the starting and ending revisions in the range, respectively.

- -q --quiet]

  Output the minimum amount of output; usually output consists of the revision numbers, the author of the revision, and the date of the revision (see --verbose). The log messages are not output.

- -v --verbose]

  Tell Subversion to output the files that were changed, and what action was performed on them in addition to the normal output for each log message. File actions include whether the file was modified (M), added (A), or deleted (D). If used in conjunction with --quiet, the files that have changed are output in addition to the usual output when using --quiet.

- --targets arg

  Parse the files pointed to by arg, and add them to the list of arguments for the command.

- --stop-on-copy

  Tell Subversion to stop outputting log messages as soon as it reaches a revision where the file or directory was copied from another location.

- `--incremental`

  Format the output so that it can be concatenated with the output from another run of `svn log`. In normal output, this leaves the final separator line off of the output. When `--xml` is used, it leaves off an XML header and enclosing `<log>` element.

- `--xml`

  Format the output in an XML format.

- `--username arg`

  Use the username `arg` when contacting the repository. If a username is not given, Subversion uses the username that has been cached in the current working copy, or if a URL is given instead of a PATH, it uses the current login username.

- `--password arg`

  Use the password `arg` when contacting the repository. If a password is needed and not supplied, Subversion prompts for one.

- `--no-auth-cache`

  Don't keep the authentication information for use with future repository connections.

- `--non-interactive`

  Don't ask the user for any additional information. Useful for running the command in a script.

- `--config-dir arg`

  Load the user configuration files from the directory pointed to by `arg`, instead of the default directory.

15.1.16   svn merge

This command takes the differences between two revisions of a repository (or a working copy and a repository revision) and merges them into a working copy.

Basic Usage

```
$ svn merge SOURCE_URL1[@N] SOURCE_URL2[@M] [WC_PATH]
```

   or

```
$ svn merge SOURCE_PATH1@N SOURCE_PATH2@M [WC_PATH]
```

   or

```
$ svn merge -r N:M SOURCE [WC_PATH]
```

In the first and second usages, two sources are given for comparison, with the differences merged into the WC_PATH in the working copy. If the sources are URLs, the revisions can be omitted (and Subversion uses the HEAD revisions). If the sources are given as paths in the working copy, a revision must be given, and the comparisons are made against the corresponding URLs to each working copy path.

In the third form, the SOURCE can be either a URL or a working copy path. The revision range is required in this case to give two different versions to compare. The differences are merged into WC_PATH as in the first two usage forms.

In Subversion 1.1 and later, the use of the @ sign indicates peg revisions. If a peg revision is used, Subversion takes the file of the given URL at that particular revision. If the normal --revision option is used, Subversion instead looks for the file of the given URL in the HEAD revision and follows it back to the requested revision. Normally, the distinction is unimportant, but if a file was moved or deleted and then later replaced by a file of the same name, using the wrong form might not give you the file that you really want.

Options

- -r --revision] arg

  Give the two revisions to be merged between, in the form -r N:M, where N is the older revision and M is the newer revision. The revision numbers can be reversed to reverse the merge direction.

- -N --non-recursive]

  Don't recurse into subdirectories and process their contents.

- -q --quiet]

  Supply the minimum output possible.

- --force

  Turn off any precautions meant to ensure that you don't accidentally lose data. This can be useful in some instances, if you know what you're doing, but use it with caution.

- --dry-run

  Run the command without actually modifying anything. Outputs which files will change, as well as any expected conflicts.

- --diff3-cmd arg

  Use the command pointed to by arg for performing two- and three-way diffs, instead of the built-in functions.

- --ignore-ancestry

  Cause Subversion to ignore the ancestry of the files involved in the merge.

- `--username arg`

  Use the username `arg` when contacting the repository. If a username is not given, Subversion uses the username that has been cached in the current working copy, or if a URL is given instead of a PATH, it uses the current login username.

- `--password arg`

  Use the password `arg` when contacting the repository. If a password is needed and not supplied, Subversion prompts for one.

- `--no-auth-cache`

  Don't keep the authentication information for use with future repository connections.

- `--non-interactive`

  Don't ask the user for any additional information. Useful for running the command in a script.

- `--config-dir arg`

  Load the user configuration files from the directory pointed to by `arg`, instead of the default directory.

15.1.17   svn mkdir

This command creates a new versioned directory, either in a working copy or directly on the repository. If the directory is created in the working copy, it is scheduled for addition to the repository on the next commit (just as if you'd created a local directory and then done an `svn add`). If the directory is created in the repository, it is committed immediately, with a new revision created (just as if you'd done an `svn commit`).

Basic Usage

`$ svn mkdir PATH...`

   or

`$ svn mkdir URL...`

   Either PATHs or URLs can be given, but PATHs and URLs cannot be mixed on the same command line.

Options

- `-m --message] arg`

  Use `arg` as the log message for the commit. On repository-side directory creation operations, if this option isn't used, an editor is opened to request the log message (if a default editor has been configured or the `--editor-cmd` option is also used).

- -F --file] arg

  Read the log message from the file arg.

- -q --quiet]

  Supply the minimum output possible.

- --username arg

  Use the username arg when contacting the repository. If a username is not given, Subversion uses the username that has been cached in the current working copy, or if a URL is given instead of a PATH, it uses the current login username.

- --password arg

  Use the password arg when contacting the repository. If a password is needed and not supplied, Subversion prompts for one.

- --no-auth-cache

  Don't keep the authentication information for use with future repository connections.

- --non-interactive

  Don't ask the user for any additional information. Useful for running the command in a script.

- --editor-cmd arg

  Use the command pointed to by arg as the editor to open when asking for a log message, rather than the system-wide default editor.

- --encoding arg

  Use to indicate that the log message is encoded in a different encoding than the system default. The encoding used is given as arg.

- --force-log

  Force the provided log message source to be accepted as valid. This may be needed if Subversion thinks that a provided log message or file containing a log message is meant as something else (for instance, if you use a versioned file as the source of your log message).

- --config-dir arg

  Load the user configuration files from the directory pointed to by arg, instead of the default directory.

15.1.18 svn move (mv, rename, ren)

This command moves a file in a repository or working copy from one location to another. If the move is done in the working copy, the change is scheduled to be applied to the repository on the next commit. If it is applied directly to a repository, the move takes place immediately, with a new revision (as if svn commit had been run).

Basic Usage

```
$ svn move SOURCE DESTINATION
```

The SOURCE and DESTINATION can either be working copy paths or URLs pointing to the repository. In either case, SOURCE and DESTINATION must be of the same form (both paths or both URLs).

Options

- -m --message] arg

  Use arg as the log message for the commit. On repository-side moves, if this option isn't used, an editor is opened to request the log message (if a default editor has been configured or the --editor-cmd option is also used).

- -F --file] arg

  Read the log message from the file arg.

- -r --revision] arg

  For all practical purposes, svn move does not really accept --revision. You can specify it as an option, but the only valid argument is HEAD.

- -q --quiet]

  Supply the minimum output possible.

- --force

  Turns off any precautions meant to ensure that you don't accidentally lose data. This can be useful in some instances, if you know what you're doing, but use it with caution.

- --username arg

  Use the username arg when contacting the repository. If a username is not given, Subversion uses the username that has been cached in the current working copy, or if a URL is given instead of a PATH, it uses the current login username.

- --password arg

  Use the password arg when contacting the repository. If a password is needed and not supplied, Subversion prompts for one.

- --no-auth-cache

  Don't keep the authentication information for use with future repository connections.

- --non-interactive

  Don't ask the user for any additional information. Useful for running the command in a script.

- `--editor-cmd arg`

  Use the command pointed to by `arg` as the editor to open when asking for a log message, rather than the system-wide default editor.

- `--encoding arg`

  Use to indicate that the log message is encoded in a different encoding than the system default. The encoding used is given as `arg`.

- `--force-log`

  Force the provided log message source to be accepted as valid. This may be needed if Subversion thinks that a provided log message or file containing a log message is meant as something else (for instance, if you use a versioned file as the source of your log message).

- `--config-dir arg`

  Load the user configuration files from the directory pointed to by `arg`, instead of the default directory.

15.1.19 svn propdel (pdel, pd)

This command deletes a property from a working copy file, or deletes a revision property. If the working copy property is deleted, the deletion is committed to the repository on the next `svn commit`. If the deletion is applied to a revision property, the change takes place immediately, and is not undoable.

Basic Usage

```
$ propdel PROP_NAME [PATH...]
```

or

```
$ propdel PROP_NAME --revprop -r REVISION [URL]
```

If no PATHs are given, the property is deleted from the current working directory. Otherwise, it is deleted from all files or directories pointed to by the PATHs. For revision properties, the URL of the current working copy is used if a URL is not given.

Options

- `-q --quiet]`

  Supply the minimum output possible.

- `-R --recursive]`

  Recursively descend into any directories supplied in the path, and process all of the files contained therein.

- -r --revision] arg

  Indicate the revision that should be modified when deleting a revision property. Must be used in conjunction with --revprop.

- --revprop

  Indicate that the property referred to is a revision property, not a versioned property.

- --username arg

  Use the username arg when contacting the repository. If a username is not given, Subversion uses the username that has been cached in the current working copy, or if a URL is given instead of a PATH, it uses the current login username.

- --password arg

  Use the password arg when contacting the repository. If a password is needed and not supplied, Subversion prompts for one.

- --no-auth-cache

  Don't keep the authentication information for use with future repository connections.

- --non-interactive

  Don't ask the user for any additional information. Useful for running the command in a script.

- --config-dir arg

  Load the user configuration files from the directory pointed to by arg, instead of the default directory.

15.1.20   svn propedit (pedit, pe)

This command opens a text editor, with the contents of a versioned property in a working copy, or a revision property in the repository. If the property contents are changed and saved, the modified property value is applied to the property. For a working copy file, the property change is applied at the next commit. If the property edited is a revision property, the changes take effect immediately on saving and exiting from the text editor, and are not undoable.

Basic Usage

```
$ propedit PROP_NAME [PATH...]
```

   or

```
$ propedit PROP_NAME --revprop -r REVISION [URL]
```

   If no PATHs are given, the property is edited on the current working directory. Otherwise, it is edited for all files or directories pointed to by the PATHs (each file or directory is opened separately in the editor). For revision properties, the URL of the current working copy is used if a URL is not given.

Options

- **-r --revision] arg**

  Indicate the revision that should be modified when editing a revision property. Must be used in conjunction with --revprop.

- **--revprop**

  Indicate that the property referred to is a revision property, not a versioned property.

- **--username arg**

  Use the username arg when contacting the repository. If a username is not given, Subversion uses the username that has been cached in the current working copy, or if a URL is given instead of a PATH, it uses the current login username.

- **--password arg**

  Use the password arg when contacting the repository. If a password is needed and not supplied, Subversion prompts for one.

- **--no-auth-cache**

  Don't keep the authentication information for use with future repository connections.

- **--non-interactive**

  Don't ask the user for any additional information. Useful for running the command in a script.

- **--encoding arg**

  Use to indicate that the log message is encoded in a different encoding than the system default. The encoding used is given as arg.

- **--editor-cmd arg**

  Use the command pointed to by arg as the editor to open when asking for a log message, rather than the system-wide default editor.

- **--force**

  Turns off any precautions meant to ensure that you don't accidentally lose data. This can be useful in some instances, if you know what you're doing, but use it with caution.

- **--config-dir arg**

  Load the user configuration files from the directory pointed to by arg, instead of the default directory.

15.1.21   svn propget (pget, pg)

This command outputs the value of a versioned property on a file or directory, or a revision property.

Basic Usage

```
$ propget PROP_NAME [PATH...]
```

or

```
$ propget PROP_NAME --revprop -r REVISION [URL]
```

If no PATHs are given, the property is output for the current working directory. Otherwise, it is output from all files or directories pointed to by the PATHs. For revision properties, the URL of the current working copy is used if a URL is not given.

Options

- `-R --recursive]`

  Recursively descend into any directories supplied in the path, and process all of the files contained therein.

- `-r --revision] arg`

  Indicate the revision that the property should be retrieved from. May be used in conjunction with revision properties and versioned properties.

- `--revprop`

  Indicate that the property referred to is a revision property, not a versioned property.

- `--strict`

  Indicate that Subversion should use strict semantics, which prevents the output of an end-of-line character at the end of the output. This is useful for outputting binary files stored in properties.

- `--username arg`

  Use the username `arg` when contacting the repository. If a username is not given, Subversion uses the username that has been cached in the current working copy, or if a URL is given instead of a PATH, it uses the current login username.

- `--password arg`

  Use the password `arg` when contacting the repository. If a password is needed and not supplied, Subversion prompts for one.

- `--no-auth-cache`

  Don't keep the authentication information for use with future repository connections.

- `--non-interactive`

  Don't ask the user for any additional information. Useful for running the command in a script.

- `--config-dir arg`

  Load the user configuration files from the directory pointed to by `arg`, instead of the default directory.

15.1.22   svn proplist (plist, pl)

This command outputs all of the versioned properties that have been set for a file or directory, or all of the revision properties that have been set for a given revision.

Basic Usage

`$ propdel [PATH...]`

   or

`$ propdel --revprop -r REVISION [URL]`

If no PATHs are given, the properties set for the current working directory are listed. Otherwise, properties are listed for all files or directories pointed to by the PATHs. For revision properties, the URL of the current working copy is used if a URL is not given.

Options

- `-v --verbose]`

  Cause Subversion to output property values in addition to property names when listing set properties.

- `-R --recursive]`

  Recursively descend into any directories supplied in the path, and process all of the files contained therein.

- `-r --revision] arg`

  Indicate the revision that the properties should be retrieved from. May be used in conjunction with revision properties and versioned properties.

- `-q --quiet]`

  Supply the minimum output possible.

- `--revprop`

  Indicate that the property referred to is a revision property, not a versioned property.

- `--username arg`

  Use the username `arg` when contacting the repository. If a username is not given, Subversion uses the username that has been cached in the current working copy, or if a URL is given instead of a PATH, it uses the current login username.

- `--password arg`

  Use the password `arg` when contacting the repository. If a password is needed and not supplied, Subversion prompts for one.

- `--no-auth-cache`

  Don't keep the authentication information for use with future repository connections.

- `--non-interactive`

  Don't ask the user for any additional information. Useful for running the command in a script.

- `--config-dir arg`

  Load the user configuration files from the directory pointed to by `arg`, instead of the default directory.

15.1.23 svn propset (pset, ps)

This command sets the value of a versioned property on a working copy file or directory, or the value of a revision property in the repository (erasing any previous value). The value to set the property to is supplied on the command line. If a working copy file or directory is modified, the property change is sent to the repository on the next commit. If the change is applied to a revision property, the change is applied immediately, and is not undoable.

Basic Usage

```
$ propset PROP_NAME PROP_VAL [PATH...]
```

or

```
$ propset PROP_NAME --revprop -r REVISION PROP_VAL [URL]
```

If no PATHs are given, the property is set on the current working directory. Otherwise, it is set on all files or directories pointed to by the PATHs. For revision properties, the URL of the current working copy is used if a URL is not given.

Options

- `-F --file] arg`

- `-q --quiet]`

  Supply the minimum output possible.

- `-r --revision] arg`

  Indicate the revision that should be modified when setting a revision property. Must be used in conjunction with `--revprop`.

- `--targets arg`

  Parse the files pointed to by `arg`, and add them to the list of arguments for the command.

- `-R --recursive]`

  Recursively descend into any directories supplied in the path, and process all of the files contained therein.

- `--revprop`

  Indicate that the property referred to is a revision property, not a versioned property.

- `--username arg`

  Use the username `arg` when contacting the repository. If a username is not given, Subversion uses the username that has been cached in the current working copy, or if a URL is given instead of a PATH, it uses the current login username.

- `--password arg`

  Use the password `arg` when contacting the repository. If a password is needed and not supplied, Subversion prompts for one.

- `--no-auth-cache`

  Don't keep the authentication information for use with future repository connections.

- `--non-interactive`

  Don't ask the user for any additional information. Useful for running the command in a script.

- `--encoding arg`

  Use to indicate that the log message is encoded in a different encoding than the system default. The encoding used is given as `arg`.

- `--force`

  Turn off any precautions meant to ensure that you don't accidentally lose data. This can be useful in some instances, if you know what you're doing, but use it with caution.

- `--config-dir arg`

  Load the user configuration files from the directory pointed to by `arg`, instead of the default directory.

15.1.24 svn resolved

This command tells Subversion that a conflicted file has been fixed to resolve the conflict. This removes the conflict state from the file, and deletes any additional files generated by Subversion when the conflict was detected.

Basic Usage

```
$ svn resolved PATH...
```

Options

- `--targets arg`

  Parse the files pointed to by `arg`, and add them to the list of arguments for the command.

- `-R --recursive]`

  Recursively descend into any directories supplied in the path, and process all of the files contained therein.

- `-q --quiet]`

  Supply the minimum output possible.

- `--config-dir arg`

  Load the user configuration files from the directory pointed to by `arg`, instead of the default directory.

15.1.25   svn revert

This command reverts a file in a working copy to its last unmodified state. This permanently removes all local changes, and any scheduled actions (addition, deletion, and so on).

Basic Usage

```
$ svn revert PATH...
```

Options

- `--targets arg`

  Parse the files pointed to by `arg`, and add them to the list of arguments for the command.

- `-R --recursive]`

  Recursively descend into any directories supplied in the path, and process all of the files contained therein.

- `-q --quiet]`

  Supply the minimum output possible.

- `--config-dir arg`

  Load the user configuration files from the directory pointed to by `arg`, instead of the default directory.

15.1.26   svn status (stat, st)

This command outputs the current status of files in a working copy directory.

Basic Usage

```
$ svn status [PATH...]
```

Options

- -u --show-updates]

  Cause the output to show which files have been updated in the repository, too. This requires Subversion to contact the repository, which is not normally done when running svn status.

- -v --verbose]

  Cause Subversion to output all of the files in examined directories, regardless of whether they have been modified locally. It also outputs the current working copy revision of the file, the last committed revision of the file, and the file's last author.

- -N --non-recursive]

  Don't recurse into subdirectories and process their contents.

- -q --quiet]

  Supply the minimum output possible.

- --no-ignore

  Instruct Subversion to show files that it has been instructed to ignore through the svn:ignore property or user configuration.

- --username arg

  Use the username arg when contacting the repository. If a username is not given, Subversion uses the username that has been cached in the current working copy, or if a URL is given instead of a PATH, it uses the current login username.

- --password arg

  Use the password arg when contacting the repository. If a password is needed and not supplied, Subversion prompts for one.

- --no-auth-cache

  Don't keep the authentication information for use with future repository connections.

- --non-interactive

  Don't ask the user for any additional information. Useful for running the command in a script.

- `--config-dir arg`

  Load the user configuration files from the directory pointed to by `arg`, instead of the default directory.

15.1.27   svn switch (sw)

This command switches the current URL of a file or directory in a working copy. This can be used to switch a directory to a branch or tag, or to switch an entire working copy to a new URL, if the repository is moved.

Basic Usage

```
$ svn switch URL [PATH]
```

   or

```
$ svn switch --relocate FROM_URL TO_URL [PATH...]
```

   If no PATHs are given, the current working copy directory is switched.

Options

- `-r --revision] arg`

  Give a specific revision to place the working copy at when switching. This is equivalent to running `svn update -r N` immediately after running `svn switch`.

- `-N --non-recursive]`

  Don't recurse into subdirectories and process their contents.

- `-q --quiet]`

  Supply the minimum output possible.

- `--diff3-cmd arg`

  Use the command pointed to by `arg` for performing two- and three-way diffs, instead of the built-in functions.

- `--relocate`

  Instruct Subversion to relocate the working copy from one URL to another. This is used if the URL of the repository has changed.

- `--username arg`

  Use the username `arg` when contacting the repository. If a username is not given, Subversion uses the username that has been cached in the current working copy, or if a URL is given instead of a PATH, it uses the current login username.

- --password arg

  Use the password arg when contacting the repository. If a password is needed and not supplied, Subversion prompts for one.

- --no-auth-cache

  Don't keep the authentication information for use with future repository connections.

- --non-interactive

  Don't ask the user for any additional information. Useful for running the command in a script.

- --config-dir arg

  Load the user configuration files from the directory pointed to by arg, instead of the default directory.

15.1.28 svn update (up)

This command updates files or directories in a working copy to reflect a different revision (the HEAD revision, by default). Local modifications are kept. If a directory is given, Subversion recursively updates all of the files contained within that directory, as well as the directory itself.

Basic Usage

```
$ svn update [PATH...]
```

If no PATHs are given, the current working copy directory is used.

Options

- -r --revision] arg

  Tell Subversion to update to a revision other than HEAD. Only single revisions may be given, not ranges.

- -N --non-recursive]

  Don't recurse into subdirectories and process their contents.

- -q --quiet]

  Supply the minimum output possible.

- --diff3-cmd arg

  Use the command pointed to by arg for performing two- and three-way diffs, instead of the built-in functions.

- `--username arg`

    Use the username `arg` when contacting the repository. If a username is not given, Subversion uses the username that has been cached in the current working copy, or if a URL is given instead of a PATH, it uses the current login username.

- `--password arg`

    Use the password `arg` when contacting the repository. If a password is needed and not supplied, Subversion prompts for one.

- `--no-auth-cache`

    Don't keep the authentication information for use with future repository connections.

- `--non-interactive`

    Don't ask the user for any additional information. Useful for running the command in a script.

- `--config-dir arg`

    Load the user configuration files from the directory pointed to by `arg`, instead of the default directory.

15.2   svnadmin

The `svnadmin` program provides an interface for administrative tasks associated with the repository itself. It provides command-line tools for creating new repositories, maintaining repositories, and performing backups/migration of data.

    Online help for each of `svnadmin`'s subcommands can be obtained by running the program as: `svnadmin help [COMMAND]`.

Options

- `--version`

    Outputs version information about `svnadmin`.

Subcommands

The `svnadmin` commands (with alternate names in parenthesis) are

- `create`

- `dump`

- `help (?, h)`

- `hotcopy`

- `list-dblogs`

- list-unused-dblogs

- load

- lstxns

- recover

- rmtxns

- setlog

- verify

15.2.1 svnadmin create

This command creates a new repository.

Basic Usage

$ svnadmin create --fs-type bdb REPOSITORY_NAME

    or

$ svnadming create --fs-type fsfs REPOSITORY_NAME

Options

- --bdb-txn-nosync

  Cause the newly created repository to disable fsync when a transaction is being committed. This command is Berkeley DB specific, and does nothing when creating an FSFS repository.

- --bdb-log-keep

  Tell a newly created repository to keep all of its logs, instead of periodically removing them. This command is Berkeley DB specific, and does nothing when creating an FSFS repository.

- --config-dir arg

  Load the user configuration files from the directory pointed to by arg, instead of the default directory.

- --fs-type arg (1.1 only)

  Tell svnadmin which type of repository backend to use when creating the repository. Currently, the valid values are bdb for a Berkeley DB backend and fsfs for a filesystem backend.

15.2.2   svnadmin dump

This command outputs the contents of a repository (or selected range or revisions), in a format that is portable across Subversion versions. This can be useful for creating backups of a repository, or when upgrading across major version changes (the only ones allowed to change the database format).

Basic Usage

$ svnadmin dump REPOSITORY > REPOSITORY.dump

Options

- -r --revision] arg

    List the range of revisions to dump, in the form -r N:M where N is the lower revision and M is the upper revision.

- --incremental

    Output the repository dump in a form that can be concatenated onto a previous dump-file.

- --deltas (1.1 only)

    Tell Subversion to output deltas for file changes, instead of the full file contents. This makes dumpfiles much smaller, at the cost of the dump's speed.

- -q --quiet]

    Supply the minimum output possible.

15.2.3   svnadmin help (?, h)

This command outputs documentation for the svnadmin command. To get help on a specific subcommand, run help with the name of the command.

Basic Usage

$ svnadmin help [COMMAND]

Options

None

15.2.4   svnadmin hotcopy

This command makes a copy of a repository, without requiring exclusive access.

Basic Usage

$ svnadmin hotcopy REPOSITORY REPOSITORY_BACKUP

Options

- --clean-logs

  Tell Subversion to remove any redundant log files from the repository when it is copied.

15.2.5 svnadmin list-dblogs

This command lists all of the log files associated with a Berkeley DB backend for the given repository. Be very careful though. You should never delete logfiles that are still in use (see svnadmin list-unused-dblogs).

This command only applies to Berkeley DB-based repositories.

Basic Usage

```
$ svnadmin list-dblogs REPOSITORY
```

Options

None

15.2.6 svnadmin list-unused-dblogs

This command lists all of the *unused* log files associated with a Berkeley DB backend for the given repository. Deleting these files does not harm your repository.

Basic Usage

```
$ svnadmin list-unused-dblogs
```

Options

None

15.2.7 svnadmin load

This command loads the contents of a dumpfile (created with svnadmin dump) into the given repository. If the repository already contains data, the data in the dumpfile is added as new revisions. If the repository is empty, the UUID of the repository is changed to match the UUID in the dumpfile.

Basic Usage

```
$ cat OLD_REPOSITORY.dump | svnadmin load REPOSITORY
```

Options

- `-q --quiet]`

  Supply the minimum output possible.

- `--ignore-uuid`

  Ignore any UUIDs provided by the input, and leave the UUID of the repository intact.

- `--force-uuid`

  Force Subversion to set the repository's UUID to that found in the input, regardless of whether there is already data in the repository.

- `--parent-dir arg`

  Use a specific directory in the repository as the base path for all data loaded in. This allows you to load a dumpfile in relative to somewhere other than the root directory.

15.2.8   svnadmin lstxns

This command lists all of the transactions currently in the repository, which have not yet been completely committed.

Basic Usage

`$ svnadmin lstxns REPOSITORY`

Options

None

15.2.9   svnadmin recover

This command runs a Berkeley DB recovery on the supplied repository. It only applies to a Berkeley DB-based repository, and does nothing on an FSFS repository. Make sure that you have exclusive access to the repository when this is run, as any other access during the recovery procedure could result in a corrupted repository. In Subversion 1.1 or later, if recover detects another process accessing the repository when it is run, it automatically exits.

Basic Usage

`$ svnadmin recover REPOSITORY`

Options

- `--wait` (1.1 only)

  Don't exit if another process is accessing the repository. Instead, wait for it to exit.

15.2.10   svnadmin rmtxns

This command removes the given transaction(s) from the repository.

Basic Usage

```
$ svnadmin rmtxns REPOSITORY TRANSACTION...
```

Options

- -q --quiet]

  Supply the minimum output possible.

15.2.11   svnadmin setlog

This command sets the log message for a given revision to the contents of the supplied file. This change is immediate and permanent. Because Subversion doesn't version revision properties, the old message is lost. This triggers any pre-revprop-change or post-revprop-change hook scripts.

Basic Usage

```
$ svnadmin setlog REPOSITORY -r REVISION FILE
```

Options

- -r --revision] arg

  The revision that the log should be set on.

- --bypass-hooks

  Tell Subversion not to execute any hook scripts when changing the property.

15.2.12   svnadmin verify

This command runs a verification procedure on the repository to check the integrity of the data contained therein.

Basic Usage

```
$ svnadmin verify REPOSITORY
```

Options

None

15.3   svnlook

The svnlook program provides an interface for *server-side* examination of a repository. None of the svnlook commands modify the repository in any way. Most commands can look at both committed revisions and transactions. All commands operate directly on the repository and cannot access the repository remotely.

Online help for each of svnlook's subcommands can be obtained by running the program as: svnlook help [COMMAND].

Options

- --version

    Outputs version information about svnlook.

Subcommands

The svnlook commands (with alternate names in parenthesis) are

- author

- cat

- changed

- date

- diff

- dirs-changed

- help (?, h)

- history

- info

- log

- propget (pget, pg)

- proplist (plist, pl)

- tree

- uuid

- youngest

15.3.1   svnlook author

Prints out the username of the author of the given revision or transaction.

Basic Usage

```
$ svnlook author -r REVISION REPOSITORY
```

Options

- -r --revision] arg

  Indicate the revision that the command should look at. This option and --transaction are mutually exclusive.

- -t --transaction] arg

  Indicate the transaction that the command should look at. This option and --revision are mutually exclusive.

15.3.2   svnlook cat

Outputs the contents of the given file in the repository.

Basic Usage

```
$ svnlook cat REPOSITORY FILE
```

Options

- -r --revision] arg

  Indicate the revision that the command should look at. This option and --transaction are mutually exclusive.

- -t --transaction] arg

  Indicate the transaction that the command should look at. This option and --revision are mutually exclusive.

15.3.3   svnlook changed

Prints out all of the paths that were changed in a given revision or transaction.

Basic Usage

```
$ svnlook changed -r REVISION REPOSITORY
```

Options

- -r --revision] arg

  Indicate the revision that the command should look at. This option and --transaction are mutually exclusive.

- -t --transaction] arg

  Indicate the transaction that the command should look at. This option and --revision are mutually exclusive.

15.3.4 svnlook date

Prints out the date when a revision or transaction was created.

Basic Usage

```
$ svnlook date -r REVISION REPOSITORY
```

Options

- -r --revision] arg

  Indicate the revision that the command should look at. This option and --transaction are mutually exclusive.

- -t --transaction] arg

  Indicate the transaction that the command should look at. This option and --revision are mutually exclusive.

15.3.5 svnlook diff

Prints out a diff of all the changes that occurred in a given revision or transaction.

Basic Usage

```
$ svnlook diff -r REVISION REPOSITORY
```

Options

- -r --revision] arg

  Indicate the revision that the command should look at. This option and --transaction are mutually exclusive.

- -t --transaction] arg

  Indicate the transaction that the command should look at. This option and --revision are mutually exclusive.

- --no-diff-deleted

  If a file has been deleted, don't print the differences. This prevents an entire file from being dumped if it has been deleted.

15.3.6 svnlook dirs-changed

Prints out all of the directories that had their properties modified, or had files contained therein modified, in the given revision or transaction.

Basic Usage

$ svnlook dirs-changed -r REVISION REPOSITORY

Options

- -r --revision] arg

  Indicate the revision that the command should look at. This option and --transaction are mutually exclusive.

- -t --transaction] arg

  Indicate the transaction that the command should look at. This option and --revision are mutually exclusive.

15.3.7 svnlook help (?, h)

This command outputs documentation for the svnlook command. To get help on a specific sub-command, run help with the name of the command.

Basic Usage

$ svnlook help [COMMAND]

Options

None

15.3.8 svnlook history

Shows the revisions where changes were made to the supplied path in the repository.

Basic Usage

$ svnlook history REPOSITORY [PATH]

  If no PATH is given, the history for the root of the repository is shown.

Options

- -r --revision] arg

  Indicate the revision that the command should look at.

- `--show-ids`

  Tell Subversion to show the node revision IDs for each entry listed in the history output.

15.3.9   svnlook info

Prints out information about the given revision. Information consists of the author of the revision, the datestamp, the size of the log message, and the log message.

Basic Usage

```
$ svnlook info -r REVISION REPOSITORY
```

Options

- `-r --revision] arg`

  Indicate the revision that the command should look at. This option and `--transaction` are mutually exclusive.

- `-t --transaction] arg`

  Indicate the transaction that the command should look at. This option and `--revision` are mutually exclusive.

15.3.10   svnlook log

Prints out the log message for a given revision.

Basic Usage

```
$ svnlook log -r REVISION REPOSITORY
```

Options

- `-r --revision] arg`

  Indicate the revision that the command should look at. This option and `--transaction` are mutually exclusive.

- `-t --transaction] arg`

  Indicate the transaction that the command should look at. This option and `--revision` are mutually exclusive.

15.3.11   svnlook propget (pget, pg)

Prints out the value for a given property (prints versioned properties only, not revision properties).

Basic Usage

```
$ svnlook propget -r REVISION REPOSITORY PROP_NAME PATH
```

Options

- -r --revision] arg

  Indicate the revision that the command should look at. This option and --transaction are mutually exclusive.

- -t --transaction] arg

  Indicate the transaction that the command should look at. This option and --revision are mutually exclusive.

15.3.12 svnlook proplist (plist, pl)

Lists all of the properties that have been set for a given file or directory in the repository. This command only works to list versioned properties. It does not have a way to list the revision properties set on a specific revision.

Basic Usage

```
$ svnlook proplist -r REVISION REPOSITORY PATH
```

Options

- -r --revision] arg

  Indicate the revision that the command should look at. This option and --transaction are mutually exclusive.

- -t --transaction] arg

  Indicate the transaction that the command should look at. This option and --revision are mutually exclusive.

- -v --verbose]

  Print out the property values, in addition to the property names.

15.3.13 svnlook tree

Prints out the file/directory tree for a repository, at a given revision. If a path is supplied, the tree relative to that path is shown.

Basic Usage

```
$ svnlook tree -r REVISION REPOSITORY [PATH]
```

If no PATH is given, the tree is shown for the root of the repository.

Options

- `-r --revision] arg`

  Indicate the revision that the command should look at. This option and `--transaction` are mutually exclusive.

- `-t --transaction] arg`

  Indicate the transaction that the command should look at. This option and `--revision` are mutually exclusive.

- `--show-ids`

  Tell Subversion to show the node revision IDs for each entry listed in the tree output.

15.3.14   svnlook uuid

Prints out the universal unique identifier (UUID) for the given repository.

Each repository has a UUID, which is used by the Subversion client to uniquely identify a given repository. This allows the Subversion client to know if it is accessing the same repository, even after the URL changes. It also allows the Subversion client to prevent you from running a Subversion command that crosses repository boundaries (inter-repository communication is not supported by Subversion).

Basic Usage

`$ svnlook uuid REPOSITORY`

Options

None

15.3.15   svnlook youngest

Prints out the most recently committed revision in the given repository.

Basic Usage

`$ svnlook youngest REPOSITORY`

Options

None

15.4   svnversion

Outputs a version number for a file or directory in a working copy. If the working copy has been modified, the version number has a trailing M. If it has been switched, there is a trailing S. If the working copy contains multiple revisions, the revision number is given as a range, in the form N:M, where N is the lowest revision and M is the highest.

Switched directories are detected automatically for all files and directories except the one specifically given on the command line as the base path. To determine whether the base path has been switched, you have to provide a URL on the command line that gives the unswitched URL.

Basic Usage

```
$ svnversion WC_PATH [URL]
```

Options

- -n

  Tell svnversion not to output a trailing newline at the end of the output.

- -c

  Tell svnversion to output the last changed revision numbers, instead of the revision numbers of the current revision.

- --version

  Outputs version information for the svnversion program.

15.5   svndumpfilter

This program works as a filter for the output of svnadmin dump, and allows you to exclude specific paths, or alternately specify only certain paths in the output.

Online help for each of svndumpfilter's subcommands can be obtained by running the program as: svndumpfilter help [COMMAND].

Options

- --version

  Outputs version information about svndumpfilter.

Subcommands

The svndumpfilter commands (with alternate names in parentheses) are

- exclude

- include

- help (?, h)

15.5.1   `svndumpfilter exclude`

Allows you to specify path prefixes that should be excluded from the dump stream output.

Basic Usage

`$ svnadmin dump REPOS | svndumpfilter exclude PREFIX... > REPOS.dump`

Options

- `--drop-empty-revs`

  Remove any revisions that end up empty after the filtered paths are removed.

- `--renumber-revs`

  Renumber the revisions that remain after filtering out paths, so that all revisions are sequential.

- `--preserve-revprops`

  Don't filter out any revision properties.

- `--quiet`

  Don't display any statistical information about the filtered output.

15.5.2   `svndumpfilter include`

Allows you to specify specific path prefixes and exclude all paths that don't match.

Basic Usage

`$ svnadmin dump REPOS | svndumpfilter include PREFIX... > REPOS.dump`

Options

- `--drop-empty-revs`

  Remove any revisions that end up empty after the filtered paths are removed.

- `--renumber-revs`

  Renumber the revisions that remain after filtering out paths, so that all revisions are sequential.

- `--preserve-revprops`

  Don't filter out any revision properties.

- `--quiet`

  Don't display any statistical information about the filtered output.

15.5.3 svndumpfilter help (?, h)

This command outputs documentation for the svndumpfilter command. To get help on a specific subcommand, run help with the name of the command.

Basic Usage

```
$ svndumpfilter help [COMMAND]
```

Options

None

Index

A status indicator, 60, 67-68

Access control, 137

    Apache configuration for, 32-33

    certificates for, 103-104, 142-144

    direct, 138

    svnserve, 20, 138-140

    Windows Domain Controller authentication, 146-148

Accountability, version control for, 5

`AcquireLockFile` function, 173, 177-178

add command

    reference for, 275

    for repository files, 63-64

AnkhSVN project, 111-112

`annotate` command, 276-277

`anon-access` option, 139

Apache Portable Runtime (APR) libraries, 26, 201-202

Apache Web server, 26

    configuration, 31, 146-147

        access setup, 32-33

        Apache 1 and Apache 2 together, 33-34

        authentication, 140-141

        certificates, 144

        loading modules, 31-32

        parent paths, 33

API in Subversion, 21, 198-206

Appending issue tracking messages, 247

APR (Apache Portable Runtime) libraries, 26, 201-202

`apr_psprintf` function, 203

Archival e-mails, automating, 168-169

`AssembleThePieces` function, 175-176, 180, 183-184

Atomic commits, 18

`[auth]` section in config, 98

`AuthDigestDomain` entry, 141

`AuthDigestFile` entry, 141

Authentication

    in Apache, 140-141

    in Windows Domain Controller, 146-148

`AuthName` entry

    in Apache configuration, 33

    in password protection, 141

Author

    printing, 195

    property for, 95

author command

    reference for, 314-315

    for revisions and transactions, 195

Author keyword, 93

Authorization retention setting, 98

`AuthType` entry

    in Apache configuration, 33

    in password protection, 141

`AuthUserFile` entry, 33

`AuthzSVNAccessFile` option, 144

`[auto-props]` section in config, 101

`Autoexec.bat` file, 31

Automation, 159-160

    API for, 198-206

informIT

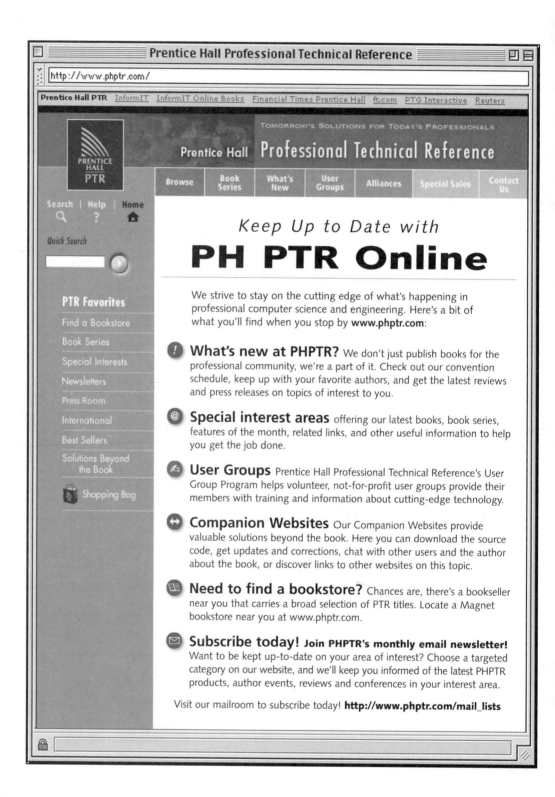